ebXML

THE NEW GLOBAL STANDARD FOR DOING BUSINESS OVER THE INTERNET

CONTENTS AT A GLANCE

ebXML

THE NEW GLOBAL STANDARD FOR DOING BUSINESS OVER THE INTERNET

ALAN KOTOK & DAVID R.R. WEBBER

New Riders

www.newriders.com

201 West 103rd Street, Indianapolis, Indiana 46290
An Imprint of Pearson Education
Boston • Indianapolis • London • Munich • New York • San Francisco

ebXML: The New Global Standard for Doing Business over the Internet

International Standard Book Number: 0-7357-1117-8

Library of Congress Catalog Card Number: 00-100522

06 05 04 03 02   7 6 5 4 3 2 1

Interpretation of the printing code: The rightmost double-digit number is the year of the book's printing; the rightmost single-digit number is the number of the book's printing. For example, the printing code 02-1 shows that the first printing of the book occurred in 2002.

Printed in the United States of America

Trademarks

Warning and Disclaimer

Publisher
David Dwyer

Associate Publisher
Al Valvano

Executive Editor
Stephanie Wall

Managing Editor
Kristy Knoop

Acquisitions Editor
Ann Quinn

Editor
Robin Drake

Product Marketing Manager
Stephanie Layton

Publicity Manager
Susan Nixon

Indexer
Angie Bess

Manufacturing Coordinator
Jim Conway

Book Designer
Suzanne Pettypiece

Cover Designer
Aren Howell

Composition
Suzanne Pettypiece

Media Developer
Michael Hughes

To Rhoda Kotok and the late Teddy Kotok, who never let me forget that all I ever wanted to be was a writer.

—A.K.

To John Redvers Webber, who always walks the other way around the mountain, and the British Army, which taught me nothing is impossible.

—D.R.R.W.

Table of Contents

About the Authors

Alan Kotok is a Washington, DC-based reporter and writer on technology, business, and public policy, and editor of *E-Business Standards Today*, published by Data Interchange Standards Association (DISA), and of U.S. Techno-Politics on Suite101.com. He writes frequently for the information technology trade press, including *Electronic Commerce World* magazine, XML.com, and CMP TechWeb. He is the lead author of *Print Communications and the Electronic Media Challenge* (Jelmar Publishing Co, 1997). Kotok serves on the ebXML Marketing-Awareness-Education project team and the W3C advisory council.

Kotok previously served as DISA's Director of Education, responsible for conferences, training, and information resources. He joined DISA in October 1999 as standards manager for the OpenTravel Alliance, helping this worldwide organization establish its first XML-based message specifications.

Before joining DISA, Kotok served 10 years with Graphic Communications Association (GCA) as Director of Management Technologies and then as Vice President for Electronic Business. Before joining GCA, Kotok founded Overseas Technology, a high-tech export company, and served 15 years with the U.S. Information Agency on assignment in the U.S., Middle East, Africa, and Japan.

Kotok has a B. A. in journalism from the University of Iowa and a Master of Science in communications from Boston University. He completed postgraduate work in Technology of Management at The American University in 1981–82.

David R.R. Webber is Vice-President for Business Development for XML Global Technologies, in Vancouver, BC, Canada. He is a cofounder of the XML/edi Group and an acknowledged authority on XML. Webber lectures frequently in the U.S., Europe, and Asia, has more than 20 years' experience implementing business systems in a broad spectrum of industries, and is a U.S. patent holder for advanced EDI software technologies.

Webber has published numerous articles and multimedia on requirements for developing XML/EDI business solutions, and is currently involved in an advisory role with a wide variety of industry initiatives developing XML business schemas. He is also participating with the RELAX Schema Working Group and is heavily involved in ebXML interoperability standards development.

Most recently, Webber has been focusing on facilitating the development and deployment of semantic registry systems by government and industry organizations.

He received his degree in physics with computing from the University of Kent, Canterbury, UK, in 1976.

About the Technical Reviewers

These reviewers contributed their considerable hands-on expertise to the entire development process for *ebXML*. As the book was being written, these dedicated professionals reviewed all the material for technical content, organization, and flow. Their feedback was critical to ensuring that *ebXML* fits our reader's need for the highest-quality technical information.

Benoît Marchal is a consultant and writer who has worked extensively on XML and e-commerce. He is a cofounding member of the XML/edi Group. Benoît is the author of *XML by Example* (Que, 2000, ISBN 0-7897-2242-9) and *Applied XML Solutions* (Sams, 2001, ISBN 0-672-32054-1) and a columnist for Gamelan. Details of his latest projects can be found at www.marchal.com.

Duane Nickull is the Chief Technical Officer (CTO) of XML Global Technologies, Inc. He is a co-inventor of the first context-sensitive XML search engine, GoXML™, and the first web-based XML e-commerce ASP. In addition to his work with XML Global, Duane is the technical director for XSLT.com and actively participates in a number of standards bodies. He sits on the ebXML Steering Committee and serves as the co-Chief Editor of the technical architecture team. He also participates in UDDI, OAG, and OMG. Duane is a regular contributor of technical articles to a wide variety of established industry publications. He lives in Vancouver, B.C., and is a snowboarder and competitive mountain biker.

Acknowledgments

In this book, we frequently use the term *process* to describe a sequence of events and activities undertaken by businesses in partnership with each other. That word also describes how we came to write this book. We would like to briefly describe those processes, which will provide a way of expressing our genuine gratitude to the many people who helped us.

One of those processes involves our interactions with New Riders Publishing (NRP). In late 1999, David Webber proposed a comprehensive book written for businesspeople on XML business strategies, and brought in Alan Kotok as co-author. One of the publishers we contacted was New Riders Publishing, which led us to Stephanie Wall, NRP's Executive Editor.

We had to reengineer our original plans into something more feasible for us to deliver, but the fact that you're reading this page is a testimony to Stephanie's persistence and leadership on this entire project. Throughout the entire process, Stephanie kept in contact with us; when we saw an opportunity to focus the project on the (then) very new ebXML idea, she led the effort to make it happen. Stephanie combined effective encouragement with the occasional slap-upside-the-head to keep our work on track, and we sincerely thank her for being the godmother of this enterprise.

Stephanie got plenty of help from NRP colleague Ann Quinn and freelance editor Robin Drake, who together we dubbed *las tres amigas,* and we are genuinely grateful for all of their help. Robin gave both of us clear guidance on format and usage that made it possible to deliver the text in a style with which she could work. Robin also handled all of the technical editor contacts and corrected the inevitable inconsistencies that arise over the six months of copy preparation. Ann, our acquisitions editor, served as our main day-to-day contact with NRP, keeping the project on track, answering all of our questions, and providing much-needed morale building and support.

The stunning design of the book came about because of Suzanne Pettypiece, one of NRP's compositors/project editors. During this project, we came to appreciate the premium that NRP puts on good design and the attention to detail on human factors when interacting with a printed work.

The content of this book came about because of another process, the development of the ebXML specifications. We need to first acknowledge the incredible job of leadership by Klaus-Dieter Naujok, the chief technical officer of IONA Technologies and chair of ebXML. Klaus led an all-volunteer army of hundreds of organizations and thousands of individuals. The fact that ebXML completed its work on time and in good quality, and followed a process completely open to anyone with an email account, is a testimony to Klaus's leadership.

As we discuss in Chapter 5, "The Road Toward ebXML," the ebXML initiative divided into several project teams, and we divided our efforts among some of those teams over the 18 months of ebXML's development. We would like to cite several individuals whom we found helpful to understanding the ebXML specifications or who stimulated ideas that we worked into the content of the book.

David took part in the Registry-Repository (acting team lead of this group at one meeting), Requirements, and Technical Coordination teams during this period. Lisa Carnahan and Len Gallagher from National Institute of Standards and Technology provided much of the intellectual firepower in the Registry-Repository Group, with important ideas for this very important part of the ebXML architecture. Martin Bryan and Chris Nelson, both XML consultants based in England, performed seminal work on the information models of core components and classifications and how they link into the registry system.

Mike Rawlings of Rawlings EC Consulting and Mark Crawford of Logistics Management Institute directed a team of requirements writers who crafted a document that gave the technical specialists a clear path forward for developing the technical documents. Tim McGrath led the technical coordination team and had the unenviable task of fitting the different pieces together, in which he succeeded admirably.

In the ebXML Marketing, Awareness, and Education team, Alan and the rest of the team struggled with the task of explaining a complex technical product in understandable terms to businesspeople. Many of the ideas in this book resulted in part from those discussions, and we need to thank project team leads Simon Nicholson of Sun Microsystems and Michael Weiner of IBM, and earlier Ann Bullen of PriceWaterhouseCooper and Rachel Foerster of Rachel Foerster and Associates. Also on the team were three excellent writers on e-business technology: Carol Geyer of OASIS, Ed Julson of Sun Microsystems, and William (Willie Joe) Kammerer of Foresight Corp. provided brilliant ideas and encouragement on communicating these complex ideas.

In developing material for the book, we called on several professional colleagues who deserve mention. Anthony Dutton, a colleague of David's at XML Global, prepared much of the CatXML material in Chapter 9, "Moving from Theory to Practice," which shows a working system that implements many of the ebXML ideas. Of course, CatXML itself would not have happened without the sheer determination of Bruce Peat of eProcess Solutions, who developed the EMall application for the Department of Defense, from which CatXML is derived. Bruce is a cofounder of the XML/edi Group (along with David Webber) and a participant in ebXML. We thank as well another leading XML/edi colleague, Betty Harvey of Electronic Commerce Connection, who is also an ebXML participant and who compiled the e-business/XML glossary in Appendix A, "Acronyms."

We would not have had the chance to establish our credentials on the topic of ebXML without opportunities to write about ebXML for leading technology web sites, and we need to recognize editors who gave Alan this opportunity: Edd Dumbill of XML.com and Larry Laing of PlanetIT.com, a part of CMP TechWeb. We also need to thank Alan's colleagues at Data Interchange Standards Association (DISA) and its affiliates, who provided the support and opportunity to take part in the ebXML effort: Jerry Connors and Tim Cochran of the DISA staff, Jim Young of Continental Airlines, and Nick Lanyon of Lanyon, Inc., both of the OpenTravel Alliance (OTA) Board, early and strong ebXML supporters.

A special thanks goes to Don McCubbrey of the Daniels College of Business at University of Denver, a true pioneer in the use of XML in business, for providing the preface to this book. Don was one of the early proponents in the academic world for using XML for business data.

A heartfelt thanks also goes to our technical editors, Duane Nickull of XML Global Technologies and Benoît Marchal of PineappleSoft in Belgium, who kept the content of the book true to the technology. Duane served as editor of the ebXML Technical Architecture specifications, from which we drew a fair amount of the content of this book. Ben has become one of the very best writers on XML; his book *XML by Example* continues to be a bestseller on XML.

Alan needs to thank his wife Sharon for patiently enduring six months of incessant chatter of XML technical minutiae, lost weekends devoted to producing text, and for learning more about the book publishing business than she (or anyone, for that matter) would want to hear. If, after 25 years, our marriage can survive the processes of writing a book (my second one of these exercises), then anything is possible.

David, in the meantime, has to thank his wife Marjorie for tirelessly wrestling with three actively growing young children and explaining why Dad has to spend most of his life staring at a computer, talking on the phone, and surrounded by piles of paper litter in an effort to better the human condition globally and here at home.

Tell Us What You Think

As the reader of this book, you are the most important critic and commentator. We value your opinion and want to know what we're doing right, what we could do better, what areas you'd like to see us publish in, and any other words of wisdom you're willing to pass our way.

As the Executive Editor for the web development team at New Riders Publishing, I welcome your comments. You can fax, email, or write me directly to let me know what you did or didn't like about this book—as well as what we can do to make our books stronger.

Please note that I cannot help you with technical problems related to the topic of this book, and that due to the high volume of mail I receive, I might not be able to reply to every message.

When you write, please be sure to include this book's title and author as well as your name and phone or fax number. I will carefully review your comments and share them with the author and editors who worked on the book.

Fax: 317-581-4663

Email: stephanie.wall@newriders.com

Mail: Stephanie Wall
           Executive Editor
           New Riders Publishing
           201 West 103rd Street
           Indianapolis, IN 46290 USA

Preface

With this book, Alan Kotok and David Webber have made an important contribution to the understanding of ebXML from both a managerial and technical perspective. ebXML holds great promise for helping to facilitate global e-business for small and large players alike. It may well be the solution the EC community has been seeking for some time.

Traditional EDI has worked well for more than 30 years. In particular, it has worked well for the large hub companies who often coerced their smaller suppliers (known as "spokes") into using EDI if they wanted to keep the hubs as customers. For the hubs, EDI was faster, cheaper, and more accurate than exchanging paper business documents. It proved to be essential for supporting such supply chain partnerships as Just in Time manufacturing; Quick Response; and Collaborative Planning, Forecasting, and Replenishment. As evidence of its value, some 95% of the Fortune 1000 companies in the U.S. use EDI. On the other hand, as evidence that small and medium-sized enterprises (SMEs) used it only because of the hubs' insistence, only about 2% of SMEs are traditional EDI users. Traditional EDI can be complicated to set up and administer, and, as practitioners well know, EDI standards are standard in name only.

For some time, the search has been on for a "new EDI," a method of exchanging standard business documents that would be simple and cheap enough that the benefits of EDI would be opened up to large and small companies alike, no matter where in the world they were located. The vision of the new solution was one in which the intelligence needed to interpret electronic business documents could be somehow encapsulated with the documents themselves. This would permit a company to create an electronic purchase order, for example, and send it over the Internet to a company it had never done business with before, and have that purchase order be interpreted and processed at the receiving end. Many schemes have been advanced. Alan and David review most of them in their book. Indeed, they were personally involved with some of the research efforts, as was our Center.

In 1999, for example, one of our graduate students, René Kasan, developed a prototype operating environment for XML/EDI under the aegis of the XML/edi Group. David was one of our external advisors on the project. Some elements of that work were carried forward to the ebXML Registry and Repository specifications.

As of this writing, there seems to be a consensus building around ebXML as being the most promising of the candidate solutions. The web site, ebXML.org, describes it as follows:

[A] set of specifications that together enable a modular electronic business framework. The vision of ebXML is to enable a global electronic marketplace where enterprises of any size and in any geographical location can meet and conduct business with each other through the exchange of XML based messages. ebXML is a joint initiative of the United Nations (UN/CEFACT) and OASIS, developed with global participation for global usage.

As with any emerging technology, practitioners need to ask themselves whether ebXML will become a viable option. They also need to determine whether now is the right time to make an investment in learning more about it, developing a pilot installation, and perhaps even becoming involved in the collective effort to help bring it into widespread usage. These are important questions, and this book provides answers.

ebXML could be exactly what the EC community has been waiting for. Alan and David explain it in very clear terms and position it for the reader in its proper historical and technical context. They give us a much-needed platform of understanding of the potential benefits that ebXML can bring to global e-business: a consistent pathway openly supported by the leading vendors in the field.

—Donald J. McCubbrey, Ph.D.
Director, Center for the Study of Electronic Commerce
Daniels College of Business
University of Denver
Denver, Colorado, USA

Prologue

Over 25 years ago, the idea of electronic business was born to eliminate the use of paper documents for exchanging business data, by linking computer systems together so that the data could be sent from one system to the other. This concept became known as *Electronic Data Interchange (EDI)*. The advantages of EDI are still valid today: no reentering of data and therefore fewer errors, if any. However, looking at the numbers of companies with EDI, one must wonder why every business is not using it. Among the top 10,000 companies in the world (the Fortune 1000 in the top 10 countries), almost all are using EDI, 98%, to be exact. However, for the rest of the world only 5% of the companies are EDI users. In other words, millions of companies are still using faxes and paper documents instead of e-business. Why? The answer is well known: startup cost. EDI saves a lot of money, but only over time.

In order to reduce the cost of EDI so its implementation becomes routine and inexpensive, one would have to agree to a single data format for a particular EDI message. This step would allow software vendors to create an EDI application that would have a large enough market to reduce the cost for small and medium-sized companies to be able to afford. This situation will never happen. So what does it take for software companies to build software that's not tailored for each of the different EDI message implementations, but is able to adapt to the different data requirements for a particular customer and its trading partners?

The answer is to capture the business processes and associated information needs for a particular business goal in an unambiguous way that can be processed by a computer program. Instead of looking at the data requirements based on internal legacy database records, business experts identify the collaborations with other parties in order to achieve a certain business goal. Those collaborations are then documented in business process and information models. This book describes the latest efforts that followed this path of e-business standards called *ebXML* (Electronic Business XML).

The United Nations Centre for Trade Facilitation and Electronic Business, known as UN/CEFACT, saw the potential for such an initiative (ebXML) by making the dream of business data exchange a reality for millions of smaller businesses. In partnering with OASIS, business knowledge was merged with XML experience. ebXML gave UN/CEFACT the chance to apply its rich experience in business semantics—the data exchanged between parties in transactions—as well as its more recent work in crafting a methodology for describing businesses processes.

These business aspects of ebXML offer more businesses more opportunities for exchanging more data, more easily and with more business partners than ever before. This book tells the story about ebXML for businesspeople, outlining the issues facing business of all sizes and how ebXML can address them. Unlike other specifications generated by a few companies, usually technology vendors, the ebXML specifications represent a global consensus across industry and geographic boundaries, taking in the views of vendors and business users alike.

The ebXML initiative released the first version of its specifications following the plenary meetings held in May 2001 in Vienna, Austria. As of production of this book, software vendors are expected to deliver ebXML-compliant products very soon. One of the other key drivers will be the creation and adoption by industry bodies and associations of registries of business semantic information that will allow their members to build consistent application software systems. Particularly important is how well legacy EDI formats can be migrated to and based around the ebXML registry and associated core component business information guidelines.

While all this is important, perhaps the most important factor is that of mindshare or commitment. That mindshare means the will to succeed and the confidence to inspire businesses around the world to commit to using the ebXML specifications and stepping from the current paradigm to a new world and a new age in the chapter of world trade and human endeavor.

The next moves now are up to the businesspeople who want to take advantage of these powerful technologies to reap the benefits of exchanging data with their business partners, as the larger companies have done so well. This book describes in compelling terms the ebXML ideas and shows how you can use them in your business. As business managers, your job is to make the important decisions that affect the future of your business. Along with Alan and David, the authors of this book, I urge you to consider the benefits of ebXML compliance in your next e-business systems. It will be a decision that will pay off well for your business for many years to come.

—*Klaus-Dieter Naujok*
Chief Scientific Officer, IONA Technologies Inc.
Chair of ebXML

Introduction

Doing business electronically became quite the vogue in the late 1990s, as the idea captured the attention and imaginations of everyone from business and political leaders to individual consumers. To most people, the term *electronic business* (or just *e-business*) meant having to develop a presence on the web, sometimes with a sound business strategy and execution, but many times just to keep up with consumer expectations and competitors. In 1999, *Time Magazine* named Jeff Bezos, founder of Amazon.com, as its Man of the Year, joining such notables as Charles Lindberg and Martin Luther King, Jr. The technology dazzled and the possibilities seemed endless.

By the year 2001, however, a new sense of realism replaced the initial hype as the dot.com bubble deflated. With the sharp drop in value of technology stock prices, and closing or consolidation of hundreds of web-based businesses that had seemed so promising just a few months earlier, it became increasingly clear that using the Internet for business required as much good business sense as new technology.

E-Business Is Business First

This book is about a worldwide project built on good business sense and experience that takes advantage of these new technological innovations. The *Electronic Business XML (ebXML)* initiative brought together business as well as technology experts to craft a common set of specifications to make e-business possible anywhere on the globe, for any company, in any industry, of any size.

E-business is of course based on technology, but the experience of the dot.com boom and bust shows that successful e-business starts with good business. This book describes how the ebXML specifications can open new markets and higher productivity for all businesses, using the significant improvements and innovations that result from the intelligent use of these technologies.

This book also talks about a process that brought together representatives of hundreds of companies, industry organizations, vendors of software and services, and standards bodies for 18 months from November 1999 through May 2001. The ebXML specifications developed as a result of a total worldwide volunteer effort, and a completely open and transparent process, where anyone with a computer, Internet connection, and email address could take part. ebXML is a testament to the open standards process and the quality of its results. ebXML is also a credit to the foresight and dedication of the two organizations that made it all happen: the Organization for the Advancement of Structured Information Standards (OASIS) and the United Nations Centre for Trade Facilitation and Electronic Business (which uses the acronym UN/CEFACT).

The Goal: Enable Businesses of Any Size to Do Business Electronically with Anyone Else

The international consortium that developed ebXML made it clear from the outset that the only way this effort could succeed is to address the needs of businesses large and small—smaller enterprises up to now having largely been left out of the e-business boom. The participation of UN/CEFACT also made it imperative that the specifications encourage e-business anywhere in the world. As a result, the goal of ebXML is a standard that makes e-business almost as ubiquitous as the telephone and as interoperable as a fax transmission.

At this stage, ebXML is a set of documents, with several prototypes completed, but with many companies now building systems to support it. To show how ebXML can work, we need to introduce you to some real people and organizations that hope to benefit from it.

Alexander and Yelena Vilshinetskaya are painters in
Moscow. Alexander is also a physician and Yelena a
physicist. They both love their art, but because of
deflated professional salaries in modern Russia, they
need to sell their works in order to survive. Alexander
and Yelena, while both talented, found they needed a
way to distinguish their work from other painters. As
a result, Yelena paints delicate designs on mother-of-
pearl brooches that she sells through PEOPLink, a
not-for-profit organization that connects artisans with
buyers worldwide over the web.[1]

PEOPLink partners with development organizations
that organize local artisans such as the Vilshinetskayas
and teaches them business skills. They provide the
basic technology to capture digital photographs of the
merchandise, which they then post for sale on the
PEOPLink web site.

One of PEOPLink's partner organizations, in
Guatemala, has the improbable name of Out of the
Dump. In 1991, a photojournalist named Nancy
McGirr began photographing children living in abject
poverty in the central garbage dump of Guatemala
City. Families living in the dump scavenge for food
and scrap materials to sell; as you might expect, this
existence represents their last hope for survival.
McGirr found that children in the dump were fasci-
nated with her camera, and she got the idea of letting
the children there photograph themselves.

McGirr acquired eight cameras. Returning to
Guatemala, she gave the cameras to the children living in the dump, to shoot pictures of their world. The
results startled everyone who saw these prints. The
children's photographs captured the daily life of the
dump, offering gripping images of children playing
among grinding poverty, drug abuse, and random
violence.

As word of this unusual project grew, Nancy was able
to line up sponsors to provide cameras, film, paper,
and batteries. The donations enabled the children to
take more photos for note cards and prints, sold first

through UNICEF and now PEOPLink. Revenues from sales pay for basic schooling for the children, as well as more advanced skills in English, creative writing, and computer systems.[2]

PEOPLink sells the items of these and hundreds of other artisans and organizations directly, as well as through auctions on eBay. But they want to be able to open other distribution channels, using existing networks of resellers and galleries, not just the web. PEOPLink is developing a combination of web-based service and software called *Catgen* that would give small businesses a way of developing catalogs and offering their goods to potential buyers worldwide.[3]

Marc Beneteau, the chief technology officer of PEOPLink, expressed an interest in ebXML as a way of helping meet this objective. ebXML can supplement Catgen by providing the ability for trading partners to exchange standard electronic business messages such as orders, delivery schedules, receipts, and invoices. With ebXML, these small businesses, just like their larger counterparts, can concentrate on production and marketing, and devote less of their precious resources to administration.[4] You don't have to be a big business to worry about overhead and opportunity costs.

Another business cataloging system plans to use the ebXML specifications, but this one can serve the needs of larger, more sophisticated vendors as well as smaller businesses. The U.S. Department of Defense sponsored an early business application of *Extensible Markup Language* (*XML*) to create a single requisitioning system for the four military services—Army, Navy, Air Force, and Marines—designed for common non-weapons supplies and spare parts. The system integrates with the services' established back-end systems, using a simple web form that the smallest businesses can handle.

The developer of the system has since generalized this work into a more comprehensive CatXML specification that uses cataloging interchange formats from the Open Applications Group and the connectivity specifications from ebXML. CatXML allows for simple query and purchase operations for small businesses but also for more complex and integrated supply-chain relationships among trading partners. Designing these applications around open standards and specifications such as ebXML allows for such scalability.[5]

ebXML created a specification that makes possible these kinds of business innovations in order to face a new business environment with a technology that meets these needs. We outline both the business needs and the technology in the following sections, and detail them later in the book.

Business Is Bigger, and Different, But Is It Better?

To put it plainly, the Internet has changed everything, and the way companies do business continues to change quickly. The roles of supplier, customer, and distributor have blurred. Competition is increasing and the nature of that competition is changing. Customers are becoming more demanding and less loyal at the same time. The pace of change has picked up to what is now called "Internet time." And the scale, scope, and potential payoff have grown along with the complexity and risk. Any e-business solution, especially a specification for exchanging messages, needs to address these metrics and conditions.

The growing realization of companies[6] that e-business covers more than just taking orders reflects an important change in recent months. Conducting business means meeting the total needs of customers. Delivery, service, payments, maintenance, warranties, and financing play significant roles in business decisions, and businesses need to configure their systems to support these functions as well as sales. Combining these functions into business processes provides ways of identifying series of related transactions, and illustrates the need for flexibility in systems and databases to move data among them.

Much of the commerce generated over the 20th century was based on stable supply chains, dictated in many respects by the needs of the producers. In the 21st century, customers now are empowered by information. Earlier, the suppliers produced the goods and services but also managed the flow of information about these goods and services. Intermediaries such as salespeople or wholesalers provided information about product characteristics, warranties, servicing, and status of deliveries. Now companies use the web to provide this kind of information, not only for retail customers but for all supply-chain partners. Customers now demand instant access to this information via a web browser, not from a telephone call.

With more information at their fingertips, customers can force suppliers to provide information on goods and services in the way that customers want to see it, not the way producers want to present it. A few years ago, only publications such as *Consumer Reports* provided apples-to-apples comparisons of products and services. Now, web-based services compete with each other to present these kinds of details on an expanding array of items. Producers have long resisted this process of commoditizing, but the web has made it routine. Both consumer and business customers want more choices, more channels, and more options before they spend their money.

The need to provide more choices has forced businesses to work in different ways with competitors and customers. The days of stable supply chains meant working with the same suppliers and distributors from one year to the next. You knew the competition, and they knew you. Now we see more *coopetition*, where companies partner with competitors on short-term projects when business opportunities arise. Companies move into new lines of business faster than before, either when new opportunities arise or as a result of mergers.

Even with the economic slowdown in the first half of 2001, the volume of e-business continues to grow over previous years. In many respects, the growth of business-to-business transactions remains as strong as ever, as companies continue to invest in systems to coordinate their activities with trading partners. While consumer sales over the web may have moderated somewhat from the torrid pace of 1999–2000, the market research company Jupiter Media Metrix still expects business-to-business trade to grow past the $6 trillion dollar mark by 2005.[7]

E-Business Technology Has a History

As we noted at the beginning of this introduction, e-business became a household word during the late 1990s, but many companies have exchanged standard electronic business documents for as long as two decades. Over this time, most of the larger manufacturing, financial services, retailing, and transportation companies have used *electronic data interchange (EDI)* for quotations, orders, ship notices, and invoices, with varying degrees of success. Those using EDI successfully could reduce inventories dramatically with substantial savings, as well as tighten supply chains and improve cash flow.

But not all companies could use EDI with this kind of success. In fact, most companies, especially smaller enterprises, found EDI too expensive, complex, and just not worth the investment. Unless forced to use EDI by their larger customers, most small and medium-sized companies ignored EDI and e-business in general until the web came along. Nonetheless, the experience with EDI provides some valuable lessons—both pro and con—for a new web-based specification.

Along with development of the web in the late 1990s came a new high-powered web language called *Extensible Markup Language (XML)*. The web pages loaded on common Netscape or Internet Explorer browsers display text and images and (with some effort) can capture data in web-based forms. XML makes it possible to send structured data—like the extensive data found in company databases—across the web, using many of the same basic tools. With XML, the idea of exchanging business data became much more of a prospect for many more companies than with EDI.

While this potential of XML for business data exchange became apparent to EDI proponents, the first applications of XML were for electronic publishing, particularly for electronic documentation. Even as a publishing tool, XML had some early business uses. For example, National Semiconductor, a manufacturer of electronic components, put its extensive parts catalogs into XML, distributing the data in an XML syndication protocol called *Information and Content Exchange (ICE)*. With ICE, National Semiconductor subscribed its many specialized distributors to customized versions of its catalogs, managed through profiles stored in XML. ICE enabled National's distributors to get only the parts data they needed and ensured that they always had the latest updated information, without National having to devote extensive resources.[8]

The key to XML's potential was its extensibility (the *X* in XML) that made it possible to define a common set of terms on which companies could agree for their business messages. On this point XML became a little too promising. By late 2000, hundreds of individual XML-based vocabularies emerged, representing different industries and individual business functions that cut across industry boundaries. It became clear that any hope for achieving interoperability across these different vocabularies required a solid universal specification that would enable companies in different industries to exchange business data.

The Task for ebXML

For the volunteers developing ebXML, these business and technology conditions presented a stiff set of requirements for a successful common e-business specification. While XML looked promising, XML by itself did not have all of the tools needed to make it ready for the business world. What does "ready for the business world" mean? ebXML set these criteria as measures of success for the new specifications:[9]

- Make electronic business simple, easy, and ubiquitous.
- Use XML to the fullest extent possible.
- Offer an open standard that enables business transactions across industry boundaries for both business-to-business and business-to-consumer commerce.
- Bring together the structure and content of various XML business vocabularies into a single specification.
- Offer a migration path from current EDI standards, as well as XML vocabularies.
- Encourage industry efforts with immediate or short-term objectives to come together under a common long-term goal.
- Avoid solutions that require end users to invest in proprietary software or impose constraints requiring specialized systems to conduct e-business with ebXML.
- Keep costs to a minimum.
- Support multiple written languages and accommodate common rules of national and international trade.

This last point shows the influence of UN/CEFACT on the ebXML initiative.

ebXML Tests, Demonstrations, and Projections

At the time of this writing, ebXML has completed its technical documents, and many vendors announced their plans and schedules for software and systems supporting ebXML. While ebXML has not yet established a user base to provide case studies, the ebXML initiative did conduct several proof-of-concept tests and demonstrations during its development. These tests and demos used business data based on realistic business scenarios.

One of the demonstrations (at the 2001 Data Interchange Standards Association conference in March 2001) used a complex supply-chain scenario involving coordinated manufacturing and deliveries, vendor-managed inventories, orders with quick production schedules and tight deadlines, and replacement of an ordered product with a substitute item. Using e-business for these issues is not unknown for larger enterprises, but this demonstration involved smaller companies, such as local paper wholesalers and printing companies. The test, using realistic business data, showed that the kinds of advanced business practices made possible in big companies by EDI are now quite possible for smaller companies using ebXML.[10]

In this book, we take the kind of business scenarios in ebXML's proof-of-concept tests and develop more comprehensive scenarios to show how ebXML can apply to different kinds of realistic business cases:

- A travel agency that moves from its traditional role as a booking service to consolidator of tour packages, using XML data in customer profiles and booking messages to conduct reverse auctions over the web to make arrangements for "instant" tour groups.

- A local runners' store that institutes vendor-managed inventories, using ebXML messages to update sales forecasts, report on inventory levels, order replacement stock, and track deliveries.
- An importer of crafts from developing countries that sells by direct-mail catalogs, using ebXML messages to manage complex print orders to generate specialized copies of the catalog for identifiable market segments, and providing detailed delivery instructions for the postal service.

In all of these projected cases, the messages and systems are used by smaller companies—not the big manufacturers, retailers, and financial services using EDI today. The technology outlined in the following sections and discussed in this book makes these kinds of improvements in business processes and practices feasible for smaller businesses.

The ebXML Technology

The ebXML technology is based on a set of building blocks designed to meet common business requirements and conditions. The ebXML technical architecture makes use of existing standards wherever possible, building on the experience of EDI while taking advantage of the increased flexibility of XML and ubiquity of the Internet. Because the architecture is modular, industries or companies can choose to implement parts of the ebXML technology rather than trying to do everything all at once.

Messaging

Most companies interested in ebXML will probably start with the messaging functions that enable companies to send and receive business data in a standard envelope-and-message format. The ebXML messages use a specification called the *Simple Object Access Protocol (SOAP)*. SOAP is an XML application that defines a message format with headers to indicate sender, receiver, routing, and security details. A recent enhancement to SOAP allows for the attachment of any digitized content, which enables ebXML messages to send engineering drawings or patient X-rays, as well as business data.

Business Processes

A basic feature of the ebXML architecture, and one that separates it from other XML frameworks, is its emphasis on business processes. The use of modeling languages and charting tools such as the Unified Modeling Language (UML) offer ways of systematically capturing the flow of business data among trading partners and representing this business knowledge in a standard format, down to a fine level of detail and independent of technical implementation. Business processes that are defined systematically can be used as the basis for defining common message sequences across industry boundaries, and offer a basis for achieving interoperability.

Trading Partner Profiles and Agreements

Another important feature of ebXML is the systematic representation of company capabilities to conduct e-business in what ebXML calls the *collaboration protocol profile* (*CPP*). With CPPs, companies can use a common XML format to list the industries, business processes, messages, and data-exchange technologies that they support. Companies then use CPPs to agree upon the business processes, messages, and technologies used to exchange business messages, in a *collaboration protocol agreement* (*CPA*), also an XML document. Companies still may need a *trading partner agreement* (*TPA*) to cover non-technical business or legal issues, but the CPA provides the technical features of the agreement in an automated form.

Registries and Repositories

The part of ebXML with which most companies will have contact early on are the *registries*, which contain the industry processes, messages, and vocabularies used to define the transactions exchanged with trading partners. Companies also will use ebXML registries to register the CPPs that list their e-business capabilities for inspection by potential trading partners, as well as search the registries for companies with the capabilities desired in trading partners. Registries index these items, but they're actually stored in corresponding *repositories*. Because these functions are critical for companies new to ebXML or those seeking to expand into new industries or find new trading partners, registries and repositories are considered the key to making ebXML work successfully.

Core Components

As well as business processes, ebXML relies on *core components* to provide interoperability among industries and business functions, but core components work at the individual data-element level. Core components identify the data items that businesses use most often and across industries, assigning them neutral names and unique identifiers. With core components, companies can relate data used in one industry to counterparts in another industry, or from an XML vocabulary to previously defined EDI transactions. Core components, as of the time of this writing, are still a work in progress. While the ebXML team responsible for core components has identified some of these key data items, much work still remains. However, the EDI standards bodies have agreed to relate their data dictionaries to the ebXML core components. Once completed, core components will have a welcome reception.

What ebXML Is Not

It's important to note the limitations of ebXML. This effort will produce a set of specifications for software and services—but not the software and services themselves, which will be generated by technology vendors. Also, at least as of spring 2001, ebXML will not produce standard message formats, say for purchase orders or invoices. The ebXML specifications will provide the building blocks and infrastructure to write those messages, but the actual development of standard messages will generally fall to industry groups and standards bodies.

Purposes and Organization of This Book

We wrote this book for business managers, to help them decide on investments in systems based on ebXML and the need for ebXML-compliant systems from developers or vendors of their systems in the future. While the book is written for managers, technical specialists who would like an introduction to ebXML and a discussion of the business rationale for its development will certainly find the book of value.

The book has two basic audiences, and we organized the contents with these two groups in mind.

Part I: Executive Overview of ebXML

Part I gives an executive overview of ebXML. Chapter 1 provides a discussion of the business conditions driving development of ebXML and Chapter 2 offers an introduction to ebXML requirements and technology. Chapter 3 gives projected cases of how ebXML will work in realistic business scenarios, as mentioned earlier in this chapter. With this part of the book, readers should be able to describe the reasons for ebXML and discuss the basics of the ebXML approach and technology.

Part II: ebXML Background and Details

Part II is written for managers and business analysts directly responsible for and involved in e-business implementation and offers more background on the requirements, development, and technology of ebXML. Chapters 4 and 5 provide background on XML and the ebXML initiative, describing the developments leading up to, and contributing to the development of ebXML. Chapter 4 also discusses some of the limitations of XML, which is important to understanding several features of ebXML.

Chapter 6 presents ebXML's business requirements that tie the business needs discussed in Chapter 1 to the specifications themselves. Chapter 7 discusses web services specifications related to ebXML, including the Simple Object Access Protocol (SOAP) used to define much of the ebXML message structure. Chapter 8 gives details of the ebXML technical architecture, in business terms to the extent possible. Chapter 9 provides a detailed example of ebXML message exchanges in a realistic business scenario.

Part III: Learning More About ebXML

This section of the book is intended for both of the book's audiences. Any new technical or business initiative will create plenty of acronyms. Thus, Appendix A, "Acronyms," provides an extensive list of the acronyms used in this book and applicable to the discussion of ebXML. For readers who need even more detail about web-based business in general and ebXML in particular, Appendix B, "Resources," lists the technical documents from ebXML for use by system specialists, as well as books, articles, and more general business information on the applicable technologies for everyone else interested in ebXML.

This Book's Web Site

Because of the dynamic nature of the material, New Riders Publishing and the authors have established a web site at www.ebxmlbook.com, where readers can get updates, links, and supplements to this book. We encourage readers to visit the site for developments on ebXML as they relate to the contents of the book.

What This Book Is Not

Just as we did with the ebXML specifications, we need to point out the limitations of this book. The reader should not consider this book a substitute for the ebXML specifications themselves. Companies that want to develop systems based on ebXML can download the specifications from the ebXML web site (www.ebxml.org), free of charge.

In this book, we summarized many of the technical details, even in Chapter 8, "ebXML Technical Architecture." We also based some of the content on specifications still in draft at the time of writing this book. While the specifications were nearing completion, it's possible that some of the details may have changed between the production of this book and issuance of the final documents.

Finally, it's important to keep in mind that e-business is as fluid as the rest of the business world, particularly in the economic slowdown of 2001. By the time of this printing, web sites or even whole businesses listed in this book may have changed—or disappeared entirely. When web-based or brick-and-mortar businesses seem to have vanished, it's always wise to employ a search engine to scour the Net for new names or URLs—or at least for press releases and other such business information that can indicate the company's new name, owner, or address.

Conventions

This book follows a few typographical conventions:

- *Italics* are used to introduce new terms and for emphasis.
- Program text, functions, URLs, and other "computer language" are set in a fixed-pitch font—for example, `RegistryService` or `www.ibm.com`.

Endnotes

[1] "Yelena Vilshinetskaya," Linkages, October 1999.
www.peoplink.org/scripts/web_store/
web_store.cgi?page=./gen/magazine/9910/index.htm.

[2] "Out of the Dump: A Children's Photographic Project of
Guatemala City," PeopLink, undated, www.peoplink.org/
scripts/web_store/web_store.cgi?page=./products/gt/
od/index.htm. The project has its own web site, with
samples of these incredible photographs. See
www.oneworld.org/media/gallery/guatemala/1.html.

[3] CatGen.Com, "How It Works," undated,
www.catgen.org/howitworks.html.

[4] Kotok-Beneteau email messages, 14 April and 23 April
2001.

[5] David Webber et al., "CatXML based interchanges for
open catalogue integration," XML Global Technologies,
Inc., June 2000, www.catxml.org/CatXMLexec.PDF.

[6] In this book, we use the term *company* to mean any
entity producing goods or services for market, including
governmental agencies and not-for-profit organizations.

[7] Jupiter Communications news release, "B-To-B
Online Trade Will Rise to $6.3 Trillion by 2005,"
2 October 2000, www.jup.com/company/
pressrelease.jsp?doc=pr001002.

[8] "National, A Publisher?" undated, National Semiconductor
Corp., http://ice.national.com/.

[9] Electronic Business XML (ebXML), Requirements
Specification Version 1.06, 8 May 2001, pp. 9–10.

[10] "DISA's Show Features First Demonstration in 2001 of
New ebXML Specifications," Data Interchange Standards
Association press release, 14 February 2001,
www.disa.org/pr_doc.cfm?Name=515.

Part I   Executive Overview of ebXML

This part of the book helps business executives understand the reasons for ebXML and enables you to discuss with confidence ebXML's main points. It gives an introduction to the business conditions driving development of ebXML, a summary of ebXML's requirements and technology, and projected cases of ebXML at work in three different business scenarios.

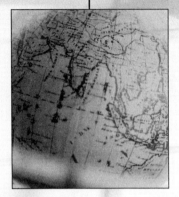

Chapter 1

There's No Business Like E-Business

The Internet and the World Wide Web have provided a wealth of new opportunities for companies[1] eager to do business electronically, and *Electronic Business XML* (or *ebXML*) provides an open standard to help make those opportunities possible. This book discusses the ebXML initiative, but to understand the reasons for ebXML and why it has attracted support from such a wide variety of industry groups, we need to first look at the basic and dramatic changes in business environment brought about by the Internet and the web.

When companies begin sharing information to improve service and product quality, they are truly conducting electronic business. This concept of electronic business, with its benefits in improved business processes and lower costs, is the goal of ebXML.

Relationships among business partners have changed, and now go beyond the common idea of just buying and selling. A few years ago, one of the authors established a database to track paper inventories in the publishing industry—known for secrecy among its companies. After about 18 months of rumored but nonexistent paper shortages resulting from hoarding, and wild gyrations in price levels that hurt both suppliers and customers, leaders in the industry agreed that they needed to share information on inventory levels to prevent further destructive swings. Printing companies agreed to furnish their inventory data in electronic form to a central database that would generate monthly summary statistics so everyone would be working from the same base of solid data on inventories.

Is this an example of electronic business? You bet it is. Were any goods bought or sold as part of this project? None whatsoever.

Companies need to use their information systems as strategic assets to move with speed and agility in this changing business environment.

This example also shows how businesses in recent years have found business climates becoming much more complex. They need to respond more quickly to changes in business conditions, a more fickle customer base, and demands by customers and stockholders to jump on new opportunities, even in new lines of business, as they become available. Companies have discovered that they need to use their information systems as strategic assets to move with more speed and agility in this environment. ebXML's specifications encourage the development of systems that address these kinds of business scenarios.

The ebXML technology (explained more fully later in the book) is built specifically for meeting these conditions:

- Because ebXML organizes business content around business processes rather than fixed documents, and interchangeable core components rather than hard-coded, predefined data elements, companies can relate their current practices and terminology more easily to changing conditions.
- Because ebXML automates many aspects of business trading agreements, companies can engage in new and innovative relationships with partners—even competitors—more easily.
- Because ebXML lists industry processes, messages, core components, and other business objects needed to conduct e-business in distributed registries and repositories, rather than in either a central store or in each user's system, the software needed to run ebXML applications can be made less complex and less expensive.

- Because ebXML takes advantage of existing Internet technical standards to develop its message structure and electronic envelopes, almost any means of Internet transport, such as the web or email, can carry ebXML messages. Thus, even the smallest companies already have much of the technology needed to begin running ebXML.

So what is this thing we call *electronic business* or *e-business*? The popular concept of electronic business is retail sales over the web—with Amazon.com perhaps the most well-known example. In the late 1990s, the success of these "e-tailers" triggered a headlong charge by established brands to secure their own web presence.

But any businessperson can tell you that doing business between companies is more than just selling consumer goods. It covers the entire panoply of interactions with suppliers, distributors, investors, staff, and customers—all of the entities that have a stake in the performance of the company. ebXML is designed to extend the benefits of e-business to a much wider audience than ever before, covering the entire potential spectrum of this panoply of interactions.

Of course, a good deal of important business activity goes on inside a company, not just between business partners. Because ebXML concentrates on the interactions among companies, this chapter discusses those kinds of business conditions.

This chapter reviews electronic business in business terms. E-business indeed depends on technology, but until very recently the "business" side of e-business has gotten less attention than the highly visible technology that has mesmerized normally skeptical businesspeople. The ebXML initiative addresses these business issues, which are the focus of this chapter. The chapter also explores how ebXML encourages development of real business solutions by making technology a simple enabler.

In Case You Hadn't Noticed, Doing Business Is Different Now

The way companies do business is changing—and quickly. The roles of supplier, customer, and distributor have blurred. Competition is increasing and the nature of that competition is changing. Customers are becoming more demanding and simultaneously less loyal. And the pace of change has picked up to what is now called *Internet time*. The scale, scope, and potential payoff have also grown, along with the complexity and risk.

Being open has become a big win for companies. Businesses that interact with more suppliers, more customers, and a larger segment of industry often see increases to the bottom line. This has resulted in a paradigm shift in corporate philosophy. Any e-business solution needs to address these metrics and conditions.

Let's start with some basic principles and some real-life examples of how e-business has changed business.

The relationship of supplier to customer has changed markedly in the customer's favor.

The first realization is that the amount of information available to customers has increased to such an extent that the relationship of supplier to customer has changed markedly in the customer's favor. During most of the 20th century, suppliers controlled the delivery of goods and services, and particularly the information associated with those goods and services. Except for highly regulated industries such as the utility industry, suppliers controlled pricing and managed expectations. Suppliers had one way of doing business, and while they often talked a good game about meeting customer needs, if you were the customer you did business the suppliers' way.

For companies, this meant higher overheads from teams of intermediaries, either independent of the suppliers or in the suppliers' employ. These intermediaries—distributors, wholesalers, jobbers, account executives, customer service representatives, or just salespeople—acted as the conduits of information between the creators of the goods or services and the customers. In many cases, these intermediaries provided important distribution services—getting the physical product into a store and on the shelves, for example. But they also served as the agents of the customers in their dealings with suppliers, and would go to bat for the customers if they had problems.

In the late 1980s, for example, one of this book's authors founded a technology export service that represented American software companies overseas, providing marketing and logistics as well as licensing, and in some cases end-user technical assistance. The clients for this service were smaller developers, often one or two persons, who couldn't afford marketing or customer support outside the United States. The export company acted as a reseller; the American suppliers sold their products to the export company, which in turn resold the software to customers (mainly dealers) overseas. The export company handled all shipping, delivery, and financial terms, such as letters of credit. The client software vendors made sales that they otherwise wouldn't have been able to handle, the dealers overseas got access to software products they wouldn't otherwise have even known about, and the export company made a little money in the process.

Today, the export company would serve little if any useful purpose.[2] American software vendors can and do sell their products to business or end-user customers in most countries in the world directly over the web—except for software with sophisticated encryption or potential military use (an increasingly rare occurrence). Other vendors of physical goods hire package-delivery services that can handle shipments to most places on the globe and provide online access to their shipping status. More U.S. banks now operate internationally and can deal with most major currencies, likewise giving almost real-time status of funds transfers. Repeat this scenario for stockbrokers and travel agents, who essentially once provided information to customers, many of whom can now get this information without the need for intermediaries.

What has happened in 15 years that made these services largely redundant? The end of the Cold War and the triumph of Western capitalism as the world's dominant business model happened, of course, which opened new markets for trade and investment worldwide. For the information technology industry, it meant a loosening of the restrictions on exporting Western (especially American) technology. All of these conditions contributed to a worldwide market for information technology, which contributed directly to the development of the World Wide Web.

In his book *The Lexus and the Olive Tree*, Thomas Friedman calls this process the *democratization of technology*,[3] which he credits to the accumulated innovations in computer systems, telecommunications, chip design, miniaturization, compression technologies, increasing bandwidth, and the dramatic drop in the price for storage capacity. He describes it this way:

> So when I say that the innovations in computerization, miniaturization, telecommunication, and digitization have democratized technology, what I mean is that they have made it possible for hundreds of millions of people around the world to get connected and exchange information, news, knowledge, money, family photos, financial trades, music or television shows in ways, and to a degree, never witnessed before.

Customers plug into suppliers' systems and get information for which they used to depend on intermediaries.

With the web and its associated client/server technology, customers can now plug right into manufacturers' internal systems and get the kinds of information for which they formerly depended on intermediaries such as brokers or clients. The ability of manufacturers to provide this level of information directly to customers changed the expectations of customers and demands on suppliers. Manufacturers could now deal directly with the end customers, lower many of the costs, and provide a higher level of customer service. Intermediaries would need to find new ways to serve their customers—or face extinction.

With the Internet and web, customers also discover that they share many of the same information needs of other customers. Online email lists and message boards enable customers with similar questions to share their questions and concerns, and compare notes on solutions. Smart companies set up their own email lists and message boards to encourage customers to share their experiences, rather than paying for extra customer support staff. These kinds of facilities free the customer support staff to solve the really difficult problems, not the routine questions.

Even where suppliers already dealt directly with their customers, the nature of business has changed drastically. Paper companies serving the graphic arts market, for example, used to rely almost exclusively on direct sales forces for their major clients, the printing companies that produced long-run magazines and catalogs, and sometimes even the publishers of those books who purchased the paper. Most paper salespeople were (and still are) as knowledgeable about graphic arts processes as the printers themselves, and could help the publishers or printers select the appropriate paper grades for the jobs they had planned. The salespeople also knew the production people in the paper mills and could track the status of production or shipping for the customer.

With the web, however, many paper mills now put their catalogs online, as well as provide real-time access to production orders. The more enterprising paper mills help manage the customers' paper inventories, cutting down the need for per-job procurement and reducing overall inventory levels.[4] As with third-party services, the job of direct salespeople changed and in many cases became more specialized, reducing the need for frequent direct contacts, and thus reducing the need for a large sales force.

These examples illustrate the changing nature of supplier/customer interactions resulting from more and better (more accurate and timely) information available to customers. This change provides customers with greater power, and the businesses that provide more of this information demanded by customers are more likely to succeed than those that try to operate in the earlier, more traditional mode.

The result of the process is a higher level of service—certainly to the customer, but in many cases with benefits to the supplier as well. Here is another example from the paper industry: The practice of some paper companies to manage their customers' inventories is based on the ability to track consumption of individual units of inventory, in this instance the large rolls of paper mounted on printing presses. By tracking the individual units, suppliers and customers can watch inventory levels more closely and with more precision. The result is less need for expensive inventory cushions and potentially lower costs to the customer.

But this same practice of tracking individual rolls of paper also lets the printing company report on the performance of the paper more precisely. The paper mill can now capture data on the amount of waste from the roll; if the roll breaks on the press, the paper mill can trace those data items directly back to its own internal production processes. With this information, paper mills can answer questions such as whether higher waste numbers from paper breaks happen because of a different kind of pulp or more acidity in the water during production. Most of the publication paper mills now have statistical process-control techniques, for which this kind of performance feedback is golden.[5] Once companies start collecting these kinds of data, new statistical tools make it possible to find patterns or interrelationships in the data that may not have been obvious before, a practice called *data mining*.[6]

The web, modern information systems, and collaborative business models can mean better service, lower cost, and a higher-quality product.

These scenarios show that with the web, modern information systems, and a more collaborative business model, you can have better service, lower cost, and at least the potential for a higher-quality product. Yes, business is different from just a few short years ago—and, in many respects, better.

One other point about these first scenarios. Look at the many and varied kinds of electronic interactions available between trading partners; they now go beyond the common idea of electronic commerce that entails just buying and selling. When companies

begin sharing more information to improve service
and product quality, they are truly conducting electronic business. This concept of electronic business,
with its benefits in improved business processes and
lower costs, is the goal of ebXML.

Business Isn't So Simple Anymore

Business may be changing for the better, but it's not
getting any simpler. The relationships among companies have even fewer clear boundaries and linear
workflows; as a result, ideas such as partnering and
competing have become less clear.

Earlier in this chapter, we discussed how companies
are using the web to create new and creative ways of
serving their customers—but they're finding that
many more other companies are trying to do the
very same thing, and with the very same customers.
Increasing competition has become a fact of life in
business, but with e-business the whole idea of competition has changed, becoming much more widespread and multidimensional. Companies used to
know their competition. Now, competitors can come
from out of the blue or even be one's own suppliers
or customers.

The complex world of 21st century business is push-
ing companies to form new and different kinds of
partnerships with suppliers, customers, and in some
cases even competitors. These new relationships can
last for a week or a lifetime, but companies need to
be prepared to respond quickly to opportunities and
shift mental gears in ways they rarely needed to
before.

Competitors and partners now can come from
almost anywhere. The global nature of the marketplace today opens new business opportunities for
companies, but it also opens your current customers
to competitors from elsewhere. With the World Wide
Web now a worldwide activity, companies providing
web-based services can sit next door or in Bora Bora,
and still (in many cases) perform equally well;
employee retention in Bora Bora may also be better.

One of the authors recently conducted a web search for companies with whom to outsource an organization's own in-house publications and web publication operations. This organization had a growing list of complex technical publications and wanted to avoid hiring more staff to handle the demand for technical content. Instead, they sought a turnkey operation that could display titles and descriptions and take orders over the web, although the organization would continue to handle physical fulfillment.

21st century business pushes new kinds of partnerships with suppliers, customers, even competitors.

The search came up with several good candidates, all of which seemed to have sound operations and attractive web sites. Only after close inspection did the organization find that the candidates included companies with operations in the U.K., Singapore, and India. Before the web, would operations in those countries have even been considered for the job? Not likely. And given the business needs, physical location really didn't matter. For many kinds of business services, the web has made national boundaries irrelevant.

Businesspeople, journalists, and politicians are calling this new phenomenon *globalization*. But globalization is much more than business and technology. Thomas Friedman identifies six different dimensions to understanding globalization: politics, culture, military, financial markets, technology, and the environment. Friedman notes that being a globalist requires understanding the interaction of all six dimensions that defines the globalized system.[7]

The outsourcing example cited above relates to another feature of 21st century business and the complex, competitive environment in which it operates. With increasing competition from offshore, or to meet investor demands for increasingly more profitable performance, companies have begun concentrating on their core competencies, which means going outside for services not directly related to the mission of the company. In many organizations, the first operation outsourced was payroll, and companies such as EDS and ADP became profitable performing these tasks for clients.

Outsourcing key functions increases the interdependency of companies. Package-delivery services, for example, have become crucial to the success of many companies serving customers over the web. When the Teamsters Unions went on strike against UPS in August 1997, President Clinton came under pressure to invoke emergency provisions of labor laws and order the striking drivers back to work. These laws had been used in the past only for vital services such as the railroads. The dependence of companies on UPS had apparently made a strike against the company almost as much of an emergency.[8]

The need to go outside the company for vital services requires more sharing of information with the outsourcing partners. More than just suppliers, they become key players in the success of your business, which means that you need to share vital business data with them. But remember that one's partner today can also be a current or potential competitor; for example, when a partner is capable of doing what you suggest as an opportunity, or can partner with another company to provide the same thing. If you haven't already deployed and put the solution in place, beware! Therefore, one of the important requirements of e-business is the need to move quickly and engage in business from a dead start with little advance warning as opportunities develop, or if companies suddenly need to terminate relationships at a moment's notice and fill the resulting gap themselves.

Another feature of the 21st century economy is the need to address markets through different means. Distribution channels using the traditional supply chains—manufacturer to distributor to dealer to customer—are under increasing pressure from customers looking to cut out the middlemen and their markups, as well as suppliers wanting to reach end users as directly as possible. A plain fact of life of 21st century business is that companies in the supply chain must add value to the process, or risk being cut out of the action.

The plight of travel agents today vividly illustrates this fact. Agents used to make commissions from their booking of inventory held by travel suppliers: airline seats, hotel rooms, rental cars, and tour packages. They justified their commissions on the volume they could produce for the suppliers, and on finding the best travel values for customers. Travel agents used third-party services called *global distribution systems* (GDSs) that aggregated the inventories of the travel suppliers and made it possible for travel agents using online terminals to search out the best travel bargains quickly and easily.

Sabre is perhaps the best-known GDS, although others such as Worldspan, Galileo, and Amadeus compete for travel services. Sabre started as the online booking engine for American Airlines, and then expanded the service to include other airlines and later other travel services. AMR Corporation, the parent company of American Airlines, spun off Sabre as a separate company in December 1999.[9]

Obviously, the web has changed the travel industry landscape. Not only can customers do their own searching for the best of posted prices; they can search out distressed inventories (empty seats, rooms, or cars) on their own or through dynamic pricing services such as Priceline.com. With this increasing computing power in the hands of customers, both travel suppliers and GDSs want the ability to reach the customer, as well as work through the traditional travel agents, for those customers who need help with bookings.[10] Sabre created its Travelocity.com service specifically for this purpose.

Making business even more interesting in the 21st century is the fluid nature of competition. Your partner in one activity today can be your competitor in another activity tomorrow, in a practice called *coopetition*. For example, companies may form joint ventures to develop specific products and services, while competing at other levels. Organizations also take part in consortia to develop industry standards and specifications. In these consortia, such as the Interactive Financial Exchange Forum or the

Customers treat their suppliers' products and services like commodities; in effect, they're interchangeable.

OpenTravel Alliance, companies that normally compete with each other pool their knowledge and experience to agree on specifications that provide the overall industry with a common platform or data-exchange specifications. (Notice that many of the ebXML participants today come from these multi-company consortia.)

But if a partner today is a competitor tomorrow, companies need to take steps to protect themselves from partners using the information gained from the relationship against the former partners. As a result, one finds greater use of a document called a *noncompete agreement*, in which partners agree not to divulge details of the joint work or use it in competitive products or services.[11]

And what about customers? Companies who took care of their customers used to be rewarded with the customers' loyalty. This is no longer the case. Now, with increased competition, companies need to continuously build value in their relationships with customers or find their former loyal customers going to the competition.

Companies want to be able to build a continuous relationship with their vendors, but still get the best quantity/quality value for the price. To meet this objective, companies try to translate their requirements into specifications that enumerate and quantify their requirements, so any vendor with the right capabilities can take its best shot for the business.

This process forces suppliers to fit their products and services into their customers' specifications, to enable the customers to make a rational selection. But once this process happens, customers can start treating their suppliers' products and services like commodities, since they become, in effect, interchangeable.

Taking the idea to the next stage, companies can post their requirements on an open exchange, and have vendors compete for the business. These *vertical exchanges* have become a common way of doing business over the web. In the beginning, vertical exchanges provided matchmaker services—essentially putting together buyers and sellers. However, exchanges have begun taking on more functions and covering more of the supply chain. Marketplaces including e-Steel, FastParts, and ChemDex have now started covering more functions than simply buying and selling, in order to compete for business.[12]

The market research company IDC categorizes exchanges as follows:

- E-distribution sites, designed to serve the sellers' interests
- E-procurement sites, designed for buyers
- E-marketplaces, which are neutral and take into account the interests of both buyers and sellers

IDC predicts that e-marketplaces will become important players in the e-business arena. The company estimates that e-marketplaces accounted for 7.5% of the world's total e-business volume in 2000, but will grow to 56% by 2004. IDC cites examples of e-marketplaces including Freemarkets and Suppliermarket.com for industrial goods and QuoteShip.com and GoCargo for logistics services.[13]

However, exchanges have raised questions about potential violations of antitrust laws. As of August 2001, these questions have not been settled conclusively, but some early signs suggest that they will pass legal scrutiny. In September 2000, Covisint, the automotive industry exchange formed by DaimlerChrysler, Ford Motor Company, General Motors, and Renault/Nissan, received antitrust clearance by the U.S. Federal Trade Commission and Germany's Bundeskartellamt.[14]

From Just-in-Case to Just-in-Time Inventories

Bar codes are an early and successful form of e-business.

Zara, a Spanish fashion retailer with almost 1,000 stores in 31 countries, takes control of inventory seriously and integrates inventory control into its overall manufacturing and merchandising strategy. The company can take a new fashion idea and have it represented in new product selections in two weeks.[15]

The company replenishes its stock twice a week, a turnover rate well ahead of the rest of the retail business. Zara outfits its store clerks with handheld computers to record sales and customer comments, then integrates the collected data with design, manufacturing, and distribution functions. As a result, the company can spot trends early on—a rather critical quality in fashion retailing—and adjust stock accordingly, within days.[16]

One of the revolutions in business thinking over the last quarter of the 20th century is the notion of inventories. Retail businesses formerly considered inventories on the books as assets; now they're viewed as liabilities. Zara exemplifies the aggressive attitude that companies now take toward inventories. Having a huge store of production inventory once signified strength and stability. It showed that a company could buy in great quantities, to feed its machines of mass production. It also provided a buffer to protect against price increases. By stockpiling inventories when prices were low, a company could protect itself when prices went up. Stockpiling also protected companies against shortages. In the printing industry, a common expression said that one could get reprimanded for having too much paper for a job, but fired for not having enough.

Today, large material inventories mean that you can't keep count of your stock. The high cost of inventories comes from the credit needed to pay for the materials, as well as storage space and service. These costs are eminently avoidable. They only require better information. In some cases, companies themselves have that information, such as sales forecasts and burn rates. In other cases, the information comes from customers and suppliers.

If the inventories are goods, a small investment in bar codes and scanners, and a little training, can provide a current count of items on hand. Bar codes are an early and successful form of e-business.

Companies, especially in the retail supply chain, have exchanged data by printing item numbers and sometimes manufacturing data on bar-coded labels that trading partners can scan. If a company has any products that end up in retail stores, they need to acquire a *Universal Product Code* (*UPC*) company code number—or *European Article Number* (*EAN*), as they're known outside North America—and assign unique identifiers to each product. Most retailers, especially in the grocery business, require scannable bar codes on product labels.[17]

Bar codes also help keep industrial inventories under control. For industrial materials, however, the information needed may exceed simple product numbers. When the quality of a manufactured product depends on the characteristics of the input materials, the data needed on the shop floor includes those about the raw materials. The Uniform Code Council that assigns UPC company codes in North America has also established a collaborative network for sharing these kinds of data, called *UCCnet*.[18]

An everyday example from modern office life demonstrates this idea. Office copiers sometimes jam when someone adds paper from a new box, especially if the new paper is made by a different manufacturer—or even the same brand but from a different shipment. Paper may have standard weights and sizes, but small differences in water content or surface characteristics can throw off the grip of the copier feeding mechanism and cause jamming, resulting in wasted paper and time. For this reason, experienced copy center operators know to run paper from the same brand and shipment on long jobs.

Some industries have defined bar coding specifications to match manufacturing data with physical goods.

Applying this principle, more control over the input of raw materials in manufacturing implies more control over the consistency and quality of the manufactured product. When subtle changes in materials can affect the consistency of goods, the people and systems running the operations need to have the data about those materials immediately at hand. Bar codes provide an easy way to match manufacturing data with physical goods, and some industries have defined bar coding specifications for this purpose.[19]

To further support the idea of e-business rather than simple e-commerce (selling to customers using a web storefront), the sharing of data on manufacturing history and product performance constitute an entirely new form of inter-enterprise cooperation made possible by new communications technologies. These exchanges have nothing to do with buying and selling goods, and to focus only on the purchasing process misses vital ways that companies help each other.

One effect of just-in-time inventories, lower customer loyalty, and reducing goods and services to simple commodities is the downward pressure on margins, or the *superstore syndrome*. Superstores are large retail stores that work on higher volumes and smaller margins, such as Wal-Mart, Sports Authority, and Circuit City, as well as discount warehouse clubs such as Costco. When customers begin to see lower prices at the retail level as a result of superstores and their practices, they expect to see the same practices and effects in their business lives. Companies need to show continually that they are taking steps to reduce costs, or at least to add value to the equation. If they don't, their competitors will. The willingness of many companies to experiment with new kinds of business models, such as vertical exchanges, auctions, or reverse auctions, shows how seriously they take this development.

What Is an Auction?

Auctions have emerged (or rather reemerged) as a viable business model for procurement of goods and services, due largely to the availability of web technology. Peter Fingar, Harsha Kumar, and Tarun Sharma describe the various kinds of auctions and the role the web has played in their recent popularity in their book *Enterprise E-Commerce:*[20]

Forrester Research anticipates U.S. business-to-business sales using dynamic online pricing models, such as those used in auctions, to reach $746 billion in 2004.[21]

Companies that sell enterprise-capable auction software are focusing on the computer and semi-conductor industries because their fast-moving product

continues

What Is an Auction? (continued)

cycles often cause inventory management problems. The auction market is also touching commodity industries like oil and gas.

For buyers, auctions offer a wide range of goods at competitive prices and low transaction costs. Sellers liquidate surplus goods or use the auction to help set prices on first-run goods. Some companies have turned to customized solutions that account for particular inventory-management needs. Media auctions let advertisers take advantage of last-minute deals and bargains as they bid for unsold media time on networks and stations around the country. In building an auction site that emulates conventional business practices, a marketer has to be prepared to do a high degree of analysis. Allowing buyers to access lists of available advertising slots—a task that previously required dozens of telephone calls—cuts administrative costs considerably. Auctions could end up cutting out the middleman in some types of transactions, and fixed pricing will most likely fade in the digital economy.

Generally auctions are segmented into four major one-sided formats: English, Dutch, first-price sealed-bid, and uniform second-price (Vickrey). In one-sided auctions, only bids are permitted, but not "asks." A double auction is not one-sided because bids and asks take place at the same time (bid/ask trading). The English auction, known also as the open-outcy auction, is the format most familiar to Americans. Here the seller announces a reserve price or some low opening bid. Bidding increases progressively until demand falls. The winning bidder pays the highest valuation. [...] The item is sold to the highest bidder unless the reserve price is not met, in which case the item may not be sold. Often, the reserve price is not revealed to thwart rings who have banded together and agreed not to outbid each other, thus effectively lowering the winning bid.

Competition and enthusiasm is at its highest in the English auction, where inexperienced participants sometimes end up paying more for an item than its value—the "winner's curse."

The descending-price auction, commonly known as the Dutch auction, uses an open format wherein the seller announces a very high opening bid. The bid is lowered progressively until demand rises to match supply. When multiple units are auctioned together, normally more takers press the button as price declines. In other words, the first winner takes his prize and pays his price and later winners pay less. When the goods are exhausted, the bidding is over. In the Dutch system, a seller tends to receive maximum value, since the bidder with the highest interest cannot afford to wait too long to enter his bid. (The world famous tulip flower market works to this system, with buyers viewing cartons of tulip flowers on conveyor belts and purchasing according to quality, color, and size).

The third auction type, known as the first-price, sealed bid, or discriminatory auction, is common when multiple items are being auctioned. This type of auction has a bidding period in which participants submit one sealed bid in ignorance of all other bids. At the resolution phase, bids are opened, and the winner, who pays exactly the amount bid, is determined. Usually, each participant is allowed one bid, which means that bid preparation is especially important. When multiple units are being auctioned, sealed bids are sorted from high to low, and items awarded at highest bid price until the supply is exhausted. The winners can, and usually do, pay different prices.

In the uniform second-price auction, commonly called the Vickrey auction, the bids are sealed, and each bidder is ignorant of other bids. The item is awarded to the highest bidder at a price equal to the highest unsuccessful bid. When auctioning multiple units, all winning bidders pay for items at the same

continues

> **What Is an Auction? (continued)**
>
> *highest losing price. The price that the winning bidder pays is determined by competitors' bids alone and does not depend upon any action the bidder undertakes. Less bid shading occurs because people do not fear the winner's curse. Bidders are less inclined to compare notes before an auction.*

Investors Want to See Your Internet Strategy

If your customers and suppliers can't convince you to take e-business seriously, what about your investors? The global investment community has become the main driver behind economic growth, what Thomas Friedman calls the *Electronic Herd*.[22] In *The Lexus and the Olive Tree,* Friedman gives this name to the anonymous cohort of traders in equities, bonds, currencies, and other financial instruments, connected through international networks and exchanges. It has no organization and no leader, with companies operating independently of and often in competition with each other. By the nature of its electronic existence, it can respond instantaneously to developments in a choreographed way.

Investors, particularly venture capitalists, continue to look favorably on Internet-related vehicles. PriceWaterhouseCoopers (PWC), in its Money Tree survey for the first quarter of 2001, found in the U.S. venture capital investments reaching $10.1 billion, down from $16.8 billion in the previous quarter. Internet-related companies represented 75% of all financing; while down from previous quarters, still the largest single segment. As Tracy T. Lefteroff of PWC noted, "Venture capital firms are reassessing their Internet strategies, just as corporate America is. But the Internet is not going away. It's now an integral part of doing business....Venture capital will continue to back promising Internet-related technologies."[23]

Since then, through mid 2001, there has been a downturn, but technology investment continues to dominate as a percentage. Venture capitalists (VCs) invested $19.6 billion in the fourth quarter of 2000, more than 30% less than the $28.3 billion they invested in the previous quarter. In fact, it was the lowest infusion of new VC money since the third quarter of 1999, according to the National Venture Capital Association (NVCA).

What if your product or service is not technology related? In May 2000, Wayne Rash reported in *Internet Week* on a meeting with investors that he attended. These investors favored companies in more traditional businesses, rather than the high-flying dot-coms. Nonetheless, they want to see a serious Internet strategy, not just a web site. Rash said that investment "…depends on a company's plans to compete in the battlefields of the future, even if that means restructuring the company so that e-commerce tools can be used effectively. No longer is the use of the Internet or e-commerce something that's nice to have. In the minds of these investors, it's mandatory."[24]

Higher Volumes, Larger Scale, Bigger Numbers

Not only is business getting more complicated, but the scale is increasing, due in large part to the world-wide markets made possible by modern technologies in the aftermath of the Cold War. This large scale of business results from the sheer scale of intra-business goods and services, one that continues to grow significantly.

The Boston Consulting Group (BCG) estimates that in the U.S., electronic procurements between businesses will grow from $1.2 trillion in the year 2000 to $4.8 trillion in 2004. By 2004, electronic procurements should account for fully 40% of total purchasing; but only 11% of all purchases will involve online price negotiations. These findings, based on survey responses from more than 260 buyers, sellers, and e-marketplaces, as well as in-depth interviews, show that despite a high level of online penetration, the vast majority of transactions will be ordering and replenishment, and not price negotiations.

BCG's research shows that the size of the B2B e-commerce market is far greater than is commonly reported, in part because it recognizes the established base of Electronic Data Interchange (EDI) over private networks and its extensions to the Internet.[25]

Compaq Computers alone is running an average of $50 million worth of business weekly through its combined EDI and Internet systems, or about $2.5 billion annually in 2000.[26]

Last year, Forrester Research predicted that B2B e-commerce in the United States alone would total $2.7 trillion in 2004.[27] Forrester wasn't alone in its bullish outlook; the Gartner Group forecasted that U.S. B2B e-commerce will total $3.7 trillion in 2004,[28] while the Boston Consulting Group predicted an even greater upside, with B2B transactions totaling up to $4.8 trillion by 2004.[29]

But more recently, continued weakness in the U.S. economy as well as the collapse of thousands of dot-com businesses appear to have dampened such enthusiasm.[30]

By contrast, the Boston Consulting Group expects the more visible business-to-consumer purchasing in North America to total $65 billion in the year 2001. While that number represents a 44% increase over 2000 ($45 billion that year),[31] it pales in comparison to the $1.2 trillion for electronic trade among businesses in the year 2000.

The market research company Jupiter Communications anticipates the volume of online business-to-business trade to grow to $6.3 trillion by 2005, representing 42% of non-service spending by that time. For the year 2000, Jupiter found online business exchanges accounted for only 3% of non-service spending. Jupiter predicted the computer and telecommunications market alone will account for over $1 trillion in volume by 2005.

> *By 2005, the traditional direct sales model may drop to 65% of business volume.*

But as important as the pure volume is the mix of trading venues. For 2000, Jupiter estimated the traditional direct sales model with products going from one supplier to many customers would account for 92% of the business-to-business volume. By 2005, according to Jupiter's research, the proportion will drop to 65% as what Jupiter calls "net and coalition markets," such as digital exchanges that have multiple suppliers and customers, grow to about 35% of the total online volume.[32]

The importance of electronic business-to-business transactions is also growing overseas. IDC estimates the volume of Internet commerce between businesses in Europe to grow by 87% to over 400 billion Euros by 2003.[33]

A good reflection of the increased financial volume is found in the sheer overall quantity of customers and transactions facing businesses today. Here are several examples of this larger scale that businesses need to support:[34]

- A power company needs to rely on 20 other providers in the power grid to maintain service during peak loads, where before the company generated all of its own power.
- A manufacturer of PCs distributes product through 27,000 resellers over the web, and the number is growing.
- A market aggregator runs a web portal with no physical inventory of its own, but uses its branding to sell other distributors' products and attract customers to that overall branding.
- A car manufacturer has some 5,000 second-tier suppliers of parts, yet still needs to track the flow of product, keep inventory levels to a minimum, and maintain quality.
- A web-based travel service aggregates offerings from 500 vacation package providers.
- An insurance company works through 20,000 field agents who need to operate one-on-one with clients.

- An office supply company has a customer list of 50,000 small businesses, ordering product over the web, from printed catalogs, and over the telephone, and still demanding next-day delivery.

Can Your Company's Systems Keep Pace?

Managing this quickly growing, increasingly complex, and highly valuable marketplace has put an enormous strain on company information systems. These profound changes hit a company's information systems with greater intensity, since the demands simultaneously raise expectations of both management and end users. In a cruel irony, companies often find that their internal information systems—designed and working fine for previous eras and business models—are not flexible or adaptable.

Figure 1.1 shows how corporate systems have evolved over the last 40 years. The first corporate systems, installed in the 1960s and 1970s, focused on basic administrative systems such as accounting for management control, and in some industries manufacturing. These systems normally served a few end users, at most a few hundred. Computer storage came with a high price tag—so high, in fact, that data files abbreviated years to the last two digits, a decision that would come back to haunt business in the year 1999. The systems were called *mainframes* or *heavy iron* by the engineers of that time.

By the 1980s, the heavy iron became a little lighter. Minicomputers by companies such as DEC, Wang, Data General, and Prime emerged to claim a large piece of the corporate computer market. These smaller machines took on additional management tasks, such as distribution, human resources, and planning functions. During this time Electronic Data Interchange (EDI) emerged as well. Despite the introduction of EDI, however, sharing of data with other companies in the supply chain remained the exception. (We discuss EDI later in the chapter.)

IT Infrastructure Landscape

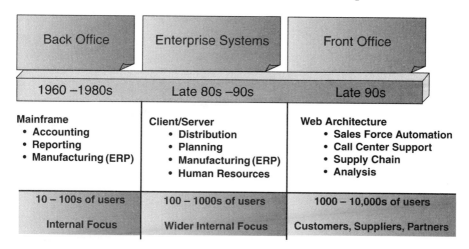

Back Office	Enterprise Systems	Front Office
1960 –1980s	Late 80s –90s	Late 90s
Mainframe • Accounting • Reporting • Manufacturing (ERP)	**Client/Server** • Distribution • Planning • Manufacturing (ERP) • Human Resources	**Web Architecture** • Sales Force Automation • Call Center Support • Supply Chain • Analysis
10 – 100s of users	100 – 1000s of users	1000 – 10,000s of users
Internal Focus	Wider Internal Focus	Customers, Suppliers, Partners

By the early 1990s, client/server architectures emerged, adding personal computers (PCs) and sometimes Apple Macintoshes to the networks supported by corporate systems. The number of users grew dramatically, into the thousands, but the focus of the systems remained internal to the enterprise.

The second half of the 1990s brought web architectures that reached outside the enterprise and brought in customers and suppliers, making the supply chain more accessible to the corporate system. Intranets enabled the sales force to keep in better touch with inventory and production, and remote call centers could now capture more sales or give real-time responses to customer inquiries. The number of system users, either direct or indirect, rose to the tens of thousands.

But the new (for the 1990s) web architectures still didn't solve the problem of integrating the systems of supply-chain partners. Suppliers either used the customer's systems or designed their own systems around the needs of the customers, whether or not they served the other needs of the supplier company.[35]

During the 1990s, several paper companies provided their better printing company customers with remote terminals to access the paper companies' order-entry

Figure 1.1
Evolution of business information technology, 1960–2000.

systems. Since few printers wanted to confine themselves to one paper company supplier, it was not unusual to find in some purchasing offices several different makes and models of remote terminals that the printers used to buy paper. The question remained, how can independent systems of trading partners relate closely with each other?

It turns out that companies can relate with their trading partners in several ways, and companies now need to be prepared to support most if not all of the arrangements described in the following sections.

Direct to Consumer

This is the most visible web approach, exemplified by the Gateway Computers model, but now practiced by many companies in imitation. You give the consumer direct access to order-entry and customer service. The customer likes the idea of buying direct from the manufacturer, and, in principle at least, this should result in lower prices for the goods. Customers also interact with other customers online through questionnaires and forms, offering ratings and reviewing goods and services. A further model is the *clicks-and-mortar* approach that takes advantage of well-known retailers' brand names to offer more service and follow-on sales.

One potential problem in this arrangement is that customer service can become a nightmare. Customers demand one-on-one service, even as the number of parties served expands to the tens or hundreds of thousands. By 1999, an idea called *customer relationship management* emerged to plan for this type of mass customization, yet remain self-maintaining systems.[36]

Disintermediation

In this approach, the supply chain disappears completely, and the customer goes directly to the manufacturer's inventory. Farmers' markets offer an example of this approach, wherein the consumer buys from the people who produce the goods. While disintermediation may seem like a worthy goal, it becomes clear that in many industries, intermediaries serve useful purposes and add considerable value to the consumer.[37] As noted earlier in this chapter, e-business puts the onus on intermediaries to add value to the business process, and those that succeed will likely thrive as a result.

Business to Business

As shown earlier, trade between businesses dwarfs the commerce between consumers and businesses. But business-to-business trade comes with its own set of rules and protocols, often varying from one industry to another. In some cases, business must learn the language and requirements of their suppliers, as in the case of small package-delivery services or healthcare claims. However, this arena has proven to be the one that lends itself most to integration through the supply chain; up to now, at least, providing much of the productivity and business process improvements, such as the vertical exchanges discussed previously.

Distributors

Another kind of business-to-business arrangement includes the use of distributors, either for marketing or customer support. Many industries still find it economical to serve end users through a dealer or distributor network. Suppliers may be too small to serve customers in remote locations, or a product may require fast deliveries, as in the case of perishable foods. Using distributors may add to the price, but they add value to the product or service for the end user. Adding another tier to the channel adds more complexity and requires more sophisticated systems in the supply chain; therefore, the services provided by the distributors need to justify these resources needed by the business partners.

References and Affiliates

The web has generated an entire new class of trading partner, the affiliate. This kind of "infomediary" adds a button or logo of the trading partner to the company web site, and then receives a nominal reward for each sale generated through that link.

Multi-Vendor Malls

Taking the modern shopping plaza as its analog, the web has generated another new form of business relationship, the mall. As with the retail Galleria, the multi-vendor mall is a collection of vendors addressing a specific market, although the electronic variety is aimed more often at business than retail customers. A good example of the multi-vendor mall is the E-Mall developed for the U.S. Defense Logistics Agency, which provides Department of Defense procurement offices a literal one-stop shop for non-weapons logistics goods.[38]

Standardizing Information Systems

One can begin to understand how a company's information systems can come under considerable strain, particularly if designed and sized in a previous era. Information systems directors cannot just toss out the older legacy systems, however. They need to make them work under these new conditions. Therefore, any solutions that address e-business need to be prepared to interface to systems created for simpler times.

Here is where trading partners can help. In some industries, notably retail, all parties in the supply chain have agreed to use the manufacturer's item number for tracking inventory or usage throughout the item's lifecycle. In the case of grocery stores, manufacturers, distributors, and retailers use the Universal Product Code (UPC) number to track sales and inventory of products. The manufacturer assigns the number to the product, and it gets bar-coded on the product label, as well as used in master carton and case bar codes.[39] The grocery industry's success shows the possibilities of standardization in an industry and the benefits that can result.

Electronic Data Interchange (EDI): E-Business as We (Used to) Know It

The idea of e-business has been around for a quarter of a century.[40] In the mid-1970s, the UPC bar codes, as described in the preceding section, began to revolutionize the way grocers and manufacturers did business, supplemented in the 1980s by Electronic Data Interchange (EDI). Both technologies are in wide use today. If these technologies have established themselves in the world of business, why do we need the new web-based forms of e-business, such as XML?

Bar codes have become a pervasive technology, but EDI has had considerably less penetration, inhibited in many ways by the overwhelming success of fax and email transmissions. The definition of EDI, according to Accredited Standards Committee X12, the standards body responsible for EDI in North America, is as follows:

> *EDI is the computer-to-computer exchange of business data in standard formats. In EDI, information is organized according to a specified format set by both parties, allowing a "hands off" computer transaction that requires no human intervention or re-keying on either end. The information contained in an EDI transaction set is, for the most part, the same as on a conventionally printed document.*[41]

With EDI, the information exchanged between trading partners is organized into *transaction sets*, as they're called by X12. Transaction sets (called *messages* in international EDI standards and XML specifications) serve as electronic equivalents of hardcopy business documents, and in most cases use the same names, such as purchase order, invoice, shipping notice, or healthcare claim.

EDI itself began in the transportation industry. The Transportation Data Coordinating Committee (TDCC) devised an electronic railroad bill of lading in 1975 and went on to establish a whole suite of electronic documents for rail, motor, ocean, and air freight. Individual companies and industries began developing their own means of exchanging data, which raised the prospect of splintering and conflicting documents that created more work for the users rather than less. The result, in 1979, was the United States Electronic Data Interchange standard, which became accredited under the American National Standards Institute as the X12 committee.[42] X12 incorporated the work of TDCC into its standard in the early 1990s.

The X12 standard had over 300 transaction sets in version 4040, released in December 2000. When the standard first began its development, X12 focused on general business documents such as the invoice. In recent years, however, the standard has released more new transaction sets for individual industries, especially in healthcare.

In 1996, the U.S. Congress passed the Health Insurance Portability and Accountability Act (HIPAA, Public Law 104-91). One of HIPAA's provisions, called *administrative simplification*, requires healthcare providers (health maintenance organizations and hospitals) and insurance companies to use standard electronic documents rather than their own hardcopy forms. In August 2000, the U.S. Department of Health and Human Services issued its rules interpreting the law to specify the X12 standard for these common electronic documents.[43] As a result, healthcare and insurance have become the single largest and fastest-growing part of the X12 Committee.

As Figure 1.2 shows, X12 transaction sets break down into *data segments*, which are collections of related data elements, many of which are interchangeable among transaction sets. This reusable data element is an important feature of EDI that offers opportunities for interoperability among applications.

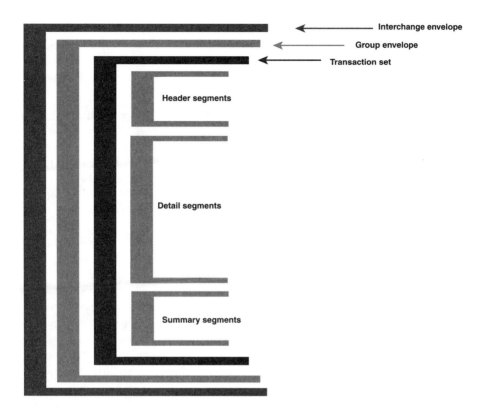

Interchange envelope

Group envelope

Transaction set

Header segments

Detail segments

Summary segments

For example, the X12 date/time data segment found in most transaction sets consists of the following data elements:[44]

- Date/time qualifier, a code indicating the type of date or time, such as date of the transaction or time of delivery
- Date, in CCYYMMDD format
- Time, in 24-hour format
- Time code or zones
- A date/time period format qualifier, indicating the date and time format—various combinations of century, year, month, date, hours, minutes, and seconds
- Date/time period, an expression of one or a range of dates and times

Figure 1.2
Hierarchy of an EDI transmission showing the position of the envelopes, as well as header, detail, and summary segments.

The data elements in the data segments can be either *simple* or *composite* elements. Simple data elements, as the name implies, are single stand-alone parent items. The date/time elements just listed are simple data elements.

Composite data elements are groups of related elements, but not with enough reason to stand alone as parent data segments. For example, a measurement element in X12 consists of related sub-elements for unit of measure and tolerances, among others. Elements can come in various types, including identifier elements consisting of codes. Some of these code lists have become voluminous as increasing numbers of industries add their own special terminologies. Code lists are quintessential to the EDI process. Each industry defines its own code lists to describe the context of a particular parent segment and its children. Understanding the context of use is therefore key to unscrambling the particular implementation of an EDI transaction, such as a purchase order, which is used across every industry and therefore has myriad flavors driven off code-list values.

Process improvements have resulted in significant productivity improvements.

Many of the companies that have successfully implemented EDI have realized significant benefits, particularly over previous use of hardcopy forms. Using forms requires people—usually many people—to handle and input the data into company systems, which is painfully slow and invariably results in errors. Not only does EDI reduce or eliminate this direct overhead, it encourages companies to use the data captured electronically to improve business processes.[45]

Some of these process improvements have resulted in significant productivity improvements. A practice called *evaluated receipts settlements (ERS)* is a good example. ERS lets trading partners do business without an invoice. Perhaps cutting out one document doesn't seem like an earthshaking achievement, but doing without an invoice means you can also use in much better ways the many people processing the documents on either end of the partnership.

ERS works where the trading partners use EDI. If the electronic purchase order provides price and desired quantity, the shipping notice provides the items shipped, and a receiving advice offers the goods accepted into inventory, an invoice (with all of the same data) becomes redundant. The receiving staff needs the authority to inspect the goods and check the received shipment against the shipping notice and purchase order; if everything matches, they authorize payment to the vendor. This is a process now used in the steel industry, for example.[46]

In many other industries, suppliers manage the inventories for their major customers. The suppliers keep close tabs on inventory levels and provide replenishment quantities when they reach predefined levels. Here again, EDI, usually with bar codes on items, keeps track of inventory levels. In some trading partnerships, the companies establish blanket purchase orders from which the buyer issues releases. The blanket order specifies the basic terms, items covered, quantity limits, locations, and prices. Agreeing to these conditions in advance and referencing them in the release keeps the actual data exchanged to a minimum.

Kodak Canada began a vendor-managed inventory program with Wal-Mart's stores in Canada, in what Kodak calls *co-managed inventories*. Kodak and Wal-Mart jointly forecast future sales and track demand levels, which reduces the number of individual orders placed. The program enables Kodak to get a better idea of Wal-Mart's needs and provide better service.[47]

Experience with process improvements such as ERS and vendor-managed inventories led Wal-Mart and other companies in the retail industry to begin work on a more comprehensive approach to squeeze as much lagging inventory as possible from the supply chain. This approach, called *Collaborative Planning, Forecasting, and Replenishment (CPFR)*, recognized that eliminating inventories at the retail level alone would not solve the problem of dislocations in the supply chain. In fact, it often forced the manufacturers or distributors to stockpile inventories to be prepared for sudden demands from the retailers. These stockpiles just moved the problem upstream, and the costs for this stockpiling would eventually find their way back to the retailer.

The CPFR project discovered that by sharing information on production and promotional plans early in the process, as well as detailed sales forecasts that reflect those plans, all parties in the supply chain can better coordinate their activities, reducing expensive inventories and costs. In response to this need for better planning and forecasting data, X12 developed the Planning Schedule with Release Capability transaction set, which enables the trading partners to exchange forecasts for specified periods of time (weeks, months, quarters). It also allows for the most current period to act as a blanket order release—refer to the earlier discussion of vendor-managed inventories—that eliminates the need for a separate purchase order.[48]

CPFR started with pilot tests in 1997, but has started attracting more attention. A survey conducted for the Voluntary Inter-industry Commerce Standards Association in late 1999 and early 2000 found more than 100 companies participating in the planning, design, or actual conduct of CPFR programs with their trading partners. Over half of the retailers plan to roll out CPFR to 25 or more trading partners within the next two years. About a quarter of the respondents have a CPFR pilot underway or planned in the next six months. Those that have started pilot projects report some impressive results:[49]

- An 80% increase in business with CPFR trading partners
- A $9 million increase in combined total sales
- Simultaneous sales growth and inventory reductions of at least 10%
- Improved fill rates with less inventory
- A 100% service level with almost 40 inventory turns a year

If EDI provides such significant benefits, why isn't it used more widely in business? Rachel Foerster, an EDI veteran and leading consultant in e-business, cites statistics showing that 95% of the Fortune 1000 companies use EDI, but only 5% of smaller enterprises.[50] The reasons indicated by Foerster and others for this lack of penetration in small business are discussed below.

Companies trying to implement EDI have run into a number of obstacles, the greatest being the high cost of systems and the extended times needed to integrate EDI into a company's overall business operations. EDI software rarely costs under $1,000 and often comes with annual maintenance fees. These high prices result from the complexity of EDI standards; see for example the earlier discussion of dates in EDI and the six different data elements needed for their representation in an EDI message. In its defense, the X12 standard covers all industries using EDI, and as a result the standard needs the flexibility to represent the wide array of business conditions. But this flexibility comes at a cost, which finds its way into the price tags for EDI products or services.

The X12 standard also changes every year. Each year, X12 adds new transaction sets, as well as additions to code lists and changes to data segments and elements. These standards changes mean that the software supporting the standards also needs to change, which requires annual updates and maintenance fees.

Because the X12 standard needs to cover all industries using EDI and because it changes every year, industry groups have stepped in to write implementation guides for their member companies. These implementation guides usually pick out the several transaction sets needed by trading partners in those industries, as well as the segments, elements, and codes needed for those exchanges. The industry guidelines also last for a few years, which gives companies some assurance of stability that enables them to develop EDI systems. But the implementation guidelines add more levels to the learning curve needed to get started, as well as increased costs to the already high price for standards, software, and networks.[51]

Another problem with using EDI is the lack of integration with a company's other business systems. EDI transactions use a neutral and efficient syntax, but one that doesn't mesh with database languages used in business. Since EDI transactions go from one trading partner's mailbox to another, systems at either end of the exchange need to translate the data to and from their native formats into the EDI syntax. The transactions carry only the data, with no instructions or routines to perform these integration steps. It's not unusual to have some companies, particularly smaller companies, finding it more economical to print and re-key the EDI data into their systems, rather than spending money or time on software development.

If companies do business internationally, they run into still another problem, one that readers may have already surmised. Two sets of EDI standards have emerged, the X12 standard for North America and the UN/EDIFACT standard for elsewhere in the world.[52] While the two standards have a similar basic design, they're not identical, and companies in the international marketplace exchanging EDI messages must support both standards, adding even further to the cost and complexity.

The accumulated effect of these obstacles is to put the whole idea of EDI out of reach of smaller companies. According to the U.S. Census Bureau's 1997 Census of U.S. Business (the latest year with available statistics), companies with 20 or more employees numbered 583,277 out of a total of 5,541,918 firms, or 10.5% of the total. Those with 500 or more employees, the traditional cutoff between larger companies and small or medium-size companies, numbered 16,079, or barely 0.3% of the total.[53]

Smaller companies, however, appear primed and ready for e-business (see Figure 1.3). According to IDC, in April 2000 less than a quarter (23.3%) of small businesses in the U.S. had web sites hosted by an Internet service provider, spending nearly $20 billion to develop and maintain a presence on the web. IDC also expects the number of small businesses engaging in business over the web to grow from about 400,000 in 1998 to almost 2.8 million by 2003, an annual increase of 47%. IDC says that "…the major distinguishing feature of small businesses that have advanced down the e-commerce track is their attitude toward technology. These small businesses already have in place much of the infrastructure to support e-commerce."[54]

What happens when small companies try to do business with EDI? A case study provides an illustration. A few years ago, Arctic Fisheries Ltd., an importer of fish and seafood from Iceland that serves stores and restaurants across the U.S., received a request from a leading supermarket chain in upstate New York—a potential major customer—to exchange purchase orders and invoices with EDI. Arctic Fisheries has nine employees, with the company's vice president doubling as the systems manager.

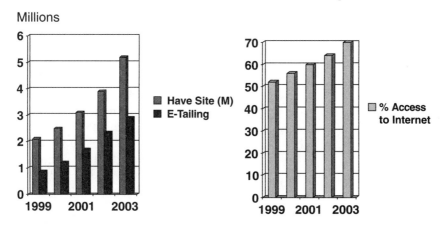

USA – Small Business Internet Adoption

Source: IDC 1999 Small Business Survey

The supermarket chain used its own flavor of X12 and offered to sell its client software for $500, a cost that Arctic Fisheries found difficult to swallow for supporting one customer; an overly aggressive software vendor didn't help the situation, either. After Arctic Fisheries asked to continue sending hardcopy

Figure 1.3
Small business Internet adoption in the U.S.

documents, the chain hit Arctic Fisheries with a $50 fine for each transaction, a price Arctic Fisheries was reluctantly willing to pay. Michael Kotok, the vice president of the company, says, "I personally felt that at the time, we would be better off waiting for an alternative on the Net that would have been no/low cost." Arctic Fisheries and the supermarket chain no longer do business, but not as a function of the EDI issue.[55]

Nonetheless, 25 years of EDI transactions offers some lessons that any web-based e-business technology like XML would be well advised to heed, as described in the following sections.

Aim to Improve the Business Process

Companies exchange data—including EDI data— for a reason, and more often than not those reasons involve improving the way business is conducted. If you can tie the time and effort of building e-business systems into innovations such as vendor-managed inventories, the payoff gets magnified many times over.

Sweat the Details

The more detail you can include with business messages, the more valuable the data will be to your trading partners. As seen with CPFR, identifying individual products down to a fine level of granularity allows for better planning and forecasting data. If a company is now identifying product at the skid level, try identifying cartons on the skids. If it gives you another few days of inventory before restocking and more turns, it's well worth the effort.

Aim for Interoperability

Include all of your business partners in the solution, including the sometimes invisible partners such as transportation companies. The OpenTravel Alliance has begun defining a travel customer's needs to include all the various services needed on a journey, in addition to the traditional airlines, hotels, and car rentals. Pet owners, for example, often need kennel services for their pets when they travel. Look at the potential business opportunity for enterprising travel services to include these auxiliary services in their package of services to travelers.

Link to Other Technologies

Consider the success that EDI has had in inventory control when combined with bar codes. Related emerging technologies, such as *biometrics* (authentication based on human physical characteristics), smart cards, and radio frequency technology have yet to be integrated on any scale with e-business. Again, great potential opportunities await the enterprising businesses that can make it happen.[56]

Endnotes

[1] We use the word *company* in this book to mean any entity—corporation, limited partnership, government agency, or not-for-profit organization—established to provide goods or services.

[2] Seeing the handwriting on the wall, the author closed the export service in the early 1990s.

[3] Thomas L. Friedman, *The Lexus and the Olive Tree* (New York: Farrar Straus Giroux, 1999), p. 45.

[4] Alan Kotok and Ralph Lyman, *Print Communications and the Electronic Media Challenge* (Plainview, NY: Jelmar Publishing, 1997), pp. 91–96.

[5] Kotok and Lyman, p. 97.

[6] For more about data mining, see the KDNuggets site at `www.kdnuggets.com/`.

[7] Friedman, pp. 16–18.

[8] CNN.com, "It's Official: Teamsters End UPS Strike," 20 August 1997. See `www.cnn.com/US/9708/20/ups.update.early/`.

[9] InformationWeek Online, "AMR to Spin Off Sabre," 14 December 1999. See `www.informationweek.com/story/IWK19991214S0004`.

[10] Nick Lanyon and Alan Kotok, Open Travel Alliance White Paper, version 2.0, February 2000, pp. 11–12. See `www.opentravel.org/opentravel/docs/OTA_WhitePaper2.pdf`.

[11] A full discussion of this complex subject goes well beyond the scope of this book. See the Antitrust Policy web site at `www.antitrust.org/` for more resources on this topic.

[12] Adam Dell, "Meeting Supplier Demand," *Business 2.0*, March 2000. See `www.impactvp.com/press/articles/b2_03_13_00.html`.

[13] IDC, "Exchanges Under Scrutiny," *eBusiness Trends* no. 14, 6 July 2000.

[14] Covisint news releases, 11 September and 26 September 2000.

[15] "Old-Line Companies Are Transforming the Rusty Supply Chain," *Mercer Management Briefs*, 2nd quarter 2000, www.mercermc.com/Press/NewsReleases/Briefs00/valuenets-2q00.html.

[16] Deb Navas, "Cutting Edge CGM," *ID Systems*, September 2000, p. 22.

[17] See the Uniform Code Council web site at www.uc-council.org/ for more information on acquiring a UPC company code.

[18] See www.uccnet.org/.

[19] See John Robertson, "Steel Identification Is Moving Toward Bar Codes," www.infosight.com/wp-sibc.htm, for a discussion of steel industry bar codes, and www2.gca.org/store/product.asp?id=219 for paper industry bar codes.

[20] Peter Fingar, Harsha Kumar, and Tarun Sharma, *Enterprise E-Commerce* (Meghan-Kiffer Press, January 2000). Reproduced with permission.

[21] Forrester Research, "B2B Auctions Go Beyond Price," May 2000. See www.forrester.com/ER/Baseline/QuickView/0,1338,9306,00.html.

[22] Friedman, pp. 93–95.

[23] PriceWaterhouseCoopers, "Venture Capital Transcends Stock Market, Q2 Investments Hit Another Record High of $19.5 Billion," *MoneyTree*, Highlights Q2 2000. See www.pwcmoneytree.com/highlights.asp.

[24] Wayne Rash, "Plot a Sound Internet Strategy and Investment Will Soon Follow," InternetWeek Online, 8 May 2000. See www.internetwk.com/columns00/rash050800.htm.

[25] Boston Consulting Group, "U.S. Business-to-Business E-Commerce to Reach $4.8 Trillion in 2004." See www.bcg.com/media_center/media_press_release_subpage22.asp.

[26] Thanks to Alice Cronquist, EDI Systems Manager of Compaq Computers, for this information.

[27] Forrester Research, "eMarketplaces Boost B2B Trade," February 2000. See www.forrester.com/ER/Research/Report/0,1338,8919,FF.html.

[28] Gartner Group, "Worldwide Business-to-Business Internet Commerce to Reach $8.5 Trillion in 2005," 13 March 2001. See `www4.gartner.com/5_about/press_room/pr20010313a.html`.

[29] Boston Consulting Group, "U.S. Business-to-Business E-Commerce to Reach $4.8 Trillion in 2004," 6 September 2000. See `www.bcg.com/media_center/media_press_release_subpage22.asp`.

[30] Ken Popovich for eWEEK, February 6, 2001 10:56 AM ET. See `www.eweek.com/a/pcwt0102063/2682559/`.

[31] Boston Consulting Group, "Online Retail Market in North America to Reach $65 Billion in 2001," 2 May 2001. See `www.bcg.com/media_center/media_press_release_subpage44.asp`.

[32] Jupiter Communications, "Jupiter: US Internet B-to-B Trade Soars to $6 Trillion in 2005, Businesses Must Invest in Multiple Selling Models or Risk Market Share," 26 June 2000. See `www.jup.com/company/pressrelease.jsp?doc=pr000626`.

[33] IDC, "Forget B2C, B2B Is the Real Driver of eCommerce in Europe," 31 July 2000. See `www.idcresearch.com/emea/press/PR/EIN073100PR.stm`.

[34] David R.R. Webber, "Practical ebXML." Presentation to XML World, Boston, Massachusetts, 5 September 2000.

[35] Webber, XML World, 5 September 2000.

[36] For an excellent discussion of CRM, see a white paper by Tony Zingale, "The Death of Customer Satisfaction— CRM in the Internet Age," with links to more resources on the subject, at `http://zingale.crmproject.com/`.

[37] Dylan Tweney, "Red Gorilla Plays Monkey in the Middle," *eCompany Now*, 31 August 2000, `www.ecompanynow.com/articles/web/1,1653,7525,00.html`.

[38] The DLA E-Mall web site is `https://www.emallmom01.dla.mil/scripts/default.asp`.

[39] See `www.uc-council.org/` for more information about UPC bar codes.

[40] In this section, we discuss EDI mainly from the North American standpoint, focusing on the X12 standard used in the U.S. and Canada. The principles behind EDI in North America apply equally to its practice elsewhere in the world.

[41] ASC X12, "What is EDI?" See www.x12.org/x12org/about/index.html?whatis.html.

[42] Computer Advocacy Inc., "EDI—Some History." See www.computeradvocacy.com/edi/history.htm.

[43] For the text of the final rules and more information about the HIPAA law, see the Department of Health and Human Services' HIPAA web site at http://aspe.os.dhhs.gov/admnsimp/.

[44] Alan Kotok, "XML and EDI: Lessons Learned and Baggage to Leave Behind," XML.com, 4 August 1999. See www.xml.com/pub/1999/08/edi/index.html.

[45] Alan Kotok, "XML for Business Data—the Next Step for the Internet or a Technology Out of Control?" UN Economic Commission for Europe, World Markets Research Centre (U.K.), 22 June 2000, pp. 199–201.

[46] AISI/OP Council. "Recommended Evaluated Receipts Settlement (ERS) Process. Standard Business Practices Guideline for Trade Between Steel Producers, Outside Processors and Warehouses," November 1998. See www.steel.org/op/Erssop4.htm.

[47] "About Kodak Canada, Vendor Managed Inventory." See www.kodak.com/country/CA/en/corp/engVendorManagedInventory.shtml.

[48] "CPFR Introduction." See www.cpfr.org/Intro.html.

[49] Industry Directions Inc. and Synchra Systems Inc., "The Next Wave of Supply Chain Advantage: Collaborative Planning, Forecasting, and Replenishment," April 2000, pp. 2–3.

[50] Rachel Foerster, "The Next Generation EC/EDI Standards," *The Executive Summary,* January 1999. See www.rfa-edi.com/00-edi.htm.

[51] The systems manager for a publishing company told one of the authors that after she discovered the increasing numbers of books, standards, guidelines, and consultants needed to do EDI, she felt like Groucho Marx in the classic scene in the film "A Day at the Races," in which Chico sells Groucho an entire set of reference books to make a bet on a horse race. Read the film dialogue for yourself at www.filmsite.org/daya.html.

[52] See www.unece.org/cefact/ for more information about the UN/EDIFACT standard.

[53] U.S. Census Bureau, "Statistics About Small Business and Large Business from the U.S. Census Bureau." See `www.census.gov/epcd/www/smallbus.html`.

[54] IDC, "Small Businesses Are Hip," eBusiness Trends, 7 September 2000. See `www.idc.com/ebusinesstrends/ebt20000907home.stm`.

[55] Correspondence with Michael Kotok, 23–25 September 2000. Arctic Fisheries Inc. (`www.arcticfisheries.com/`) is owned by Mark Kotok, brother of the co-author. Michael Kotok is the vice president and nephew of the co-author.

[56] Kotok, "XML and EDI: Lessons Learned and Baggage to Leave Behind."

Chapter 2

ebXML in a Nutshell

For ebXML to meet the business needs and conditions described in Chapter 1, "There's No Business Like E-Business," it had to spell out a series of requirements to directly address those needs and conditions, and then build the actual technical specifications keyed to these requirements. In this chapter, we outline both ebXML's requirements and technology, combined as the basis of understanding for a more technically detailed treatment of these topics in Chapter 6, "Business Requirements for ebXML," and Chapter 8, "ebXML Technical Architecture."

Vision and Scope

The ebXML initiative seeks to provide a common way to electronically exchange business data expressed in XML (or EDI, graphic images, or other formats), from one computer application to another, or between people and computers. This ambitious goal is summed up in the ebXML requirements specification as, "to provide an...open technical framework to enable XML to be utilized in a consistent and uniform manner for the exchange of electronic business (eb) data in application to application, application to human, and human to application environments—thus creating a single electronic global market™."[1]

In its vision statement, ebXML seeks to develop "A single set of internationally agreed upon technical specifications that consist of common XML semantics and related document structures to facilitate global trade." The vision also requires that any specifications comply with World Wide Web Consortium (W3C) Recommendations.[2] And whenever possible the specifications need to provide a migration path from previous specifications and standards involving EDI or other XML vocabularies.

The scope of the initiative covers businesses of all sizes, from the largest global enterprises to medium-size and smaller companies. However, the focus on smaller businesses provides greatest opportunities for ebXML, and the designers of the specifications kept those requirements paramount during the development period. Likewise, ebXML messages need to be open and available to any companies or industries seeking interoperability with trading partners and across industries.[3]

ebXML encourages companies to develop enduring solutions rather than quick fixes.

The general principles behind ebXML call for a single uniform interoperable base to reduce the spread of incompatible XML business vocabularies. Since the emergence of XML, literally hundreds of specialized XML vocabularies have been created to serve single industries or even single companies, as well as specific business functions. In a related objective, ebXML also encourages companies to develop more enduring solutions that improve business processes, rather than concentrating on continual quick fixes.

Another key principle is to keep deployment costs to businesses to a minimum, with the goal of plug-and-play ebXML-compatible software. Systems based on ebXML should avoid imposing conditions that require companies to invest in proprietary software to exchange messages. Programs compatible with ebXML must work with each other, no questions asked. Showing its international nature, ebXML must be a global specification and support multiple languages.[4]

Software Processes, Puzzles, and Pyramids

Before introducing the ebXML architecture and the associated process flow, we need to see how this architecture and process flow complement today's business systems. Of course, from a user's perspective, we would hope that ebXML implementations would only need to provide a control panel or dashboard and hide all the internal software "wiring" underneath. However, we need to introduce important concepts to help you understand the overall architecture of ebXML.

From a software perspective, ebXML doesn't present any new and previously undiscovered system. Any of the larger companies participating in the ebXML work could have developed the functionality provided by ebXML, and in fact some tried, such as Hewlett-Packard and its "e-Speak" work (see www.hp.com/espeak). However, each of these efforts to create an overall e-business architecture represents just one company's creation of a proprietary solution to solve some immediate and specific need. What sets ebXML apart is its goal from the beginning to write a global standard designed to work across vendors' products, and therefore provide a methodology and technology independent of any particular supplier's solutions.

To achieve this goal, ebXML based its development on commonly held software principles and a blend of emerging good business practices and design ideas. One of these basic principles is businesspeople expressing their needs, relationships, and operations in strictly business terms, and letting the technology implement from there. ebXML lets businesses capture and preserve business knowledge, but express it directly as technology, which makes it stand out among most e-business standards.

Figure 2.1 shows how business product or service interactions can be expressed in real-world business terms. Relating these terms directly to the software development process can lead to the accurate representation of those business needs in real working software. The terms we develop here are explicitly those used by ebXML itself, and we present more detailed discussions of these terms later in the chapter. We introduce the terms here to show how they relate to each other, and more specifically their use in actual business situations.

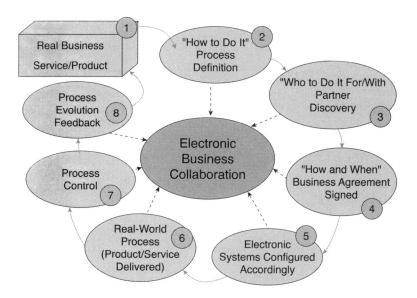

Figure 2.1
Business as a set of steps.

The numbering in the diagram represents the sequence in which this scenario unfolds, starting with step 1, where the actual product, service, or product/service combination is defined by the company providing it, and ending up at step 8. At that point, the overall process starts again, using feedback from real-world implementation, market forces, and customer demands.

From Figure 2.1, we can analyze each step, and, as ebXML has done, represent in the specifications those pieces that relate to each step. These steps then become the business processes that describe in detail each of the many pieces that go into making electronic business work. At this point, we still use

generic terms and haven't yet descended too far
down into the layers of systems engineering. Figure
2.2 shows how these pieces relate to a physical business product or service system model.

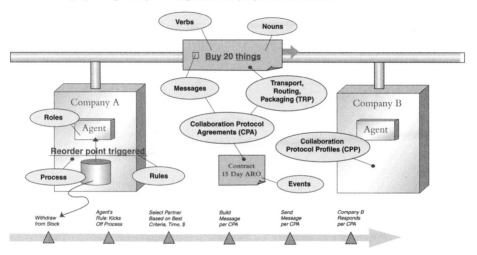

The bottom of the diagram shows a timeline with
explicit events that happen during the process. This is
not a complete set of all events, but a fragment of an
overall timeline to show the processes conceptually.
The boxes marked *Agent* represent some software
component acting in a predetermined role on behalf
of the company to direct and orchestrate the electronic execution of the physical business process. The
pipes along the top connecting Company A and
Company B represent the Internet network that con-
trols the delivery of messages by the transport, routing, and packaging software components.

Next we can structure these pieces and group them
together by purpose. In the ebXML work, this step
was critical to providing the overall technical architecture. Notice that ebXML could not define architectures for every conceivable business process, but
instead focused on the most common repeatable and
sustainable model on which to build global electronic

Figure 2.2
Business language and
processes.

business. Figure 2.3 therefore shows how these items can be grouped logically, which then form the basis of the ebXML methodology.

Next, ebXML must also provide a means to classify, associate, and manage these items through the use of a common dictionary registry. It needs as well a labeling scheme to provide a consistent global base of these terms, and can therefore ensure consistent interpretation and interoperability across geographic and industry boundaries (see our later discussion of Bizcodes, used much like bar codes for this purpose).

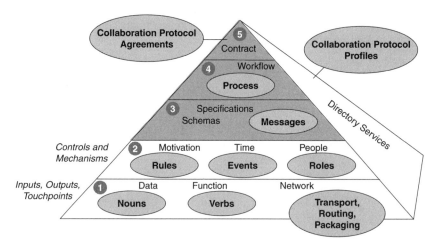

Artifacts Are Our Building Blocks for Communication

Figure 2.3
Business language artifacts.

The use of the pyramid shows how an overall electronic business collaboration is structured and fits together. Layer 1 of the pyramid contains the pieces of data needed to deliver information electronically between businesses. Layer 2 has the control mechanisms. In Layer 3, the information itself is grouped and organized into discrete messages that relate to the overall workflow and business process steps in Layer 4. The top layer has the business contract that governs the interactions between the parties and ultimately defines how the messages are delivered.

ebXML Process Flow

We now move from the generic definitions in the previous section to the specific model that ebXML has adopted for the foundation of its first specifications. Figure 2.4 provides a view of the overall ebXML approach, showing how two companies with no previous contact first establish a relationship and then begin exchanging e-business data, using the automated flow and sequence of interactions that ebXML prescribes.

As a preliminary step in Figure 2.4, notice that an industry must collect its business processes, scenarios, and company business profiles, and make them available through an industry ebXML registry. Company A is shown, and typically Company A has business software it has developed. Thus Company A, in planning to do business with other firms in this industry, requests these current and relevant specifications (step 1). Company A then acquires corresponding packaged software components or builds any additional features needed in the company's internal systems to accommodate these requirements (step 2). For example, a company wanting to sell consumable items to most hospitals will need to have product identifiers that meet the requirements of the Health Industry Bar Code specification and the systems to generate those bar codes.

After making any adjustments needed in its own business systems, Company A files the details about its systems into the industry registry using an ebXML-standard *collaboration protocol profile* (*CPP*), an XML document that provides a description of its ability to do e-business (step 3). Company A only needs to perform steps 1–3 once to do business in the industry, although it will need to update its capabilities in the company profile as the capabilities develop further.

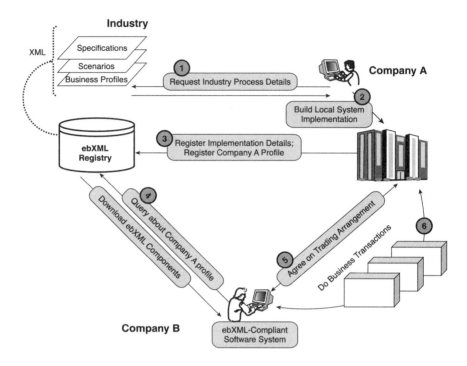

Figure 2.4
ebXML process flow, from zero to doing e-business.[5]

Next, Company A and Company B discover each other's capabilities, decide to become business partners, and develop a business partner relationship. With its ebXML-enabled system, Company B queries the registry and verifies the capabilities of Company A's collaboration protocol profile (step 4). The two companies work out the details of a relationship, including a *collaboration protocol agreement* (*CPA*)—an XML document that spells out the technical aspects of the relationship (step 5). Once this arrangement is in place, the two companies can begin exchanging ebXML data, using transactions that drive the actual business process, shown as step 6 in the figure.

Looking at this process more closely uncovers three phases for companies to use ebXML: implementation, discovery, and runtime.

1. The *implementation phase* covers the steps needed to get the company's relevant applications compliant with ebXML (portrayed in steps 1–3 in Figure 2.4). Companies request—from the appropriate registry—the

ebXML specifications and the business process models for that industry, along with the industry vocabulary and associated business objects. The industry vocabulary includes what ebXML calls *core components*, which provide the business terms (the "nouns" and "verbs") used across industries and provide interoperability with lines of business outside the industry. In this phase, companies also file their collaboration protocol profiles with the registries.

2. The *discovery phase* covers discovery of e-business capabilities and completion of the collaboration protocol agreement. The collaboration protocol profiles describe potential partners' technical capabilities, as well as the business processes and scenarios they support. In Figure 2.4, step 4 shows this process, which provides important details that companies need before deciding on their trading arrangements. Step 5 covers the actual agreement to establish technical aspects of the business relationship.

3. In the *runtime phase*, companies—or, more accurately, the company systems—run the electronic business processing by exchanging messages and data compliant with ebXML, as portrayed in step 6 in Figure 2.4. In the diagram, the messages go directly from one company system to another, but they can also include third parties, such as financial institutions or web-based services such as industry exchanges that provide message transfers and routing.[6]

A Look at the ebXML Technical Architecture

To achieve the ambitious goals of ebXML and thus perform the steps in Figure 2.4 and the cases in Chapter 3, "ebXML at Work," ebXML needs a robust, yet flexible architecture. This overall design needs to take advantage of the distributed nature of the web, capture specific definitions of business processes, encourage interoperability through common core components, and provide a way for companies to interact with each other, even if they have never done business before. Later in the book, we describe these business requirements more fully, but as already described in Chapter 1, the needs of business (not just e-business) demand that they be met.

The ebXML technology consists of the following major features:

- Definition of *business processes* by capturing the business functions and the parties, message exchanges, terminology, and data elements representing business practices for industries.

- Creation of *core components* that identify common business terms, nouns, and concepts and give them a neutral name and unique identifier. With core components, different industries can relate their own terms and thus offer a way for companies in different industries to interact with each other.

- Establishment of machine-readable *company profiles* capturing capabilities of companies to support various industry processes and the technical features of their e-business systems. These profiles become the basis of *technical agreements* between companies to exchange e-business messages, as part of more comprehensive physical trading arrangements.

- A system of distributed standard *registries* that most companies will use to get started in ebXML, and that provide indexed access to *repositories* of industry processes, messages, and business data, as well as company profiles with their technical capabilities to exchange e-business messages.

- A standard *message package* that allows for transporting ebXML data over the web, email, or file transfers; allows for acknowledgments and recovery if problems occur; and provides for various levels of secure transmissions if the business needs demand them.

The following sections discuss each of these features in more detail.

Business Processes and Objects

The business ideas and knowledge in ebXML are expressed in the business process models that describe the activities and interactions among businesses and in associated business terms. These processes define the overall business services and individual messages exchanged, as well as the data contained in the messages. Some processes may be nearly identical from one industry to the next; for example, financial reporting functions for publicly traded companies. For most industries, however, business processes will vary to reflect the peculiarities of the industry. For example, the RosettaNet Partner Interface Processes (PIPs) described in Chapter 5, "The Road Toward ebXML," include detailed supply-chain processes that undoubtedly resemble supply-chain interactions in other industries. However, the PIPs for transactions specifically involving electronic components contain items that are likely to be unique to that business sector.

As shown by the scenario in Figure 2.4 in the preceding section, business processes contain the models of the interactions describing the services shared among trading partners. They identify the trading partners and their roles in the interactions, detail the associated messages exchanged among trading partners, including the data content within such messages, and indicate the sequence of the messages (called *choreographies*).

The business processes used in ebXML can be captured as XML documents or represented in the UN's modeling methodology, which uses the *Unified Modeling Language (UML)* described further in Chapters 5 and 8. UML provides an alternate visual way to represent and portray the connections of the real-world business processes to the XML code exchanged among trading partners. This ability to connect the business process directly to the technology gives the ebXML specifications a great deal of power.[7]

Because ebXML provides the ability to consistently describe and apply these processes and transactions, businesses will probably learn to reuse them in similar situations as the opportunities arise. An example is a credit card billing process using one of the major credit card companies, which a company can extend to other credit card processors.

UML and other modeling techniques provide for a detailed analysis and description of business processes and objects. This extends down to the level of individual data elements expressed in messages exchanged between trading partners, and the related information objects needed to deliver the desired services.

> *Core components provide a way for the various industries to continue using their own terms in business messages, yet relate them to common business processes and neutral identifiers provided by ebXML.*

Note that ebXML doesn't require the use of UML or any formal modeling methods for this purpose. Industries or organizations may derive simple business process definitions by creating the XML structures and content directly from existing established business processes. For example, existing EDI transaction-based business processes that are documented and well known can be directly rendered as ebXML business process definitions in XML, and then stored in an ebXML registry for access and use.

Core Components

As described in Chapter 1, the need for companies to do business in multiple industries has become an important requirement of any e-business technology. Therefore, ebXML gives special attention to business objects that appear in multiple business domains, and calls the common reusable data items that cut across many industries *core components*. It is these core components that help ebXML achieve much of its interoperability.

To illustrate the use of core components, consider how different businesses and industries use different terminology to represent the same idea, and in some cases even the same person. Imagine a typical traveler named Xerxes Melb. Surrendering his boarding pass at the gate and entering the plane, Mr. Melb is called a *passenger*. Buying a gift at a retail outlet within minutes of landing, he becomes a *customer*. When he sends the gift home with a package-delivery service, he's a *shipper*, with the help of a hotel concierge who calls Mr. Melb a *guest*. Each time, this same individual, with the same set of identification data (street address, telephone, email), may pay for these items with the same credit card.

Thus, the same person engages in several different transactions with several different businesses, and with much the same kind of data, but is called by a different name each time *based on the business context*. A common set of data items can help bridge these semantic hurdles when the various processes and messages need to interact with each other. Yet each industry still talks in its own language, and it would be highly unrealistic to expect industries to change. Core components provide a way for the various industries to continue using their own terms in business messages, yet relate them to common business processes and neutral identifiers provided by ebXML. As long as trading partners can relate their own terminology to neutral ebXML syntax, businesses have a basis for achieving interoperability.[8]

An important feature of core components is the context in which they are used. One important type of context is the role a company plays in a business process. In a supply chain, a wholesaler will purchase goods from a manufacturer, and thus be a buyer in one set of messages. But that same company will act as a supplier to retailers, selling the very same goods (although in smaller quantities) in another set of messages. The wholesaler company and the goods involved stay the same, but the role in the process significantly changes the representation of that wholesaler, as viewed by the manufacturer and retailer.

In ebXML, the context for core components can be defined in various ways. In some cases, such as this example, the business domain can provide the context. In other cases, the context can be more complex, with the structure of components nested within other components, either sharing a context or having different contexts.

Core components can exist as individual pieces of data or be linked together in combinations. For example, a clock time and time zone together make up a time component. Note how the time zone also provides a context for the clock time. A data item with a value of 02:25:30 means something much different when followed by GMT or EST than when it measures a runner's time in a marathon. Aggregate components can take on more complex forms, depending on the relationships of the basic components to each other.[9]

Figure 2.5 shows how such core components are assembled to deliver the business transactional information required for ebXML business processes.

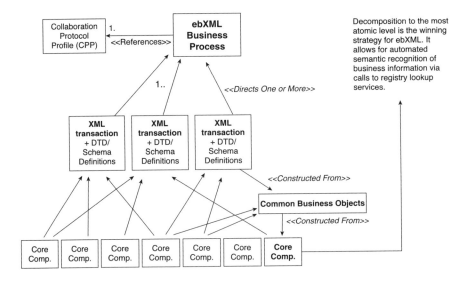

Decomposition to the most atomic level is the winning strategy for ebXML. It allows for automated semantic recognition of business information via calls to registry lookup services.

Figure 2.5
Assembling ebXML content using core components.

Another benefit of the neutral labeling and identification of commonly used quantities as core components is the ability to create basic transactions and map data between industry domains. The term *basic* (or *lightweight*) *transactions* refers to the actual XML syntax used in creating the information structures that are exchanged electronically between businesses; they don't contain any unnecessary markup details. In fact, the message details are optimized by using reference codes that uniquely identify each individual piece of information in the transaction.

ebXML calls these reference codes *Universal Identifier* (*UID*) references, and relates them to pieces of business information about a product or service. Another non-technical term for this idea is *Bizcodes*. In Figure 2.6, we see how a pair of pliers is described in an ebXML catalogue transaction that a customer receives from a supplier. Each piece of information about the pliers has a UID associated with it, as a Bizcode. Note that suppliers of these kinds of items often use bar codes in a similar way to identify the product itself.

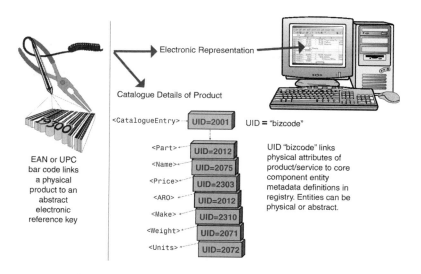

Electronic Representation

Catalogue Details of Product

EAN or UPC bar code links a physical product to an abstract electronic reference key

`<CatalogueEntry>` → UID=2001

`<Part>` → UID=2012
`<Name>` → UID=2075
`<Price>` → UID=2303
`<ARO>` → UID=2012
`<Make>` → UID=2310
`<Weight>` → UID=2071
`<Units>` → UID=2072

UID = "bizcode"

UID "bizcode" links physical attributes of product/service to core component entity metadata definitions in registry. Entities can be physical or abstract.

Because each piece of information is labeled in this way, companies can consistently and accurately exchange information across industry domains. For example, an accounting system may generically refer to a price as *Item Price*, while the catalogue system may refer to various prices as *Tools Price*, *Parts Price*, or *Product Price*. Using the UID reference system allows the associations between equivalent items to be determined and implemented by software processes (see Figure 2.7 for an example). The ebXML registry services (described in more detail in the later section "Registries and Repositories") provide the means for lookups by software of such definitions that are

Figure 2.6

Labeling product information using UID descriptors.

stored into the registry itself, using the UID as a unique reference key. A further important note here is that by using the registry in this way, ebXML greatly simplifies the process of maintenance and updating the business semantics about information content when things inevitably change.

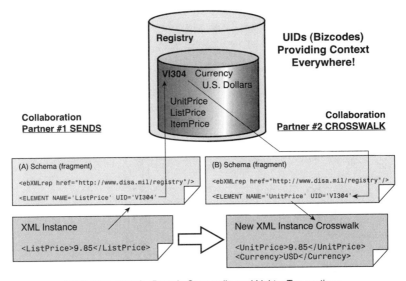

ebXML UIDs Allow for Domain Crosswalks and Lighter Transactions

Figure 2.7
Cross-referencing data between industry domains with information content.

Now that we've described how core components are used to create units of business information and then referenced in XML-based business transactions, we're ready to proceed to the next piece of the overall ebXML architecture.

Trading Partner Profiles and Agreements

Before companies can do business, they need to understand the rules under which the parties interact with each other. The discussion of EDI in Chapter 5 outlines how trading partners need these agreements to spell out responsibilities, provide the common legal boilerplate language to which the parties can refer, and clear up any misunderstandings before the messages start moving. These same functions appear in ebXML, only ebXML automates the technical aspects of the overall agreement, in an XML document called the *collaboration protocol agreement* (*CPA*).

In ebXML, each company publishes a *collaboration protocol profile* (*CPP*) that contains a basic description of its capabilities in terms of the ebXML business processes it supports, along with details about its e-business system's points of access and technologies. For companies that haven't done business together, CPPs offer a way of outlining these capabilities in XML documents, and therefore are machine-readable and -processible. These profiles are essential to finding other companies with the needed capabilities to do e-business. They also provide the raw material for trading partners to develop and negotiate a CPA.

The CPPs list the business processes as defined by one or more industries and supported by the company. Companies developing a CPA will match the business processes they support to those of the prospective trading partner and agree on the common set of processes and messages that they will exchange.[10]

As a further extension of this model, the business process specifications provide an explicit *business process specification schema* (*BPSS*) in XML that gives the details needed to describe and create a binding agreement. Figure 2.8 shows how an interaction sequence plays out between two partners seeking to do business together. Notice that all relationships are reduced to sets of collaborations between two partners, even if they may actually be part of a broader marketplace and associated agreements.

For these agreements to achieve the desired legal and economic effects, they must have the following:

- A computable success or failure state for every transaction
- Permitted means for parties to exchange legally binding statements and terms
- Permitted non-binding statements and terms
- Permitted ways of arranging messages into exchange patterns or sequences that allow for agreements about these patterns in a business process

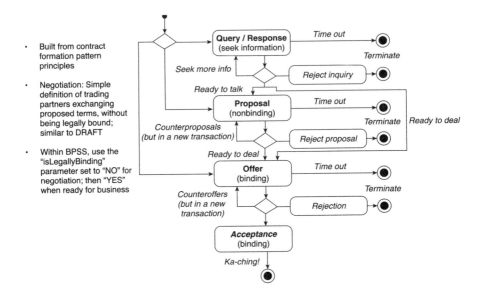

- Built from contract formation pattern principles

- Negotiation: Simple definition of trading partners exchanging proposed terms, without being legally bound; similar to DRAFT

- Within BPSS, use the "isLegallyBinding" parameter set to "NO" for negotiation; then "YES" when ready for business

Figure 2.8
The ebXML contract-negotiation process.

This diagram has an annotated set of normal items encountered during a business negotiation that leads to a formal agreement of the terms and conditions. The BPSS structure then contains and stores those items and shows how they relate to the business process definitions and messages exchanged. As mentioned earlier, the ebXML registry provides the means to store and retrieve these items and to reuse them between partners.

Registries and Repositories

Web-based registries are perhaps the most critical parts of the ebXML architecture, as well as the ebXML functions with which companies have the most contact as they get started with ebXML. As Figure 2.4 showed earlier, the ebXML registry is the place for industries to file their business process models and objects, and for companies to file their collaboration protocol profiles. Thus, the registry serves as the main point of contact for companies with little or no experience in the industry to get these details.

The actual storage of the business models expressed in XML and profiles associated with the registry are referred to as the *corresponding repository content*.

Repositories may be physically part of the registry, or may refer to remotely located content stored separately. From the user's point of view, this is mostly just a technical nuance; the user connects to the registry only, and the physical storage associated with the registry is what returns the requested content.

The registry itself provides an index to the items in the repository as well as automated routines for human and machine access to the repository.[11] The registry can also refer to other registries that index related specifications or metadata used by those companies or industries. And it must have the capacity to be continuously updated with new processes, components, and profiles.

Physically, the registry can list any other static software objects and associated processes required to do business in that industry, such as the following items:

- XML *document type definitions (DTDs)* or *schemas* ("nouns")
- Software programs and scripts ("verbs")
- Tables and lists of values and codes, such as ISO country codes, currency codes, and special packaging or labeling specifications (for example, for hazardous materials)
- Definitions of unique terms
- Industry EDI implementation guides or earlier XML vocabularies

Repositories, on the other hand, store dynamic and transactional information, and retrieval of these objects occurs when using the registry as a lookup index.

Since each item referenced in a registry needs to be accessed by systems over the web, each of these items needs a unique identifier. As shown earlier, companies need to do business both within and outside their industries; therefore, they may access registries in multiple industries, and thus need to relate items from different domains.

Individuals and companies access ebXML registries through both automated and human-readable interfaces. Underneath these access points, the XML-based interactions with registries use the same kind of XML messages as those used to exchange business messages with trading partners. Also, because not all types of content are completely open to everyone, CPAs may be required between companies accessing the registries, as business needs demand. Figure 2.9 shows the functions provided by a registry in orchestrating the various pieces of the ebXML architecture.

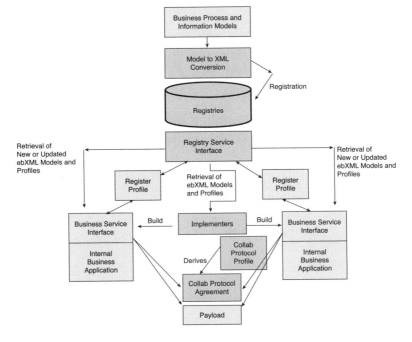

Figure 2.9

Functional service view of the ebXML architecture.[12]

Defining specifications for a registry's index is tricky, because ebXML needs to support a wide range of businesses and picking one scheme over another may make the index difficult to use for entire industries or groups of industries. With ebXML, the registry stores *metadata*, which describes or identifies an object. The registry is connected to the actual items in the repository that contains the objects themselves. Since the metadata for an object includes a globally unique identifier, it provides a way of tracking each item stored. The specifications also list a set of data to describe each registry object, including name, identification codes, and various descriptions, as well as the organizations submitting the item and those responsible for maintaining it.

As noted earlier, ebXML defines the interactions
with the registry system in somewhat the same terms
as interactions using ebXML itself. It specifies a collaboration protocol agreement (CPA) between the
party providing the registry and its clients. It also
defines a set of processes for interactions with the
registry and separate messages within the processes.
And it specifies a mechanism for queries to a registry
and responses to those queries. ebXML also outlines
processes for registry-to-registry interactions, including a CPA between registries themselves. Finally, it
identifies error conditions and messages with remedial actions.

The specifications recommend appropriate security
features to limit access to authorized users, but they
also note that registries are by nature public facilities.
As a result, a company would want to register its
overall generic business CPP, but certainly not the
definitions of its own private arrangements with
customers and partners. Security is needed particularly to control the ability to change the contents of a
registry itself and provide librarian management
facilities.

While companies need to keep their business CPP
details current, registries need to restrict access to
only those parties with proper authorization and
ownership rights to update the actual profiles. The
specifications also recommend digital signatures to
provide non-repudiation of authenticity—a guarantee
that the filing took place—and thus the company
cannot claim that it's a forgery.

Registries need to support both human and machine
queries. For human queries, registries need to provide
the capacity to browse the items based on classifications and intuitive visual groupings, and then allow
drill-down for more detail if needed, preferably using
a simple web browser interface. Also, traditional web-
based arbitrary keyword searching is required, such as
the popular search engines already provide for web
page content.

Machine queries, on the other hand, are likely to directly reference content itself, using the explicit ebXML unique identifiers or UIDs, either with or without its metadata, for retrieval to a remote computer application.

As a result, registry objects and their metadata need to be accessible as standard XML-based resources over the web. The proposed identification schemes for registry objects meet this requirement. With each registry object having a globally unique identifier, a valid query on that identifier should return that specific repository object, and no more.[13]

The remaining sections of this chapter focus on the specifications that provide the transport, security, and delivery functions in the overall ebXML technical architecture.

The ability of two or more parties to communicate in a distributed network using XML has become one of the hot topics in the XML community, and one from which we will hear much more.

Messaging Functions

The ebXML specifications describe in detail the structure of messages sent among trading partners, as well as the routing and transport mechanisms. These specifications are fundamental to any business data-exchange framework, since they define basic interconnectivity—the ability to send and receive messages with trading partners, or between trading partners and registries. These messaging specifications were also the first ebXML draft technical documents developed and subjected to several proof-of-concept tests.[14]

Business messages need to be secure and reliable. As a result, ebXML messages include security components and allow for exchange over common leading Internet protocols:[15]

- Hypertext Transport Protocol (HTTP) and Secure Hypertext Transport Protocol (HTTP/S), used on the web
- Simple Mail Transport Protocol (SMTP), used with email

Messaging Specifications

The messaging specifications outline the basic functions for transferring documents among e-business services that comply with ebXML. The specifications enable trading partners to use existing communications methods, and allow for reliable delivery, security, persistence, and extensibility as spelled out in the requirements described earlier. To meet these requirements, ebXML adopted the *Simple Object Access Protocol (SOAP)*, an XML messaging vocabulary used in several other leading web services. The specific version of SOAP used by ebXML allows for attachments, and thus has the name *SOAP with Attachments*.[16]

ebXML Message Package

ebXML messages are carried in a package defined by SOAP using the *Multipurpose Internet Mail Extensions (MIME)* protocol as well as XML documents. The Internet Engineering Task Force developed MIME as a packaging protocol for email, but because of its ability to carry messages with different kinds of file formats, it has been increasingly used with web-based transfers over HTTP. MIME not only offers a way of transporting messages in multiple formats, but also can carry encrypted content.

The ability of two or more parties to communicate in a distributed network using XML has become one of the hot topics in the XML community, and one from which we will hear much more. The W3C has established a separate XML protocol activity and working group to address these issues.[17]

Figure 2.10 shows the components of the ebXML/ SOAP message package.[18] The communications protocol, such as HTTP over the web or SMTP with email, provides the outer layer of the package. Then the outer SOAP envelope uses MIME, as do the two main parts of the message—headers and payload—to specify message length and formatting details. XML message headers inside the SOAP-based envelope provide the addressing and management information, while the payload has the business content of the message—the whole reason for the message.

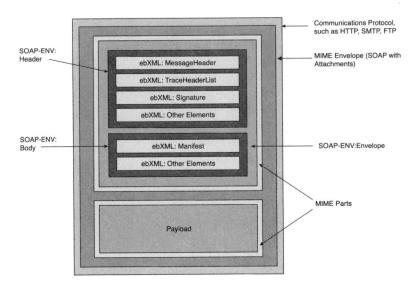

Figure 2.10
ebXML message components
and structure.

Here's where the terminology gets a little tricky. The basic SOAP message in this package has the ebXML message headers. In Figure 2.10, the SOAP envelope with the SOAP message has two parts, what SOAP calls its *Header* and *Body*, although for ebXML it's all considered just part of the message headers. The ebXML message payloads (messages can have more than one payload) reside in the attachment part of the message. Payloads can be in any digitized format, which allows for attaching content such as patient X-rays or engineering drawings as well as simple XML-based payloads.

The ebXML message headers are defined by ebXML and supplement the SOAP specifications. The headers identify the message sender and receiver, provide date/time stamps for logging, prescribe routing if required, cite reference documents (such as collaboration protocol agreements), include digital signatures or other security objects, list the contents of the payloads in a manifest, and indicate whether the message is acknowledging a previous message.[19]

Reliable Message Flow

As noted earlier, ebXML emphasizes the need for reliable messaging service. The specifications define reliable messaging as having the following characteristics:

- For any given message generated by the sender, the receiving message service will deliver at most one copy to the receiver.
- The receiving message service will send an acknowledgment to the sending service, to indicate receipt and persistent storage of the message. The sending message service will also notify the sender if it doesn't receive this acknowledgment.
- Both the sender and receiving message services will use persistent storage for recovery.

The acknowledgment and persistent storage help improve the reliability of delivery. The ebXML header document has an attribute that indicates whether the message is a normal data transfer, an acknowledgment, or an error message. Acknowledgments also are sparse and simple; they contain no business payload, service interface, or action data in the header. They must contain the reference to the original message identifier, however.

The persistent storage feature holds the message by the sending message service, even before sending the message. The receiving message service likewise holds a copy of the message in persistent storage, in case it's needed for recovery. Once the appropriate acknowledgments are received and the need for recovery has passed, the respective messaging services can remove the message from persistent storage.[20]

Getting Started with ebXML

The overall process for getting started with ebXML was portrayed in Figure 2.4 earlier in this chapter. Since this book doesn't give all of the precise technical details about ebXML, you first need to acquire the ebXML specifications and technical reports, downloadable free of charge from the `www.ebxml.org` web site.

Your company will first need to build or acquire the technical capability to reflect the business practices in your industry. Industries or individual companies may decide to implement ebXML in stages, which the modular nature of the specifications supports. Many industries and companies will find the messaging specifications, based largely on existing Internet standard protocols, the easiest way to get started. The messaging specifications provide the ability to send and receive business messages in a common and secure package, and offer best practices for the management, processing, and control of message traffic.

The next step, if not yet accomplished, is to align your company's systems with your industry's business processes. Many industries, through their industry associations, have identified the major business processes and defined standard messages, either in EDI or in XML vocabularies. If your industry association hasn't yet reached that stage, the ebXML business process specifications provide a useful method for taking this step.

If your industry group has reached the stage of establishing an ebXML-compliant registry and repository, you can download the processes, standard messages, and other objects such as standard product or location codes needed to conduct e-business in your industry. The registry will also be the place where you register your company's collaboration protocol profile (CPP), which lists the processes you support and the technical details of your e-business systems. Once your profile is in a registry, you can start seeking other companies with which you can conduct e-business.

Most companies, particularly smaller companies, need to acquire new software to generate, send, receive, and process ebXML messages. Your insistence on software compliant with ebXML and other open standards will send a powerful message to the vendor community. Systems based on open standards benefit from a full airing of user requirements and solutions based on consensus, rather than dictated by a few large players or vendors. The result often is better representation of end-user needs and lower costs.

As of the time of this writing, packaged software supporting the full ebXML specifications is only just appearing as early prerelease systems, but many vendors have announced their intent to add support for ebXML to existing products. Building working libraries of core components specifications will take time; such libraries are very detailed and require working with a wide range of business scenarios and applications.

ebXML doesn't provide standard messages for specific business documents such as purchase orders, invoices, or ship notices. These items are left to the individual industries, as they can vary widely from one industry to another. These too will be evolved and documented in ebXML registries as the basis for broad adoption of ebXML methods.

Endnotes

1 "Creating a single electronic global market" is a registered trademark of the ebXML Working Group.

2 The W3C calls its technical standards *Recommendations*, but the documents are respected and referenced as legitimate standards.

3 Electronic Business XML (ebXML) Requirements Specification Version 1.06, 8 May 2001, pp. 8–9.

4 "General ebXML Principles," Electronic Business XML (ebXML) Requirements Specification Version 1.06, 8 May 2001, pp. 9–10.

5 David Webber and Anthony Dutton, "Understanding ebXML, UDDI and XML/EDI," XML Global, October 2000, http://xml.org/feature_articles/ 2000_1107_miller.shtml.

6 "ebXML Functional Phases," ebXML Technical Architecture Specification, version 1.04, 16 February 2001, pp. 14–16.

7 Webber and Dutton, http://xml.org/ feature_articles/2000_1107_miller.shtml.

8 Alan Kotok, "ebXML: Assembling the Rubik's Cube," XML.com, 16 August 2000, www.xml.com/pub/2000/08/16/ ebxml/index.html.

9 "Core Components and Core Library Functionality," ebXML Technical Architecture Specification, version 1.04, 16 February 2001, pp. 23–25.

10 "Trading Partner Information [CPPs and CPAs]," ebXML Technical Architecture Specification, version 1.04, 16 February 2001, pp. 16–18.

11 Webber and Dutton, http://xml.org/ feature_articles/2000_1107_miller.shtml.

12 "Functional Service View," ebXML Technical Architecture Specification, version 1.04, 16 February 2001, p. 13.

13 "Registry Functionality," ebXML Technical Architecture Specification, version 1.04, 16 February 2001, pp. 25–28.

14 Alan Kotok, "ebXML Gathers Pace," XML.com, 24 May 2000, www.xml.com/pub/2000/05/24/ebXML/index.html.

[15] "Messaging Service Functionality," ebXML Technical Architecture Specification, version 1.04, 16 February 2001, p. 30.

[16] SOAP Messages with Attachments, John J. Barton, Hewlett-Packard Labs; Satish Thatte and Henrik Frystyk Nielsen, Microsoft, 9 October 2000, www.w3.org/TR/SOAP-attachments.

[17] "XML Protocol Activity," World Wide Web Consortium, 9 April 2001, www.w3.org/2000/xp/.

[18] "Packaging Specification," Messaging Service Specification, ebXML Transport, Routing & Packaging, Version 1.0, 11 May 2001, p. 13.

[19] "ebXML SOAP Extensions," Messaging Service Specification, ebXML Transport, Routing & Packaging, Version 1.0, 11 May 2001, p. 18.

[20] "Reliable Messaging," Messaging Service Specification, ebXML Transport, Routing & Packaging, Version 1.0, 11 May 2001, p. 43.

Chapter 3

ebXML at Work

Perhaps the best way to discuss the potential for ebXML in e-business is to show examples of how the international consortium of business and technical experts intends the specification to work. This chapter presents three scenarios and relates each to the changing business conditions discussed in Chapter 1, "There's No Business Like E-Business."

All of these examples are projections of how companies might interact with the specification and with each other, as ebXML gives rise to more (and more innovative) e-business opportunities. Our goal as authors is to illustrate very real business needs based on our combined 40+ years of industry experience, and the realistic and achievable results offered by ebXML-compliant technology. All the companies presented in this chapter are fictitious; we intend no similarity to any past or present enterprises.

Case 1: Go-Go Travel, in Search of a New Business Model—and Survival

As Chapter 1 points out, the web has made life difficult for many travel agencies. In April 2000, the investment company Bear Stearns & Co. Inc. (www.bearstearns.com) predicted:[1]

As customers turn to the Internet to make their travel plans, the role of the travel agent will diminish. According to Bear Stearns' analysis, 25% of all travel agents could eventually lose their jobs as Internet Travel expands… According to industry research, in the first half of 1999 approximately 1,800 travel agencies went out of business due in part to their inability to generate revenue. According to the report, in order for traditional travel agents to survive they should fill a certain niche such as luxury travel or adventure travel, and they must focus on customer service.

With online travel sites proliferating, the future for traditional travel business seems bleak. It's increasingly difficult to argue with customers who can get a lower ticket price over the web.

For Go-Go Travel, a local travel agency, the web indeed seems threatening. Much of Go-Go Travel's business comes from corporate accounts, which hire Go-Go for bookings with airlines and hotels, and from which the agency earns commissions. In the past few years, many airlines have reduced their commissions, and others threaten to do so. With online travel sites proliferating, the future for traditional travel business seems bleak.

For these corporate accounts, travel agencies can provide a few benefits such as travel profiles, frequent flyer mileage accounting, enforcement of corporate travel policies, and payment with company credit cards. But despite those benefits, and often against stated policies, company employees search for flights with online services and sometimes find fares lower than those quoted by travel agencies. Go-Go Travel finds it increasingly difficult to argue with customers who can get a lower ticket price over the web.

Some agencies have started charging fees, such as flat service charges for bookings, but Go-Go Travel is leery of going down that road. In theory, adding fees for service should help recover the lost commissions, but it may also drive away the customers to no-fee web sites.

The company determined that leisure travel, including high-ticket items such as cruises and tour packages, could provide an opportunity to make up the volume lost from business travel. With the population

aging and the Baby Boom generation reaching retire-
ment age, the demographics look promising. And
industry research indicates that cruise and tour package customers still use travel agencies for bookings.[2]

It doesn't take long, however, for Go-Go Travel to
discover that many other agencies had much the
same idea, and they all would soon compete for the
same pool of business in the same way. Go-Go Travel
needs to position itself for leisure-travel business, but
in a way that differentiates Go-Go from the rest of
the pack. The company needs more than a gimmick;
it needs a whole new business model.

In doing this bit of strategic soul-searching, Go-Go
Travel discovers the changes in business conditions
brought about by the web. Customers often want to
deal directly with suppliers (in this case, cruise lines
or package providers), unless intermediaries such as
travel agencies can provide extra benefits or lower
prices. And without corporate policies requiring use
of the official travel agency—policies with decreasing
effectiveness—customers could on their own use the
web to match services and find the best bargains.

Go-Go Travel makes a strategic decision to join the
web rather than fight it. To distinguish itself from
other travel companies, Go-Go will develop a web
presence and provide a unique collection of services
using the power of the web.

In its research, Go-Go Travel discovers the
OpenTravel Alliance (www.opentravel.org), a travel-
industry vocabulary based on XML that defines a
common customer profile, a traditional part of the
agency business. With these tools, Go-Go Travel can
change the way it does business, provide a completely
new product mix to customers, and offer its services
to anyone on the web, which offers infinitely more
opportunities than its static local market.[3]

The *OpenTravel Alliance* (*OTA*) is a consortium of
most leading airlines, hotel chains, car rental companies, tour package vendors, passenger rail, technology
companies serving the travel industry, and travel
agents. OTA developed its common customer profile

in 1999–2000, which captures and exchanges data on a traveler's identity, affiliations (including employer), loyalty programs, forms of payment, travel documents, and detailed travel preferences. The detailed preferences include common preferences, or those that apply across travel services. For example, a vegetarian will likely want vegetarian meals on an airplane, at restaurants, and on cruises. Travelers can also define preferences for specific travel services. If the traveler belongs to airline, hotel, and car rental loyalty programs (frequent flier, guest, or renter), account numbers could be captured as part of the air, hotel, or car rental preferences.

One of the OTA customer profile's features allows customers to define collections of travel preferences in any way they like. This feature lets customers—or travel agents working on their behalf—identify preferences in terms of the customers' own plans and experiences, rather than predefined categories determined by the travel services.[4] For example, a traveler may have a certain set of preferences for business travel in general, but different preferences for business travel outside the country. The same traveler may have still another set of preferences for the annual golfing trip with pals. When visiting the in-laws every year at holiday time, yet another set of preferences applies. This ability for travelers to collect preferences on their own terms gives the OTA specification a great deal of flexibility and power.

The designers of the OTA specification noticed early on that the kinds of data being collected got quite personal. As a result, the group recommended strict privacy protections that allow sharing of data from the profiles—even for updating files at various suppliers—only with the explicit permission of the customer.[5] However, this ability to share preferences, with the customer's permission, offers one of the unique opportunities that Go-Go Travel seeks to exploit.

One way that the web has changed people's lives is its ability to create instant communities of people anywhere in the world who have web access. The

> One way that the web has changed people's lives is its ability to create instant communities of people anywhere in the world who have web access.

rise of chat rooms and instant messaging, for better or worse, has made it possible for people with like-minded interests to find each other and interact. The OTA specification's ability for customers to define travel preferences in their own terms has the potential effect of allowing customers with similar interests to find each other over the web. With this ability to put together instant groups of people with common travel interests, these new-found friends could in principle bargain with travel suppliers for lower prices and added features in their tour packages.

Go-Go Travel realizes that it could offer a valuable service to leisure travelers, by serving as an aggregator of these travel preferences over the web, and as a broker of travel services to meet those preferences. Market research indicates that customers still prefer using travel agents for cruises and tour packages, so it would not need to fight a trend away from these kind of services.[6] However, Go-Go Travel needs a way of collecting the customer preferences, putting together ad hoc groups looking for similar kinds of travel, and negotiating with travel services for deals.

The concept sounds great to Go-Go Travel, but putting together a web-based service to handle the large potential scale of customers and wide variety of interests presents a number of hurdles. The model that offers the most promise is the *online vertical exchange*, which allows buyers and sellers to come together in a neutral arena and negotiate prices and features.[7] This travel exchange would also use reverse auctions, which work like regular auctions, except that sellers chase buyers rather than the other way around. Priceline.com has become probably the most well-known reverse auction site and is active in the travel business, but others have emerged as well.[8]

While Priceline.com focuses on price, the reverse auction process can also apply to finding the right mix of product or service features. In May 2000, the U.S. Army's *Communications-Electronics Command* (*Cecom*) tested a reverse auction that used software from Frictionless Commerce Inc. to purchase off-the-shelf electronics equipment. The software analyzed sellers, their performance, compliance with previous contacts, and equipment capabilities. Cecom not only found the most reliable sellers and optimal mix of features—it also realized a 50% cost savings.[9]

Go-Go Travel planned its web service to work as follows:

1.   Customers or their travel agents post their requirements on the Go-Go Travel exchange for certain destinations and features—for example, an expedition through the Costa Rican rain forest—during a particular period of time. The customers or travel agents can post these requirements as well any other important preferences, such as hotel class, desired airlines, smoking or nonsmoking rooms, families included or no children, vegetarian meals, or whatever the customer deems important. The OTA customer profile specification can provide the medium for customers or travel agencies to capture these preferences and share them with the exchange.

2.   Customers or travel agents can also use automated search agents to indicate when entries with similar interests appear in the exchange, and then decide whether to join these ad hoc groups.

3.   Travel service aggregators, such as tour providers, can put together and propose packages that meet the preferences posted on the exchange, indicating travel dates, destinations, itineraries, airlines, lodging, and special features (for example, side trips), as well as prices. The providers pay Go-Go Travel a membership fee to bid in these reverse auctions.

4.   The Go-Go Travel exchange can use analytical software, like the kind used by the Army's Cecom (described earlier), to rank the order of the proposals and list costs.

5. Customers or their travel agents can decide which of the packages to accept. If customers cannot agree on a single provider, the group can go back to a subset of the bidders and ask for best-and-final offers. If none of the bids is deemed acceptable, customers can decide to wait for more offers or disband.

    ▪ When the customers decide to accept a bid, they can book the package with the winning provider through Go-Go Travel, which would receive a commission from the provider.

    ▪ Go-Go Travel would also handle the financial settlements. In the travel business, financial settlement is no longer a simple matter, with the combination of credit cards, electronic funds transfers, and loyalty program points used for payment.

As Go-Go Travel prepares its new web services, it recognizes that the system must provide several critical functions and support a high volume of requests, many of them from companies with which Go-Go has not done business before. No single XML vocabulary can provide all of the necessary features. (See Chapter 4, "The Promise of XML," for an introduction to XML syntax.) The OTA customer service specification can capture and exchange travel preferences. Later OTA versions plan to include bookings as well. But Go-Go Travel also needs bid postings and acceptances or rejections of bids, as well as financial transfers and commission payments. The company will need to do business with perhaps thousands of travel agencies and hundreds of tour packages, and probably thousands if not tens of thousands of individual travelers.

Here is where ebXML can provide much of the solution.[10] Travel agencies will use the ebXML specifications to define and exchange messages containing their customers' profiles and preferences, book tour packages, send confirmations, and transfer payments.

Go-Go Travel will also use ebXML methodology to exchange bookings and confirmations, as well as financial transfers with tour package providers. Go-Go Travel's site will ask individual travelers to register with the site and complete a customer profile based on the OTA specification.

Travel agencies with customers who want to register their travel preferences with Go-Go Travel can send in new or update existing customer profiles using ebXML messages. Once customers form their own virtual group for a holiday this way, Go-Go Travel can alert tour package providers with a request-for-bid message, and the tour package providers can respond with bids, using ebXML message formats in both cases.

As this process continues over time, Go-Go Travel and its associates are effectively building up a registry of reusable exchange components. The ebXML approach provides a formal registry component in which to store and exchange the vital pieces of these interchange pictures. Details of the registry interactions are covered in depth in Chapter 8, "ebXML Technical Architecture."

Financial transaction messages illustrate the concept of core components. Messages used to exchange details on invoicing and remittances would follow good financial practices used across businesses.

More messages, if needed, with further bid requests and best-and-final offers, can be exchanged using the ebXML message specifications. Bookings and confirmations with the tour package providers and travel agencies representing the travelers can also use standard messages in the ebXML format. Financial transactions, including invoices and remittances, can use the ebXML message formats as well.

The financial transaction messages illustrate another important feature of ebXML, namely the core components. The messages used to exchange details on invoicing and remittances would not likely be unique to the travel business, but follow good financial practices used across businesses. Moreover, banks and credit card processors will deal with more than just travel companies, and want messages from travel companies dealing with financial matters to be compatible with those from other customers. As a result, the ebXML-based travel-industry standard messages defined for financial transactions will use the same financial data elements as used throughout the business world. This use of common components—*core components*, as they're called in ebXML—provides for interoperability across industry groups, a critical objective of the whole ebXML exercise.

Case 2: Marathoner, a Runners' Store That Goes the Distance on Inventory Control

For runners—the people you see getting their daily exercise on streets and trails at all hours of the day and night and in all kinds of weather—running shoes are the most important piece of equipment.[11] Stores that serve the market for serious runners devote most of their work space and inventory to running shoes. Marathoner is one of those stores. In addition to its storefront location, Marathoner buys booth space at expos held in conjunction with major road races, such as the New York or Chicago marathons or the Philadelphia Distance Race.

Running shoes come in many different models to meet a wide variety of running needs, foot types, body weights, and surface conditions. Shoes also come in men's and women's styles. Manufacturers make shoes to provide more motion control and to prevent *over-pronation*, a condition in which the foot strikes the surface heel first and turns inward excessively. Most runners have feet that pronate or turn inward a little, which provides natural shock absorption, but over-pronation requires more control to prevent a higher risk of injury. Motion-control shoes, because of their reinforced construction, also provide the most durability. Other types of running shoes focus on stability, which is often the best choice for runners not needing pronation control, but still provide durability. Still others feature greater cushioning, the choice of less-demanding or less-efficient runners, and of under-pronators with rigid, immobile feet. Flat feet and high arches require special shoes or inserts.

Running stores often stock shoes for special running conditions, including trail shoes for cross-country running and lightweight shoes for road racing, that are favored by more experienced and faster runners.[12]

Running shoe manufacturers rely on stores such as Marathoner to reach the serious runners who train thousands of kilometers per year and take part in distance races. Serious runners often buy multiple pairs of shoes per year. Specialty stores like Marathoner often hire runners to provide field reports that meet these customers' special and changing needs, and runners respond with loyalty. As a result, Marathoner and stores like it provide a significant and continuing market and research feedback for the shoe manufacturers.

Marathoner started doing business during the fitness craze of the 1970s and 1980s, but as the Baby Boom generation aged and its clientele began running less, the store's sales began to flatten out. Competition from superstores such as Sports Authority that serve the sporting goods market, and giant retailers like Wal-Mart, have put pressure on specialty stores like our imagined Marathoner to keep costs down and prices competitive. Unless Marathoner can keep control of costs, it will have a difficult time growing its business against the superstores' lower margins.

One way superstores keep inventory costs low is by sharing plans and forecasts with manufacturers. Manufacturers find the retailers' forecasts helpful in planning their production and keeping their own stocks under control.

A big part of Marathoner's overhead is tied up in inventory. In addition to models that meet the different kinds of running and foot conditions described above, Marathoner needs to stock a range of sizes. Road Runner Sports, a mail-order dealer, offers shoes in U.S. sizes 5–16, in half-size increments, as well as widths from extra narrow to extra wide.[13]

To keep inventory under control, Marathoner has started scanning the manufacturers' bar codes on the box labels, which gives the store current readings on its inventories and helps to avoid disruptive periodic physical inventories, which tie up staff time and require the store to close. While the bar codes help, it still isn't enough. Stocking large numbers of all of these varieties has become a difficult burden to bear. The store needs a better process.

A little research from past sales showed which brands, models, and sizes experience the greatest demand, and the use of bar codes helps the store predict precisely which models and sizes it will likely need over the next year. Marathoner discovered that one way superstores keep their inventory costs low is by sharing these plans and forecasts with manufacturers and placing orders based on the most current period's requirements to replenish the inventories. The manufacturers find the retailers' forecasts helpful in planning their production and keeping their stocks under control, and therefore are happy to oblige. [14]

Marathoner also discovered that superstores use EDI transactions to share sales forecast data, but research showed the costs of EDI to be prohibitive for a small retailer. Manufacturers, who are serving an increasing number of distribution channels and outlets requiring EDI (such as superstores), can easily justify the cost of the expensive software and dedicated systems. Small retailers, however, have neither the money nor staff to devote to EDI. Yet the need to control inventory is just as real.

How can Marathoner meet a real need for e-business, but without the resources to put into EDI? The ebXML specifications offer an answer for Marathoner and millions of small stores like it. Just as in the OpenTravel Alliance example, publicly accessible sporting goods industry transaction standards are required. Unlike with EDI, however, where these implementation details are hidden in the large vendors' back-end systems, with the ebXML approach this data can be fully shared automatically by software via the Internet. Here again, the particular industry will first need to establish a registry to store the business process definitions for inventory control, including the sharing of forecasts, as well as online inventory levels, replenishment orders based on the forecasts, ship notices, activity, and receiving reports that tell the manufacturer that the items shipped are entered into inventory.

The trading partners can exchange ebXML messages with the following sequence:

1. Marathoner prepares an annual sales forecast showing the models and sizes for each model projected each month for each manufacturer, and sends it to the manufacturer. The store updates the forecast each month. The forecasts take into account planned price promotions and special events such as local distance races that attract large numbers of serious runners.

2. Marathoner and the manufacturers agree on prices and terms based on the sales forecasts. Any significant changes in the forecasts could affect prices.

3. The store sends the manufacturers a periodic inventory activity report with the updated plan. When stock levels for each model reach a prearranged point, representing a specified number of days of inventory, the manufacturers ship Marathoner the numbers of units needed to meet the desired stock levels in the plan.

4. The manufacturers ship the goods needed to replenish Marathoner's inventories and send the store a ship notice listing the items in detail (quantity, model, size).

5. When each shipment arrives, Marathoner scans the bar codes on the new units to increment its inventory records, and sends the manufacturer a receiving report.

6. Marathoner authorizes payment to the manufacturer for the goods shipped, based on the agreed-upon prices. The manufacturer doesn't need to send an invoice.

Marked changes in forecasts can affect the transportation companies used by manufacturers, as well as the manufacturers' production processes.

Also part of this process is an affiliation program for direct sales generated from the Marathoner web site, in which out-of-stock items are shipped directly from the manufacturer's facilities.

This case involving inventory control illustrates the need to include transportation and financial services in the supply-chain planning. Best practices such as just-in-time or vendor-managed inventories can result in more frequent inventory turns but also require more frequent deliveries. Transportation companies, of course, deal with a wide range of industries and thus with the vocabularies of each industry served. Transportation companies therefore will likely use core components to relate their vocabularies to the basic terminology of their customers. (See Chapter 8 for a discussion of the ebXML core components concept.)

The manufacturers also develop transportation forecasts based on the customers' sales forecasts. Should Marathoner's forecasts change markedly, the changes could have an effect on the transportation companies used by the manufacturers, as well as on the manufacturers' production processes.

Both Marathoner and the manufacturers want to plan their cash flow and use electronic funds transfers for payments. Therefore, if Marathoner or any of the manufacturers' other regular customers forecast significant changes in sales, they want to alert their banks to adjust credit lines or prepare for a change in the level of transactions through the banks.

Case 3: World Beat, a Direct-Mail Catalog Company Using the Web to Compete with the Web

With all of the attention given to retail business over the web, it's easy to forget that printed direct mail advertising, otherwise known as "sale mail," continues to thrive. The Direct Marketing Association estimated that in 1999, overall spending on direct marketing totaled $176.5 billion, generating more than $1.5 trillion in sales. Of that total figure, direct mail advertising totaled $42.2 billion, or about a quarter of all direct marketing expenditures. By comparison, spending on online marketing amounted to $14.2 billion in 1999.[15]

For printers, according to Printing Industries of America, advertising accounts for almost half (44.8%) of the total demand for commercial printing,[16] and direct mail printing was estimated to grow some 7.6% in the year 2000. Volumes for related catalog and marketing/promotional collateral jobs growth were 5.4% and 8.0%, respectively.[17]

For World Beat, a specialty catalog company featuring apparel, jewelry, and crafts imported from Africa, Asia, and the Caribbean, online purchasing offers great potential, but World Beat still has a customer base that likes printed catalogs and purchases a significant volume of goods from the printed material. The company has noted a critical trend in direct marketing, driven in large part by the web—specifically, customization of content. While World Beat anticipates keeping its print catalog customers, it needs a strategy to better tailor its offerings to the various tastes of its eclectic clientele. By producing specialized versions of its catalogs, World Beat can increase merchandise sales and reduce production costs. The reduced costs come from producing smaller catalogs that cut down on paper, manufacturing, and postage.

One real company, Experian, offers a service called *Visitor Solutions* that helps make web customization happen. The company is one of the largest vendors of consumer data, and Visitor Solutions lets web marketers combine the data collected from web sites with the data in the Experian databases.[18]

The ability of the web to produce customized content gives it an important marketing advantage over print catalogs. Web customization can take place in either push or pull modes. In *push mode*, vendors tailor their messages and deliver advertising that meets certain demographic criteria.

The *pull strategy* lets users select content based on preferences and show that content on a web site when users log on. While many individual sites offer a "My" feature for customization, a service called *Octopus* can also aggregate data from many sites based on user preferences.[19]

> *While many individual sites offer a "My" feature for customization, a service called Octopus can also aggregate data from many sites based on user preferences.*

Web services based on the *Information and Content Exchange (ICE)* protocol, an XML vocabulary for syndication, can easily deliver customized content over the web to subscriber sites.[20]

Sites like SierraTrading.com and Amazon.com also track customer purchases and show further items in those same categories via on-site or email promotions.

World Beat's research shows that generating print catalogs with customized content is feasible but takes a good deal of planning and control. When designing a catalog, any variable change in content requires a separately identified edition so the printer can change the images running on press and assemble the catalogs accordingly.

Versioning in catalogs and magazines is nothing new. Top circulating publications and high-end catalogs such as Lands End or Nieman-Marcus create regional and demographic editions. An apparel catalog like Lands End sent to Florida customers in November will look considerably different than the version sent to Minnesota addresses at the same time. Agricultural publications such as *Farm Journal* have for some time been able to deliver segments of readership based on acreage, crop mix, and recent heavy equipment purchases.[21] Except for the agricultural publications, most print publications using complex targeting are larger publishers such as Time Inc. or Conde Nast.

If World Beat plans to publish various versions of its catalogs based on demographics or past purchasing behavior, they'll need a printer with technology as sophisticated as their customer database information. However, most printing companies are small operations, with fewer than 20 employees.[22]

The core of World Beat's catalog content is the merchandise copy. The company's customization strategy calls for each catalog issue to have a common set of items, plus others that vary according to the known tastes of the audience segments. Therefore, each issue of the catalog will have a number of special versions designed for the various market segments. To keep the effort manageable, however, each version of the catalog will have the same basic format; only the pages with the variable content will change from one version to the next.

To keep costs for this new and more complex product under control, World Beat needs to get estimates of production costs for each version before making a decision on printing the copies. To get these estimates, World Beat needs to provide the printer with specifications early in the process. With the company using the same basic format for each issue, and with variations in content based on audience demographics or profiles, the printer should be able to provide World Beat with these estimates.

A major part of World Beat's costs (or those of any cataloger) is postage. Fortunately, World Beat can take advantage of discounts offered by postal authorities for presorting and bundling the printed books according to ZIP code. By sorting the books by carrier route ZIP code (ZIP plus four), World Beat can realize even larger discounts. As a result, the company needs to provide its printer with precise sorting and bundling instructions as well as the editorial copy.

Of Standards and Things

World Beat concludes that it must rely on existing standards and technology as much as possible, since they don't have the resources to develop the technology, nor does the company want to rely too much on the printer to develop the new product. In short, World Beat wants to maintain control over the final product, but not go broke in the process.

In the graphic arts industry, guidelines such as *General Requirements for Applications in Offset Lithography* (*GRACoL*) enable print buyers such as World Beat to present their specifications more comprehensively and specifically. The guidelines cover planning, design, image capture, page layout, preflighting (tests of electronic delivery of copy), proofing and related print outputs, and binding and finishing.[23]

For ordering complex print products, an EDI specification from Graphic Communications Association called *Production Order Specification/EDI* (*PROSE*) offers standard file formats for defining these items:

- Components on pages, such as individual merchandise items
- Pages themselves
- Signatures (individual sheets printed on presses, then folded and cut for binding)
- Sections (one or more unique signatures bound in a specific location in the publication)
- Editions
- Groups of editions
- Issues of publications or catalogs[24]

PROSE also specifies supplied inserts and instructions for wraps or other items added after the publication is bound. Like other EDI specifications, PROSE requires expensive software and significant staff time to set up and operate effectively. However, a consortium of magazine publishers and printers has begun developing an XML vocabulary called *XML for Publishers and Printers* (*XPP*) that contains PROSE's functionality but promises to be cheaper to use because of the wider availability of XML-capable technologies.[25]

Another GCA specification called *Mail.Dat* defines a relational database of some 14 tables for communications between the magazine or catalog publisher and the mailing facility (usually the printer) who assembles the pieces for mailing. The Mail.Dat files contain everything about the mailing except for the names and addresses themselves, and enable the printer to sort and package the pieces to take maximum advantage of business mail discounts offered by the U.S. and Canadian postal authorities.[26]

World Beat has found some XML vocabularies other than XPP for print production, but no full open standards—at least, not yet. A company called printCafe has developed a specification called *eProduction eCommerce eXchange* (*PCX*) for interactions among print buyers, printing companies, and third-party vendors such as pre-press service bureaus. According to printCafe, PCX can exchange data among a print buyer's enterprise resource planning system, content management tools, digital asset management systems, pre-press systems, raw materials providers, and printing companies' management systems. PCX supports processes for quotations, orders, job status inquiries, inventory, and pre-press.[27]

A consortium of vendors in the graphic arts has introduced a draft specification called *PrintTalk* that supports an industry standard Job Definition Format as well as *Commerce XML (cXML)*, developed by Ariba Corp.[28] In September 2000, PrintTalk released its first specifications covering requests for quotes, orders, and order acknowledgments. PrintTalk uses the Job Definition Format to define the graphic arts aspects of the exchanges, and cXML for the business factors.[29]

None of the XML specifications gives World Beat all that they need. World Beat finds PCX a more comprehensive solution, but not a standard. PrintTalk has broader backing in the industry, but so far covers only quotations and orders. XPP is still in development. World Beat needs a specification that enables web-based commerce among smaller companies, defines the various catalog versions, and provides precise production instructions as well as the distribution data for mailing.

> *With ebXML, trading partners can exchange messages over the web covering the entire quotation, order, production, proofing, distribution, and financial processes.*

What's Next?

Faced with this plethora of proprietary and mutually exclusive formats, World Beat must turn to the ebXML approach to provide simple and effective interoperability. With ebXML, World Beat and its trading partners can exchange messages over the web covering the entire quotation, order, production, proofing, distribution, and financial processes. However, the printing industry will need to establish common process definitions, message formats, and vocabularies, settling its specification conflicts. If the industry can agree on common specifications and establish an ebXML-compliant registry (see Chapter 2, "ebXML in a Nutshell," for a discussion of ebXML's registry key enabling roles), World Beat and its trading partners can exchange messages, and World Beat can in turn provide its readers with more customized content, which can improve merchandise sales and reduce costs.

The sequence of ebXML messages in this scenario would be as follows:

1. World Beat downloads industry-specified processes for quotations, production orders, proofs, mailing data, and invoicing.

2. World Beat sends to the printer the print specifications (based on GRACoL) and templates for its catalog—defining the issues, editions, sections, signatures, and pages, as well as print quantities, page trim sizes, and paper weights.

3. The printer returns a quotation for the work.

4. World Beat accepts the quotation or returns revised specifications and templates, with the printer returning new quotations, until the trading partners agree on pricing.

5. World Beat sends to the printer the publication makeup files with the copy for common versions and alternative versions. World Beat also sends the distribution specifications (based on Mail.Dat) for each version of the catalog issue.

6. The printer assembles the copy and sends World Beat soft (electronic) proofs.

7. World Beat approves the proofs or makes changes; exchanges continue until World Beat approves all versions.

8. The printer generates press proofs. World Beat's production director reviews the proofs on-site at the printing plant, and, if the product is acceptable, approves full-scale production.

9. The printer produces and mails the copies ordered by World Beat and sends to the Postal Service a manifest detailing the number and weight of catalogs for each ZIP code, with a pro forma invoice giving the mailing costs, copied to World Beat.

10. The Postal Service approves or amends the pro forma invoice; if approved, World Beat approves an electronic funds transfer to the Postal Service.

11. World Beat sends payment to the printer based on the postal service manifest and agreed-upon pricing in the quotation. No invoice is needed.

Conclusions About ebXML at Work

Although they're projections, these cases reflect realistic business scenarios based on real-life needs. They indicate ways in which ebXML can help businesses meet the new conditions spelled out in the first chapter as well as improve the ways they conduct business for the benefit of the customers and themselves.

These cases have important common features:

- **Small companies.** Travel agencies, local retailers, and specialty catalog publishers are primarily small businesses. Yet ebXML provides feasible solutions in each case. With EDI, the companies involved would find it difficult or even impossible to succeed.

- **Ad hoc and high-volume exchanges.** The travel agency case uses vertical exchanges and reverse auctions, which create opportunities that can happen at any time; the company must be ready to respond. The running store has an annual plan with periodic updates, plus inventory reports that generate vendor replenishment. The catalog retailer has periodic issues with an indeterminate number of special versions. These kind of opportunistic data exchanges need a technology that allows for quick response rather than a regular exchange of data between long-time trading partners.

- **Business-to-business and business-to-consumer transactions.** While ebXML focuses mainly on data exchanges between businesses, it recognizes the need to support exchanges with consumers as well. The travel agency case provides an example of that scenario.

- **Multiple industries.** All of the cases involve payments, which means data exchanges with banks as well as the trading partners in the supply chain. The running store case also brings in transportation services, and the catalog has interactions with postal authorities. Because of the need for exchanges among different industries, any new e-business framework must squarely address this interoperability issue. In none of these cases would a single industry vocabulary provide the solution.

- **Improve processes or create new opportunities.** In all cases, the companies benefit from new opportunities (Go-Go Travel), improved business processes (Marathoner), or both (World Beat). The companies didn't invest in business data exchange to save incrementally from reduced staff time and errors of human processing, but to do business in new or better ways.

Making the case for ebXML requires looking at this bigger picture and providing a technology that lets these visions for better business really happen. Notice also that ebXML technologies are being adopted in a phased way, with the simpler, more immediate aspects being adopted initially, and then paving the way for extended implementations from that base. This also ameliorates the risk factors involved in adopting new technology and new business paradigms. Clearly, smaller businesses will need openly available low-cost components to enable their adoption of ebXML-based systems. In the next chapter we look at XML, one of the key technologies in the ebXML repertoire that can help make these visions a reality.

Endnotes

[1] "Bear Stearns Initiates Coverage of the Internet Travel Industry," Press release, 17 April 2000, www.bearstearns.com/corporate/corpinfo/pressrel/2000/apr/041700.htm.

[2] "Travel Agency Trends," Travelfuture, Inc., April 2000, www.travelfuture.com/new_page_2.htm.

[3] One of the authors served as the OTA's first standards manager when the group developed its customer profile specifications (www.opentravel.org). OTA soon became an early and enthusiastic supporter of ebXML.

[4] Chapter 1 discusses how the web and the information it provides to customers transferred power from the supplier to the customer. This feature of the OTA specification provides a good example of that phenomenon.

[5] OpenTravel Alliance Message Specifications—Version 1, Volume 1, Specifications Document, version 2001A, www.opentravel.org/opentravel/Docs/OTA_v2001A.pdf.

[6] "Travel Agency Trends," Travelfuture, Inc., April 2000, www.travelfuture.com/new_page_2.htm.

[7] See the discussion in Chapter 1 about exchanges.

[8] Joseph McKendrick, "Priceline.com: An Inside Look at the Reverse Auction Master," *EcomWorld,* January 2000, www.ecomworld.com/search/author/article.cfm?ContentId=51.

[9] George I. Seffers, "Army advances reverse auction," *Federal Computer Week,* 30 May 2000, www.fcw.com/fcw/articles/2000/0529/web-auction-05-30-00.asp.

[10] See Chapter 6 for a more complete discussion of ebXML features and processes.

[11] Both authors have run marathons; therefore, to us running shoes are hardly a hypothetical issue, particularly as one author ran much faster than the other.

[12] "Choosing the Right Shoe," *Runner's World Online,* www.runnersworld.com/shoes/chooser.html.

[13] See www.roadrunnersports.com.

[14] See the discussion in Chapter 1 about Collaborative Planning Forecasting and Replenishment that describes these processes and benefits in more detail.

[15] "1999 Economic Impact: U.S. Direct Marketing Today," Direct Marketing Association, www.the-dma.org/ library/publications/libres-ecoimpact2.shtml.

[16] Ron Davis, Ph.D. "What Drives Print Demand?" Printing Industries of America, www.gain.org/servlet/ gateway/industry/print_markets/demand/index.html.

[17] Ron Davis and Steve Kodey, "Print Markets Reflect Hot Economy," Printing Industries of America, July 2000, www.gain.org/servlet/gateway/PIA_GATF/articles/ econadv0700.html.

[18] "Visitor Solution," Experian, www.experian.com/ visitor_solutions/index.html.

[19] Tom Spring, "Octopus Revamps Web Customization Service," *PC World,* 7 July 2000, www.pcworld.com/ news/article.asp?aid=17577.

[20] "What are the Benefits of Using ICE?" Information & Content Exchange, www.icestandard.org/join.asp.

[21] Alan Kotok and Ralph Lyman, *Print Communications and the Electronic Media Challenge,* Jelmar Publishing, 1997, pp. 70–71.

[22] "Industry Trends," Printing Industries of America, www.gain.org/servlet/gateway/industry/index.html.

[23] Described in more detail at www.gracol.com.

[24] *Production Order Specification/EDI (PROSE), GCA Standard 125–1992, Release 1.3,* 1997.

[25] "Publishers Join Printers in XML Effort," Quad/Graphics, 5 July 2000, www.qg.com/ whatsnew/070500.htm.

[26] "Spotlight on Mail.Dat 00-1," Graphic Communications Association, www2.gca.org/store/.

[27] "E-Commerce Technologies," printCafe, www.printcafe.com/html/services_frame.html.

[28] For more information about cXML, see www.cxml.org.

[29] "PrintTalk Technical Briefing Paper," PrintTalk, www.printtalk.org/briefpaper04.pdf.

Part II   ebXML Background and Details

This part of the book explains more of the finer points of ebXML, as well as some of the background to its underlying technologies, and is designed for business analysts and managers responsible for implementing e-business in their companies. The chapters include a discussion of the business requirements, the process used to develop the ebXML specifications (a fascinating story in itself), the relationship between ebXML and other web services technologies, a look at the ebXML technical architecture, and example of an ebXML application.

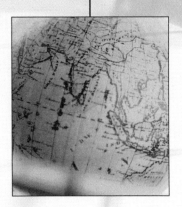

Chapter 4

The Promise of XML

With this chapter, we begin discussing ebXML's background and underlying technology, starting with the *Extensible Markup Language (XML)*. We will provide an overview of XML technologies, and discuss various features related to e-business, as well as its limitations for business purposes. This chapter is mostly technical in nature, to explain the raw technology itself and how the various components relate together. Our goal is to provide the reader enough of a sense of XML so that its overall use for business is clarified. The reader should view this chapter as a roadmap to the salient features of XML itself; however, it is not intended to be a tutorial in XML syntax.

What Is XML?

XML makes possible the entire idea of using the World Wide Web and the Internet for exchanging business messages. XML is a generic *markup language*, which means that it provides instructions that only define the message or document content, not how that content is displayed or printed. For example, the instructions can say, "This block of text contains a business shipping address."

By focusing on the content and detailing the precise business context, XML makes it possible for systems in remote locations to exchange and interpret such documents without human intervention. This ability to automatically send, retrieve, interpret, transform, and process the data in electronic messages is of course critical to the conduct of electronic business itself.

The *World Wide Web Consortium* (*W3C*) developed XML in 1996–97, and officially released version 1.0 in February 1998.[1] While XML is widely recognized as a technology and the W3C is a highly respected organization, drawing its membership from both major software vendors and academic institutions, the W3C chooses to call its fully approved technical documents *recommendations* rather than *standards*, to avoid anti-competitive lawsuits in the U.S. Recommendations represent a consensus within the W3C as well as the approval of the W3C director, now Tim Berners-Lee. As recommendations, documents such as the XML specifications demonstrate stability and are considered ready for widespread implementation and business use.[2]

Markup: Seeing Is Believing

The World Wide Web emerged as a common communications medium once the *Hypertext Markup Language* (*HTML*) became available in the early 1990s.[3] HTML is also a recommendation of the W3C (the latest version is 4.01, December 1999), and now there is also an XHTML recommendation (February 2001). HTML provides a good example of a markup language in wide use, and makes a convincing case study for the importance of consistent standards.

You can see HTML markup by opening any web page with Internet Explorer or Netscape Communicator. Using the top-level menu in the browser, select View, Source (Internet Explorer) or View, Page Source (Netscape). What you see displayed is the internal HTML syntax that the browser uses to render the page content you see onscreen. The familiar web page with its human-readable text and images are exposed as machine-readable computer markup code. Notice that the code contains a lot of instructions in angle brackets, such as <HTML>, <BODY>, <HEAD>, <TITLE>, <TABLE>, and so on. (See Listing 4.1 for an example.)

Enclosing the syntax text within angle brackets creates a *tag* or *element*. Close to the top of the web page's HTML markup source is the tag <HTML>. This tag tells the web browser that the page is coded in HTML; the web browser responds by displaying the information as directed by the rest of the tags on the page. At the bottom of the page is a similar tag, </HTML>. The slash after the opening angle bracket in the tag tells the browser that it has reached the end of the HTML page. The <HTML> tag is called an *open tag*, and the </HTML> tag is a *close tag*. The markup also contains other tag pairs: <HEAD> and </HEAD>, <TITLE> and </TITLE>, <BODY> and </BODY>. These tags define parts and functions of the HTML document.

Listing 4.1   Sample of HTML Markup

```
<HTML>
<HEAD>
<TITLE>Dynamiks Research Center News
Homepage</TITLE>
<meta http-equiv="Content-Type"
content="text/html; charset=iso-8859-1">
<meta name="keywords" content="press releases,
wind tunnels, aerospace".>
</HEAD>
<BODY bgcolor="#FFFFFF">
<TABLE width="100%" border="0" cellpadding="0"
cellspacing="0">
</TABLE>
</BODY>
</HTML>
```

The power of HTML is that it's very simple to use, as the HTML software excuses most obvious mistakes by human editors—unclosed tags, orphaned tags, mistyped tags—by always displaying something, not just a blank page. This leads to very complex HTML software, but ease of use for content creators. HTML has a fixed set of markup tags and most HTML software readily understands such commonly used tags. Because HTML is a standard more or less recognized by the browser manufacturers,[4] millions of people and companies worldwide have found new and innovative ways of communicating over the web—and in many cases doing good business—without worrying about too many technical details.

XML takes a different approach, first by allowing its users to create their own tags (hence the *extensible* part of its name). As a result, XML is highly suited to describing your own particular business data in messages and exchanging those messages with trading partners. Listing 4.2 shows the XML markup of a customer's telephone number, using the XML vocabulary from version 3.0 of the xCBL syntax:[5]

Listing 4.2   Sample XML Content for a Supplier Mailing Address

```
<?xml version="1.0" encoding="UTF-8"?>

<Supplier>
 <NameAddress>
  <Name1>ABC Wholesale</Name1>
  <Address1>1222 Industrial Park Way
  </Address1>
  <City>South San Francisco</City>
  <StateOrProvince>California</StateOrProvince>
  <PostalCode codetype='ZIP'>96045</PostalCode>
  <Country>US</Country>
 </NameAddress>
</Supplier>
```

XML elements use start and end tags as in HTML. However, the elements also contain attributes such as `codetype` within the `<PostalCode>` tag. *Attributes* act as qualifiers of the elements, providing more definition or direction to the trading partners exchanging the messages. Attributes are familiar in HTML too, such as the `<FONT typeface="italic">I said hello!</FONT>` instruction, where `italic` qualifies the style of presentation font for the text. Similarly, in the case of the XML postal code number shown in Listing 4.2, the attribute tells us that this is a U.S.-style numeric-based ZIP code.

HTML uses a fixed set of tags for display of text, not for the definition of data. Listing 4.3 shows the same information as in Listing 4.2, but coded in HTML.

You may notice another characteristic of XML from this example—its readability. XML doesn't restrict tag writers to specific string lengths; tags can be labeled to confer hierarchy, context, and meaning.

Listing 4.3   HTML Content for a Supplier Mailing
               Address

```
<!DOCTYPE HTML PUBLIC "-//W3C//DTD HTML 4.0
Transitional//EN">
<HTML>
<HEAD>
   <META HTTP-EQUIV="Content-Type"
   CONTENT="text/html; charset=iso-8859-1">
   <META NAME="Author" CONTENT="Alan Kotok">
   <META NAME="GENERATOR"
   CONTENT="Mozilla/4.06 [en]C-gatewaynet
   (Win95; I) [Netscape]">
</HEAD>
<BODY>

<ADDRESS>
Supplier name and address:</ADDRESS>

<ADDRESS>
Name: ABC Wholesale</ADDRESS>

<ADDRESS>
Address: 1222 Industrial Park Way</ADDRESS>

<ADDRESS>
City: South San Francisco</ADDRESS>

<ADDRESS>
State: California</ADDRESS>

<ADDRESS>
Zip: 96045</ADDRESS>

<ADDRESS>
County: USA</ADDRESS>

<BR> 
</BODY>
</HTML>
```

XML, Where Past Is Prologue

A review of XML's background shows some further
thinking behind the development of XML, as well as
its current readiness as a tool for business.

XML is a subset of the *Standard Generalized Markup
Language* (*SGML*), a markup language first conceived
in the late 1960s. A committee of the *Graphic
Communications Association* (*GCA*) determined the
need for standard page-composition instructions sent

from publishers of books and journals to printing plants. Individual printers at the time had their own means of marking up the text with codes that translated into font sizes or effects, such as boldface or italics. They recognized that a standard means of marking up the text would make it possible for any publisher to communicate in the same way with any printer, and save the publishers the headaches of reconciling one form of markup with another.

The GCA committee proposed separating the information content from the presentation format and developing a generic code to represent the format, rather than trying to decipher each printer's specific coding scheme. The generic code would be represented in a set of descriptive tags. The tags would indicate where the information for the heading of the document resided—identification of the author, date, title, and other general details—as opposed to the body of the document that contained the intellectual product.

By 1969, Charles Goldfarb, then working at IBM, led a research project to build on the GCA committee's ideas for a *Generalized Markup Language (GML)* for text editing and formatting to enable electronic document sharing and retrieval. GCA, working first with the *American National Standards Institute (ANSI)* and then with the *International Organization of Standards (ISO)*, moved GML from an IBM proposal into a recognized international standard—the *Standard Generalized Markup Language (SGML)*, ISO 8879, in 1986.[6]

Based on this standard, the U. S. Department of Defense, the Internal Revenue Service, and other such organizations with large numbers of complex documents were able to invest in systems to help them manage their electronic publishing operations. The European Particle Physics Laboratory in Geneva (which uses the organization's original French acronym, *CERN*) became another major user of SGML. While on staff at CERN, Tim Berners-Lee developed HTML as an application of SGML in the late 1980s and early 1990s.[7]

> *HTML's large set of features was designed to handle the demanding requirements of scientific and technical documentation and went well beyond the needs of people and companies to display text and images or exchange business messages.*

The development of SGML predated the emergence of the Internet, at least as we know it in the year 2001. What attracted Berners-Lee and many of the other web pioneers to the Internet was its decentralized nature and a design that allowed any kind of computing platform to plug in, as long as it complied with the Net's protocols. The public availability of the Internet created the potential for anyone to exchange such marked-up documents with ease.[8] HTML transformed the Internet from islands of hard-to-find content into one homogeneous whole that's visible through a web browser interface.

Meanwhile, companies, agencies, and organizations with large electronic publishing operations—usually technical, scientific, engineering, financial, or legal—found SGML useful in managing their documents and re-purposing the content in those documents. Because of its nurturing in the publishing world, however, SGML contains complexity that the average user finds intractable. Its large set of features was designed to handle the demanding requirements of scientific and technical documentation and went well beyond the needs of people and companies to display text and images or exchange business messages.[9]

Figure 4.1 shows the timeline for development of XML and the other main markup languages, as well as EDI and ebXML. The development of the web-based markup languages, both HTML and XML, came about in part to provide an alternative to the highly complex and feature-rich SGML. With HTML, the ability to write web pages with simple and inexpensive tools (free, in many cases) makes everyone with a web connection a potential publisher.

And the numbers seem to point out that the world has responded accordingly. According to Whois.Net, more than 32 million domain names with .com, .net, or .org extensions were registered as of November 2000, and NetCraft's domain search engine lists nearly 1,000 domains with *XML* somewhere in the name.[10]

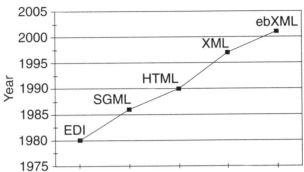

E-Business/Markup Events Timeline

Figure 4.1
Evolution of markup
technologies.

While HTML offered an effective way of presenting images, text, and multimedia content on the Internet, it still didn't meet many of the critical needs of business information dissemination. HTML has a fixed set of tags. While easy to learn, it's too generalized, and in particular doesn't provide any means to interpret the context of the information within a web page.

XML aimed to bridge the gap. Figure 4.2 shows how the needs can be viewed as four interrelated technologies: the Internet delivering content, HTML presenting it, XML identifying the data content, and Java and similar programming tools providing the process control.

Having identified the need, the World Wide Web Consortium committee convened in 1996, and, led by Jon Bosak of Sun Microsystems and Tim Bray of Textuality, designed XML for electronic publishing. The group focused on creating a simpler form of markup to overcome the obstacles to broad adoption shown by SGML. They therefore set 10 design objectives for the new language:

■ XML shall be straightforwardly usable over the Internet.

■ XML shall support a wide variety of applications.

■ XML shall be compatible with SGML.

- It shall be easy to write programs that process XML documents.
- The number of optional features in XML is to be kept to the absolute minimum, ideally zero.
- XML documents should be human-legible and reasonably clear.
- The XML design itself should be prepared quickly by the W3C team.
- The design of XML shall be formal and concise.
- XML documents shall be easy to create.
- Terseness in XML markup is of minimal importance.[11]

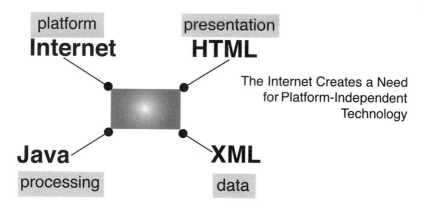

The Internet Creates a Need for Platform-Independent Technology

XML Validation and Parsing

An XML document by itself is just arbitrary text. To describe the actual rules to be followed in creating your particular type of XML content, you need an additional mechanism.

One of the features of SGML that carried over into XML version 1.0 is the concept of a *schema*, which describes the layout of a document, also known as the *Document Type Definition (DTD)*. The role of both schemas and DTDs is to allow the author to define the structure permitted for any given XML document, including the relationships among elements in the document. Think of schemas or DTDs like the instructions that come with a Lego™ bricks model for assembling the pieces in the correct order.

Figure 4.2
The role of XML: the four-legs-of-the-table metaphor.

The terms *schema* and *DTD* are often used interchangeably, but they have specific meanings. A schema is a generic term for document or data structures with a predetermined set of rules. A DTD is one type of schema, specified in SGML and XML 1.0.

The DTD also provides a way of testing the structure of a document against the prescribed structure in the DTD, a process called *validation*. This validation step, designed as a quality check for documents, also can be used to check the structure of business messages sent using XML.

The XML schema or DTD therefore performs two roles. It acts as a blueprint to allow someone who has no prior knowledge of your particular XML to create that content. It also allows software to check content to make sure it is correctly structured.

But XML allows for sending documents without such validation being required. The XML creators allowed for XML documents that are correctly tagged, but that don't have a schema DTD, and thus can't be tested for any structural validity. These documents are referred to as *well-formed documents*, indicating that they meet the basic XML markup syntax rules.

A *valid XML document* is both well-formed *and* meets the additional requirements of the schema DTD.[12] Again, the Lego model is instructive; if you lose the printed directions, you can probably still build an interesting model, but you won't know if it exactly matches the original design.

The combination of its extensibility, structure, and validation makes XML useful not only for electronic publishing but for business messages sent between companies. The ability to define the elements exchanged between companies and the structure of the elements means that trading partners can define messages in advance and thus process the messages automatically on receipt. Having validation means that trading partners can test the messages against the associated schema DTD, and thus provide a form of quality assurance.

> The combination of its extensibility, structure, and validation makes XML useful not only for electronic publishing but for business messages sent between companies.

To validate an XML message with a DTD, the message needs to be read and interpreted, in a process called *parsing*. A software component called a *parser* reads the XML message and interprets the XML tags it finds. A *validating parser* tests the message against the predefined rules of the schema DTD and then reports any errors.

To help provide software programmers using parsers with a standard connection between the message and the parser, the W3C developed the *Document Object Model (DOM)*, independent of software languages or computing platforms.[13] XML documents have a nested structure that resembles a tree with a trunk and branches. The DOM represents the XML message as an inverted hierarchical tree, starting with the root element and branching out from there. By defining this logical structure in a common application program method, parsers and other software packages can manipulate messages consistently. Software developers call this kind of tool an *Application Program Interface (API)*.

Microsoft's web browser, Internet Explorer (IE), displays XML documents using the DOM. If you open a well-formed XML document with IE 5.0 or higher, you'll see the document hierarchy clearly portrayed. The W3C approved Level 1 of the DOM in 1998, but had some enhancements approved as of November 2000.[14] Under the hood, IE 5.0 provides an automatic visual display of an XML document with another technology called the *Extensible Stylesheet Language (XSL)*, and a default stylesheet.

One limitation of the DOM approach is that the whole XML document must be stored in memory at the same time. Obviously, this doesn't work for high transaction-volume or large-sized business information flows. In a process befitting the free and open nature of the Internet, members of the XML Developers mailing list (XML-DEV) developed an event-based programming interface called *Simple API for XML (SAX)*, while waiting for the W3C to finish work on the more complex DOM specifications. SAX therefore allows programmers to process just fragments of XML content at high speed.[15]

Therefore, SAX is an event-based rather than a tree-based API. The event-based approach looks for tags and content meeting some conditional criteria that identifies the fragment within the overall information stream. The SAX API then passes that fragment to a custom event handler (software program) that the programmer has defined. SAX lets systems access and query only those parts of XML documents without loading them entirely into memory, thus working faster and more efficiently. All the major vendors providing XML parser implementations support SAX.[16]

XML's Global Reach and Accessibility

Although XML is a creation of the W3C, companies don't need the web to send and receive XML messages. XML's first design objective makes XML straightforwardly usable over the Internet, not just the web. As a result, trading partners can exchange documents with email messages or *File Transfer Protocol (FTP)* downloads, as well as over the web. With XML, the means of transporting the messages is independent of the message content.

XML Works with Non–English Character Sets

We often take the ASCII-English alphabet codeset for granted, but we forget that most of the world uses alphabets and characters not based on simple Latin (Roman) characters.

Since the Internet made the information technology business truly a worldwide endeavor, the designers of XML added an important XML feature, namely the ability to support non–English character sets. In North America and Western Europe, we often take the ASCII-English alphabet codeset for granted, but we forget that most of the world uses alphabets and characters not based on simple Latin (Roman) characters. XML supports the Unicode standard, a system for representing text characters for computer processing of all the known 50,000 written languages on the planet.

The latest version of Unicode (3.0) matches up to the international standard for character sets, ISO/IEC 10646-1:2000. It uses pairs of two bytes or 16 bits to represent characters, which allows for encoding most of the world's known character sets, including scientific and mathematical symbols. As a result, Unicode provides codes for more than 65,000 characters.[17]

With the worldwide nature of business today, this ability to represent non–English characters has become vital for many businesses.[18] Fortunately, the design of XML is backwardly compatible with today's ASCII 8-bit encoding, so regular ASCII editors and tools work just fine handling and creating what are labeled as "UTF-8 encoded" XML documents.

XML Works with Java

While the development of the Java[19] programming language preceded the development of XML, the two technologies now complement each other. Java is a high-level language used extensively in distributed applications over the web. Sun Microsystems developed Java to run on any computing platform. Programs written in Java are first compiled into an intermediate form called *bytecodes*—machine codes that are interpretable on most computing platforms.[20]

In 1997, Jon Bosak of Sun Microsystems, one of the creators of XML, wrote a white paper describing ways that the two technologies could work together. Bosak pointed out that "XML gives Java something to do." He described potential applications of XML in which the processing is distributed among client and server sites rather than centralized in a single server, using Java applets. For example, a design engineer could download XML data from a manufacturer's web site, and then use distributed Java code to try the circuits in various configurations.[21]

Matthew Fuchs notes several affinities between XML and Java that make them a productive partnership. Java uses a simple and predictable package structure that follows the structure of a typical Windows or UNIX filesystem. As a result, when sharing data with XML documents, programmers can easily route the data to the correct location thanks to this property of Java.

XML supports the use of style sheets that contain the instructions for presenting data on screens, in print, and in audio formats. Style sheets provide the formatting details for visual display or printing, such as page size, margins, and fonts.

Another feature of Java loads code dynamically at runtime, which allows for *applets*—pieces of Java code that browsers can download and run locally rather than relying on a full program at a remote site. This ability allows applets to run code that can process XML documents locally at much higher speeds and with much less overhead.

Fuchs also names Java Beans technology as an innovation that works well with XML. *Java Beans* are a set of application program interfaces that work as components with other software.[22]

XML Works with Style Sheets

Early in this chapter we discussed how markup languages such as XML separate content from its presentation format. Since business-to-business exchanges involve sending data from one computer to another, they don't require a human-readable version at either end of the exchange. But many business processes need to present the exchanged data in some human-readable presentation form. XML supports the use of *style sheets* that contain the instructions for presenting data on screens, in print, and in audio formats.[23]

Style sheets provide the formatting details for visual display or printing, such as page size, margins, and fonts. They are used frequently in word processing (but often called *templates*); for example, many organizations have a standard fax cover page template.

Style sheets have important business uses and do much more than just make data look pretty. For example, documents formatted for North American customers generally need to be printed on standard letter-size pages (8 1/2 inches by 11 inches), while other parts of the world commonly use the A4 size (210 x 297 mm).

While HTML by itself offers some ways to present text and images on a web page, its features are limited and don't provide enough power or flexibility for professional print content designers.

Another problem with HTML is consistency and reuse. This problem has been addressed in advanced word processing products by the use of *styles*; the user can apply a paragraph style, a table of contents style, an indented list style, and so on. HTML also has a need to use consistent style of text display size, font, and layout. HTML needs a separate style system, called *Cascading Style Sheets (CSS)*, to display web page content. CSS can also be used to display XML content in the same way.[24] The method CSS uses is very simple, but requires that the content of the XML already be structured in a way that matches the output layout.

The W3C has developed an even more powerful style sheet for XML documents, called the *Extensible Style Sheet Language (XSL)*, that gets around the restrictions of CSS and has two sets of core features:

- **Transformation** changes XML data according to predefined program rules.
- **Formatting** provides presentation rules and instructions to display the XML content as HTML, or some other provided target markup.

The transformation features of XSL give it extra power over CSS. With XSL, you can add or remove elements from an XML file, rearrange the elements, and make decisions about the display of the elements.[25] Figure 4.3 shows an example of XSL stylesheets displaying XML data on an HTML page.

The next need is to locate information consistently within an XML document. What if you need the second occurrence of Address, not the first? Associated with *XSL Transformations (XSLT)* is the *XML Path Language*, also called *Xpath*, which permits the location of any part of the tree branch path of an XML document hierarchy to be specified. Figure 4.3 gives an example of this capability, to find and select Database/People/Person.

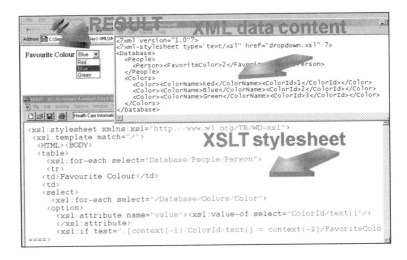

Figure 4.3

How a style sheet works to display XML as HTML.

A transformation using XSLT needs to address specific components in an XML document, and Xpath provides that ability. It works like a pair of programming tweezers to find and return the exact piece of an XML document desired. XSLT can also change the hierarchical structure of an XML document using a set of predefined XSLT syntax rules that dynamically inspect and traverse the document structure.[26] [27] [28]

Using either CSS or XSL style sheet references with an XML document provides a way to visually display XML content to end users, or to morph XML documents for input processing by business application software.[29]

Building XML Messages from Processes to Data

This section looks at the process for building business messages with XML. As we discussed earlier in this chapter, XML lets trading partners define their own elements and tags, taking advantage of XML's extensible nature—the *X* in XML. But XML messages also represent the structure of those elements, following their prescribed relationships in the hierarchy. The message schema DTD captures the names of the

elements as represented by the tags and their hierarchical structure. Messages exchanged among trading
partners therefore must represent the rules and practices of a business or industry, as captured in the
schema DTD.

For example, in Chapter 3, "ebXML at Work," the
Marathoner running store case study points out how
retailer and manufacturers can exchange product
identifiers and precise inventory levels, so that manufacturers can compare inventory levels to predefined
reorder points and decide whether they need to ship
more product. Before any of these exchanges can
happen, however, the retailer and the manufacturers—or, better yet, the entire industry—need to agree
on common terminology and structure of the messages. With this common set of rules, shoe manufacturers and retailers can use the same basic set of
messages, which promotes the use of packaged software and makes it possible for the parties to develop
their systems faster and for less money.

We call this common set of rules a *data model*
because, like a schematic drawing, it offers a skeleton
view of the messages, specifies the order of the elements in a message, and shows how the various elements relate to one another in a hierarchy. The term
comes from the database world, where database
design needs to meet the users' business requirements
as efficiently as possible, yet still allow for future
growth. The *logical model* defines the information
fields and their relationships in a database (much like
a schema DTD in an XML message), while the
physical model details field sizes and datatypes, such as
alphanumeric or date formats.[30] In fact, defining an
XML schema of information is analogous to creating
traditional row-and-column layouts for a database
design system.

The XML syntax is not just about interpreting the
content. The business process is a vital component of
the content and is helped along by XML.

Determine Processes

As shown in the case studies in Chapter 3, the parties identify business processes or actions taken by the companies to achieve their business goals. For example, the travel agency case proposes a process to decide on a tour package. This process has contingencies built in for continued bids and best-and-final offers if the customers don't want to accept one of the first offers. By working out these larger processes, the trading partners can agree on the overall conduct of the business, before trying to determine the individual messages.

A tool called *use cases* can help identify these processes. Use cases describe scenarios in which users interact with each other and the systems under development. Each scenario describes the accomplishment of a specific task or achievement of a goal. They also identify the players, steps in the process, and the messages or even the data exchanged. By describing these situations in a storytelling mode, use cases often uncover the processes underlying business practices.[31]

By working out larger processes, trading partners can agree on the overall conduct of the business, before trying to determine the individual messages.

One of the ebXML development activities involves identifying similarities in business processes across industries. While each industry has its own language and culture, using these common processes helps speed the work and improves the chances for interoperability among industries.[32]

Determine Message Flows

Each process contains a set of individual messages exchanged among the trading partners. In Chapter 3, the running store case listed a series of messages in the process of reporting inventory levels and replenishing the stock:

- Periodic inventory report sent from the store to the manufacturer
- Ship notice sent from the manufacturer to the store with the shipment details
- Receiving report sent from the store to the manufacturer once inventory is accepted

Industries defining their processes can identify the individual messages contained in those processes, as well as how and when the companies send and receive the messages. These messages may resemble EDI transaction sets (see Chapter 5, "The Road Toward ebXML," for a discussion of EDI), as in the running store case, or look nothing like EDI transactions, as in the travel agency case.

Identify Data in the Messages

Once industries identify the messages, they next need to identify the sets of business data that go into those messages. Industry organizations that have previously developed EDI transactions can use this work as the basis for identifying data for XML messages. Newer business processes must rely on information analysis between companies to determine the content required, often replacing older, paper-based documents. But the objective is to improve the way companies do business—not necessarily to follow the current EDI transactions or old paper-process documents. Industries sometimes use this exercise to test traditional assumptions and practices, which can cut out captured or exchanged data that's no longer needed. On the other hand, this process can generate *more* pieces of data needed by trading partners to meet their business requirements.

When applying this process to XML, industry groups develop XML vocabularies that put these groups of data into definable messages, also identifying the structure of the data in the messages. To aid understanding and reuse, the XML structure should link related and most-used pieces of information together as logical blocks. The messages thus embody the rules and practices of doing business in a particular industry, defined in terms of XML. In this way, industries can design common groups of data with common structures as industry-wide rules for processing XML messages.

XML vocabularies can represent more than vertical industries. Vocabularies can also define business functions found in multiple industries, or entire frameworks that provide interoperability across industries and functions. One of these frameworks is ebXML itself, which provides the underpinning for global business, not just an industry sector.[33]

Business Schema DTDs

As discussed earlier, DTDs, as specified for XML, contain the rules for both constructing and structurally validating XML messages. We'll now describe schemas in more detail to give you an understanding of how this key piece of the XML technology is used to enable consistent electronic business.

DTDs assemble information into *elements* with connected attributes. Elements are the basic building blocks of XML messages, and therefore the basic components of DTDs. Elements can contain other elements expressed in a hierarchy (*compound elements*), or they can stand alone as simple containers for character data. Compound elements for parent/child blocks can be referenced together. When the modeling process identifies the data in proposed XML messages, most of these data items will become elements, identified as such in DTDs. In XML messages themselves, elements are marked up as tags within the now familiar angle brackets (<>). Element definitions can indicate the frequency with which the elements occur—once or more than once—and whether they're required or optional.[34]

XML vocabularies can define business functions found in multiple industries, or entire frameworks that provide interoperability across industries and functions.

Then *attributes* provide additional description or qualification for elements. Using the language metaphor often applied to XML, one can think of elements as nouns and attributes as adjectives. The XML document example presented earlier and the following DTD fragment identify the `PostalCode` as an element, with the `codetype` and its use as an attribute of that element:

```
<PostalCode codetype='ZIP'>96045
</PostalCode>
```

```
<!— DTD definition for element and
attribute —>

<!ELEMENT PostalCode (#PCDATA) >
<!ATTLIST PostalCode
                  codetype CDATA #IMPLIED >
```

With the schema DTD syntax, the attributes also provide a limited form of data typing, which means that they describe the kind of data allowed for that element. Attributes can contain *strings* (character data), enumerated lists, or references to other components in the document called *tokens*.

Enumerated lists restrict the attribute to only permitted character strings. For example, an attribute to identify smoking preferences for hotel reservations would have the following as its enumerated listing: SMOKING or NONSMOKING. Attributes can likewise indicate a default response, used routinely unless the customer requests otherwise. Returning to the hotel example, the NONSMOKING response could serve as the default, unless the customer specifically requests SMOKING.[35] While schema DTD datatyping is deliberately simplistic but thereby more easily understood, the new W3C extended schema datatyping is extensive and sophisticated.[36]

The Entity Referencing System

Entities are rather misnamed. They're really aliases or substitution strings, intended to identify the reusable objects in a schema DTD, providing handy shortcuts and helping to ensure consistency in the rules expressed by the DTD. These reusable objects can consist of text strings, such as legal boilerplate, or more complex data element and attribute combinations, defined in advance and recalled when needed. Entities can be internal to the DTD or stored as fragments externally.[37]

Entities also help when placing a character inside a character data or CDATA section of an XML document that would cause confusion with the processing of the XML, such as &, <, >, and ".

Consider the telephone number in the following example. The boldfaced element **<Telephone>** is a substitution string declared as an entity in the schema DTD `telephone-usa.xml`, and then included as needed in XML documents based on that DTD. The OpenTravel Alliance uses this technique in its customer profile, which specifies several telephone numbers (customer, emergency contact, travel agency, and so on). The use of this technique simplifies the schema DTD and guarantees that all telephone numbers in the valid messages are defined consistently.[38]

```
<?xml version="1.0"?>
<!DOCTYPE Cust.Telephone SYSTEM
'http://xml.org/telephone-usa.xml' []>
<Cust.Telephone PhoneTech="Voice"
PhoneUse="Home">
   < Telephone CountryAccessCode="1">
     < Phone.AreaCityCode>703
     </Phone.AreaCityCode>
     < Phone.Number>555-9999
     </Phone.Number>
   </ Telephone>
</ Cust.Telephone>
```

Example of Building a Data Model and XML Equivalent

Using a traveler's customer profile, we can show an example of a DTD and how it helps build and validate an XML message.

Table 4.1 shows the pieces of information in a scaled-down traveler profile database, showing three levels in the data hierarchy, as well as the content of each level—element, text, or attribute—as well as single/multiple occurrences, requirement indicator, and allowable options.

The control information identifies the creator of the profile (a travel agency, for the purpose of this exercise), whether it's a new record or an update, whether the customer has given permission to share the data in the profile, and a date/time stamp that most systems can generate routinely.

Table 4.1:   Traveler Profile Database Structure

Data level 1	Data level 2	Data level 3	Content	Occurs	Required?	Options
Control info			Element	Single	Yes	
	Share permission?		Attribute			Yes No
	Agency		Element	Single	Yes	
		Agency name	Text	Single	Yes	
		Agency ID	Text	Single		
	New/Update		Text	Single	Yes	New Update
	Date-time		Text	Single	Yes	
Traveler ID			Element	Multiple	Yes	
	Traveler name		Element	Single	Yes	
		Title	Text	Multiple		
		Family name	Text	Single	Yes	
		Given names	Text	Multiple		
	Address		Element	Multiple	Yes	
		Address type	Attribute			Mailing Delivery
		Number/street	Text	Single	Yes	
		Room/floor	Text	Multiple		
		City name	Text	Single	Yes	
		Postal code	Text	Single	Yes	
		State/Province	Text	Multiple		
		Country	Text	Single		
	Telephone		Element	Multiple	Yes	
		Telephone use	Attribute			Work Home
		Country access	Text	Single		
		Area/city code	Text	Single	Yes	
		Tel. number	Text	Single	Yes	
	Email		Element	Multiple		
		Email type	Attribute			Work Personal
		Email address	Text	Single		
Form of payment			Element	Multiple	Yes	
	Payment type		Attribute			Credit card Debit card
	Payment detail		Element	Multiple	Yes	
		Card number	Text	Single	Yes	
		Exp. date	Text	Single	Yes	
		Name on card	Text	Single	Yes	

continues

Table 4.1:   Continued

Data level 1	Data level 2	Data level 3	Content	Occurs	Required?	Options
Travel preferences			Element	Multiple		
	General		Element	Multiple		
		Smoking section	Text	Single		Smoking Non-smoking
		Meal preferences	Text	Multiple		
		Special needs		Multiple		
	Loyalty programs		Element	Multiple		
		Program type	Attribute			General Airline Hotel Rental car
		Program name	Text	Single		
		Program ID	Text	Single		
	Airline		Element	Multiple		
		Departure airport	Text			
		Seat selection	Text			Aisle Center Window
	Hotel		Element	Multiple		
		City section	Text			Downtown Suburbs Airport
		Room type	Text			Single Double
	Car rental		Element	Multiple		
		Car type	Text			Compact Midsize Full SUV Truck
		Child seat	Text	Single		Yes No

The DTD for this database structure (`Traveler.dtd`) is found on this book's web site (`www.ebxmlbooks.com`). Please note that this DTD example is meant only to illustrate how a DTD works, and should not be used for normal business messages.

From this database structure, a travel agency wants to create a traveler profile record for a traveler, with the following specific data and preferences:

Administrative control data

- Agency name: GoGo Travel
- Agency ID code: ZZY98234
- Purpose of record: new
- Date/time: 21 June 2001, 3:55 pm
- Permission to share data in profile? No

Traveler identification

- Traveler's name: Ms. Phoebe P. Peabody-Beebe
- Address (delivery): 312 Sycamore St., Buffalo, NY 14204
- Telephone (work): 716-555-9999
- Email: Phoebe@PeabodyBeebe.com

Payment data

- Type of payment: Credit card
- Card number: 0000111122223333
- Expiration date: 12/2002
- Name on card: Phoebe P Peabody-Beebe

Preferences

- Nonsmoking
- Meal type: Vegetarian
- Loyalty program—airlines: US Airways, no. 24680
- Loyalty program—car rental: National Car Rental, no. 54321
- Loyalty program—general: AmEx Membership Miles, no. 09876
- Departure airport (IATA code): BUF
- Airline seat preference: Aisle
- Hotel, city section preference: downtown
- Hotel room preference: single
- Car type preference: Compact

Listing 4.4 gives a validated XML document for these entries based on the rules presented in `Traveler.dtd`.

Listing 4.4   Sample XML Document Based on Traveler.dtd

```
<Traveler>
  <Control>
        <Agency>
                <AgencyName>Go-Go Travel
                </AgencyName>
                <AgencyID>ZZY98234</AgencyID>
        </Agency>
        <Purpose>New</Purpose>
        <DateTime>20010621t15:55:00</DateTime>
  </Control>
  <TravelerID Share="No">
        <TravelerName>
                <Title>Ms</Title>
                <Family>Peabody-Beebe</Family>
                <Given>Phoebe</Given>
                <Given>P.</Given>
        </TravelerName>
        <Address AddressType="Deliver">
                <NumberStreet>312 Sycamore St
                </NumberStreet>
                <City>Buffalo</City>
                <PostalCode>14204</PostalCode>
                <StateProv>NY</StateProv>
        </Address>
        <Telephone PhoneUse="Work">
                <AreaCity>716</AreaCity>
                <PhoneNumber>555-9999
                </PhoneNumber>
        </Telephone>
        <Email>
                <EmailAddress>
                 Phoebe@PeabodyBeebe.Com
                </EmailAddress>
        </Email>
  </TravelerID>
  <Payment>
        <PayDetail>
          <CardNumber>
           0000111122223333
          </CardNumber>
          <ExpDate>12/2002</ExpDate>
          <NameOnCard>
           Phoebe P Peabody Beebe
          </NameOnCard>
        </PayDetail>
  </Payment>
```

```
<Preferences>
      <General>
            <Smoking>Non-smoking</Smoking>
            <MealPref>Vegetarian</MealPref>
      </General>
      <Loyalty LoyalType="Airline">
            <LoyalName>US Airways
            </LoyalName>
            <LoyalID>24680</LoyalID>
      </Loyalty>
      <Loyalty LoyalType="Car Rental">
            <LoyalName>National Car
            Rental</LoyalName>
            <LoyalID>54321</LoyalID>
      </Loyalty>
      <Loyalty LoyalType="General">
            <LoyalName>Amex Member
            Miles</LoyalName>
            <LoyalID>09876</LoyalID>
      </Loyalty>
      <Airline>
            <DepartAirport>BUF
            </DepartAirport>
            <SeatSelect>Aisle</SeatSelect>
      </Airline>
      <Hotel>
            <CitySection>Downtown
            </CitySection>
            <RoomType>Single</RoomType>
      </Hotel>
      <CarRent>
            <CarType>Compact</CarType>
      </CarRent>
  </Preferences>
</Traveler>
```

This message referencing the Traveler.dtd contains all of the required data, uses tags that match the element names in the DTD, presents the elements and tags in the order prescribed by the DTD, and therefore conforms as a valid structure to that DTD. Notice that the example doesn't have any data for child seat preferences listed under the XML car rentals section, but does have three different loyalty programs listed. The rules expressed in the DTD allow for such variations. However, if a message left out the traveler's name, a validating parser would return an error message accordingly.

XML Schema

The generic name for DTDs is *schemas*, a term borrowed from the database world. DTDs represent data only in a hierarchy, which works fine for documentation; remember that the W3C borrowed DTDs from SGML, designed for electronic documentation and the predecessor to XML.

However, many business databases use other kinds of structures—such as relational databases or object-oriented classes and properties—some of which don't always lend themselves to a hierarchical model. In some cases, particularly when working with a simple data structure, data architects have been able to adapt object-oriented structures or relational data models to the kind of hierarchies represented in DTDs. But business doesn't always deal a simple hand, and technologists need more robust and flexible tools than the DTD to be prepared for these more complex conditions.

The W3C has developed *XML Schema*, a major enhancement to XML that offers extended tools for representing information structures and objects, as well as providing extended datatypes beyond those in DTDs. In May 2001, XML Schema reached full recommendation status.[39]

Software and systems supporting XML Schema will need to resist the temptation to cover all of the bells and whistles, since they build in more complexity and cost than is needed.

XML Schema provides more power for defining the structure, content, and semantics of XML documents. The W3C specifications document has three parts:

- Methods for describing the structure of data
- Definition of datatypes
- A primer, explaining its features[40]

The first part of the specification deals with structures, documenting the meaning, use, and relationships of the components of an XML document, such as elements, attributes, and entities. It provides the rules for validating XML documents, based on the rules described in the schemas. It also allows for referencing partial or multiple schemas, thus providing a great deal more flexibility and power than DTDs.[41]

The second part of XML Schema covers datatypes and addresses the need for defining more kinds of data in the rules used to validate XML documents. This part of the specification identifies a group of basic (or *primitive*) datatypes such as strings, integers, dates, and sequences. The specification describes features of a datatype system, including acceptable ranges of values and valid representations of the data (such as whole numbers or scientific notation).

The specification identifies datatypes derived from those built into the basic XML recommendations, such as character data (CDATA), tokens, and entities. And it defines various components of datatypes to allow for the development of unanticipated datatypes.[42]

This greater flexibility comes with a price, however. While it's tempting to use many of these new features, many business applications require just a few of them at any time. For example, being able to validate dates and times will be a significant addition to XML's ability to support business. Few businesses, however, will need the ability to create entirely new datatypes. Software and systems supporting XML Schema will need to resist the temptation to cover all of the bells and whistles, since they build in more complexity and cost than is needed.[43]

As an alternative, work on *RELAX NG* is being developed by an OASIS Technical Committee and eventually for submission to ISO. RELAX NG is designed as a simpler and more accessible approach to providing schema functionality for XML documents.[44]

Other Details

XML Schema incorporates one of the first enhancements to the XML specification, called *XML Namespaces*. With XML Namespaces, schemas can address multiple XML vocabularies in a single document. Namespaces provide for uniqueness in element names by combining the namespace prefix (mapped to a uniform resource identifier, like a web address), and the local part or element or attribute name.[45]

Put simply, XML Namespaces allow different companies or industries to avoid name clashes where they both use the same word with different meanings or contexts, but with the same tag name. An example is the word *stock*, which has at least six possible meanings. An obvious example is using formats such as `billing:address` and `supplier:address` to clarify that *address* is being used in two different contexts.

Is XML Ready for Business?

> *The major inhibitor to the use of XML for business is its inability to provide for interoperability among the various vocabularies written for exchanging business messages.*

While the XML family of technologies goes a long way to build up the features needed for exchanging business messages, XML markup technology by itself can't do all that's needed. The major inhibitor to the use of XML for business is its inability to provide for interoperability among the various vocabularies written for exchanging business messages. The number of these vocabularies is expanding rapidly; a survey in 2000 showed these vocabularies doubling between February and August 2000.[46] Unless a way is found to allow businesses using these vocabularies to understand messages from other vocabularies, the promise of XML as a data exchange technology will go unfulfilled.

To achieve this interoperability, companies using XML need to have a common set of methods with translation among the different industry syntaxes. Also needed is a way of relating the XML messages to overall business processes that give context to the messages and the data contained within them. XML by itself also has no inherent provisions for security and privacy, although the W3C has undertaken important initiatives in these areas, notably with digital signatures and privacy preferences using extensions to the base XML specifications.

At the same time, no solution can just pile on all of these requirements without keeping an eye on the impact it will have on achieving the desired objectives—keeping within the scale and price range of the millions of smaller businesses that so far are left out of the data-exchange experience. This is the challenge laid at the feet of ebXML.

Endnotes

[1] A second edition, issued in October 2000, incorporates error corrections from the original February 1998 version.

[2] "W3C Technical Reports and Publications," World Wide Web Consortium, 3 November 2000, www.w3.org/TR/.

[3] Tim Berners-Lee with Mark Fischetti, *Weaving the Web* (New York: Harper Collins, 1999), pp. 44–45.

[4] We say "more or less recognized" because the leading browser makers have added their own features to HTML for competitive advantage. The Web Standards Project (www.webstandards.org) seeks to reduce or eliminate this variation.

[5] xCBL business language specifications, Version 3.0, January, 2001, www.xCBL.org. The xCBL syntax is derived from SimplEDI, developed originally by a UN/EDIFACT working group.

[6] Charles Goldfarb, "A Brief History of the Development of SGML," (SGML Users Group, 11 June 1990), www.sgmlsource.com/history/sgmlhist.htm.

[7] Berners-Lee, p. 4.

[8] Berners-Lee, pp. 16–17.

[9] Berners-Lee, pages 41–42.

[10] "Domain Stats", 4 November 2000, www.whois.net/, and Netcraft, www.netcraft.com/?host=codes.

[11] "1.1, Origin and Goals," Extensible Markup Language (XML) 1.0, W3C Recommendation 10 February 1998, www.w3.org/TR/1998/REC-xml-19980210.

[12] "2.8, Prolog and Document Type Declaration," Extensible Markup Language (XML) 1.0 (Second Edition), W3C Recommendation 6 October 2000, www.w3.org/TR/2000/REC-xml-20001006.

[13] The DOM applies to more than XML documents. The discussion here focuses only on the DOM's XML aspects.

[14] "Document Object Model Activity Statement," World Wide Web Consortium, 25 June 2001, www.w3.org/DOM/Activity.

[15] David Megginson, "SAX: History and Contributors" (undated), www.megginson.com/SAX/SAX1/history.html.

[16] David Megginson, "What is an Event-Based Interface?" (undated), www.megginson.com/SAX/event.html.

[17] "The UNICODE Standard: A Technical Introduction," UNICODE Consortium, December 2000, www.UNICODE.org/UNICODE/standard/principles.html.

[18] Note that XML documents don't require 16 bits per character, but can be stored in 8-bit configurations known as *Unicode Transformation Format (UTF-8)*.

[19] Java is a registered trademark of Sun Microsystems.

[20] Sun Microsystems, Inc., "About the Java Technology," The Java Tutorial, undated, http://java.sun.com/docs/books/tutorial/getStarted/intro/definition.html.

[21] Jon Bosak, "XML, Java, and the future of the Web," 10 March 1997, www.ibiblio.org/pub/sun-info/standards/xml/why/xmlapps.htm.

[22] Matthew Fuchs, "Why XML Is Meant for Java," *Web Techniques*, July 1999, www.webtechniques/1999/06/fuchs/. Reprinted in XML.com, 16 June 1999, www.xml.com/pub/a/1999/06/fuchs/fuchs.html.

[23] "What are Style Sheets," World Wide Web Consortium, 13 July 2001, www.w3.org/Style/.

[24] Matt Rotter, Charity Kahn, and Paul Anderson, "Get Started With Cascading Style Sheets: How Cascading Style Sheets Work," CNet Networks Inc., 2 November 2000, http://builder.cnet.com/webbuilding/pages/Authoring/CSS/.

[25] Jan Egil Refsnes, "Introduction to XSL," XML101 (undated), www.xml101.com/xsl/xsl_intro.asp.

[26] XML Path Language (XPath) Version 1.0, W3C Recommendation, 16 November 1999, World Wide Web Consortium, www.w3.org/TR/xpath.

[27] XSL 1.0 became a recommendation of W3C in February 2001.

[28] "Extensible Style Sheet Language (XSL)." W3C User Interface Domain, World Wide Web Consortium, 13 July 2001, www.w3.org/Style/XSL/.

[29] A good resource for anything involving XSLT is the web site www.xslt.com.

[30] Stephen Knilans, "Data Modeling Simplified: What Is Data Modeling?" 14 July 2001, Seasoned Software Inc., `http://quick-tips.com/local-search/pages/Detailed/2750.html`.

[31] Karl E. Wiegers, "Listening to the Customer's Voice," Process Impact, March 1997, `www.processimpact.com/articles/usecase.html`.

[32] "ebXML Business Process Project Team" (undated), `www.ebxml.org/project_teams/business_process/`.

[33] Alan Kotok, "Even More Extensible: An Updated Survey of XML Business Vocabularies," XML.com, 2 August 2000, `www.xml.com/pub/2000/08/02/ebiz/extensible.html`.

[34] Jan Egil Refsnes, "DTD-Elements," XML 101 (undated), `www.xml101.com/dtd/dtd_elements.asp`.

[35] "3.3, Attribute List Declarations," Extensible Markup Language (XML) 1.0 (Second Edition), World Wide Web Consortium Recommendation, 6 October 2000, `www.w3.org/TR/REC-xml`.

[36] "XML Schema Part 2: Datatypes," W3C Recommendation, 2 May 2001, `www.w3.org/TR/xmlschema-2/`.

[37] Jan Egil Refsnes, "DTD-Entities," XML 101 (undated), `www.xml101.com/dtd/dtd_entities.asp`.

[38] OpenTravel Alliance Message Specifications—version 2001A, `www.opentravel.org/opentravel/Docs/OTA_v2001A.pdf`.

[39] "XML Schema," World Wide Web Consortium, 25 May 2001, `www.w3.org/XML/Schema`.

[40] "World Wide Web Consortium Issues XML Schema as a Candidate Recommendation," World Wide Web Consortium, 24 October 2000, `www.w3.org/2000/10/xml-schema-pressrelease`.

[41] "XML Schema Part 1: Structures," W3C Candidate Recommendation, 24 October 2000, `www.w3.org/TR/xmlschema-1/`.

[42] "XML Schema Part 2: Datatypes," W3C Candidate Recommendation, 2 May 2001, `www.w3.org/TR/2000/CR-xmlschema-2-20001024/datatypes.html`.

[43] David R.R. Webber and Alan Kotok, "Less Is More in E-Business: The XML/edi Group," XML.com, 10 November 1999, www.xml.com/pub/a/1999/11/edi/index.html.

[44] See www.oasis-open.org/committees/relax-ng/.

[45] "Namespaces in XML," World Wide Web Consortium, 14 January 1999, www.w3.org/TR/REC-xml-names/.

[46] Alan Kotok, "Even More Extensible—An updated survey of XML business vocabularies," XML.com, 2 August 2000, www.xml.com/pub/2000/08/02/ebiz/extensible.html.

Chapter 5

The Road Toward ebXML

The emergence of XML raised the hopes of people seeking to supplant paper with an eventual solution enabling any company in any industry to do business electronically with any other company in the world. But, as explained in Chapter 4, "The Promise of XML," XML cannot do this alone. Any hope of using XML and the ubiquitous World Wide Web for business data exchange would require combining XML with business process models and a common message structure, translating the data exchanged among different industry vocabularies, and doing all of this economically, so that even the smallest enterprise could afford it.

Fortunately, a number of visionaries had seen the potential and limitations of XML and proposed ways of closing the gaps. This chapter discusses important technology initiatives that preceded ebXML, their influence on the ebXML specifications, the two organizations that founded the ebXML initiative, and the process used to develop the specifications.

These early examples also provided a preview of the process used by ebXML, in which hundreds of participants in a worldwide initiative collaborated in a successful complex technical project.

The XML/edi Group

The *XML/edi Group* (www.xmledi-group.org) provided much of the early thinking on the use of XML for business data exchange, and continues to serve as a grassroots advocacy and self-help movement of people worldwide who care about XML's role in business. Many of the group's ideas have found their way into the ebXML specifications.

In the late 1990s, the XML/edi Group took advantage of the use of an email list server to bring together individuals widely scattered around the world, who could share ideas and collaborate on development projects utilizing XML. The list emerged as a critical tool for building a group dynamic, even among people who had never met each other, and enabled them to work together and contribute to complex development projects. Another well-known example of this phenomenon is the XML-DEV list, founded by Peter Murray-Rust and Henry Rzepa, which generated the *Simple API for XML (SAX)* protocol. (See Chapter 4 for a discussion of SAX.)

The XML/edi Group follows much the same model. The group was founded by four individuals in Europe and the U.S., including one of the authors, in the summer of 1997, while XML itself was still in development. In June 1997, Bruce Peat, one of the group's founders, published a paper on XML/EDI, pointing out some of the advantages that XML brings to business data exchange. Peat's paper noted the following:[1]

> *While trading partners may exchange XML documents, they also need instructions for processing the documents to extract the data.*

> *[The] XML document can also be a transaction itself. XML/EDI would allow in a non-proprietary way, for structured presentation format to be included now in the transaction…Soon there will be a standard with which to share the work others have done, applications need only to simply access WWW browser objects. This object-based approach to applications will make document transaction exchange even easier. Bottom line: The EDI camp could leverage XML to aid in lowering implementation costs.*

Later that summer, Peat and David Webber outlined a framework in which XML can serve as a catalyst for e-business data exchanges. The authors noted early in the piece that "XML/EDI involves much more than just dropping EDI into an XML wrapper. An XML/EDI framework includes the use of a set of complementary and powerful technologies." These technologies include what Peat and Webber called "The Fusion of Five":

- XML
- EDI
- Templates
- Agents
- Repository

By *templates*, Peat and Webber refer to the rules expressed in a table containing the terms used in the message, supplemented by the DTD schema. The templates accompany the message, providing business meaning to the XML content. *Agents* act on the processing logic, and guide the end user through the business process (for example, with Java or ActiveX) to look up or attach the appropriate template or determine display characteristics of web-based forms. In this paper, the authors defined the *repository* as the semantic engine to connect terminology used by trading partners to a neutral syntax. This lookup function could also be assigned to the agents.

The paper noted as well the distinction between document-centric and data-centric models for exchanging business data. While trading partners may exchange XML documents, they also need instructions for processing the documents to extract the data used by the trading partners' applications.[2]

Another of the group's founders, Martin Bryan, drafted the XML/EDI Guidelines, with contributions from Peat, Webber, Benoît Marchal, and Norbert Mikula. This document provided more definition of these components and offered a process for implementing XML for EDI-style exchanges. Bryan proposed the use of *directories* to look up and verify trading partner capabilities. This discovery process became part of several later specifications, including those of ebXML.

The implementation steps recommended by Bryan included the following:[3]

- Identification of suitable data sets for electronic business transactions
- Development of DTDs that formally define the relationships of the fields that are to form a particular class of EDI messages
- Definition of application-specific extensions to standard message types
- Creation of specific types of electronic business messages
- Validation of the contents of messages
- Transmission and receipt of electronic business messages
- Processing of electronic business messages using data bots or agents

The ebXML technical architecture relies significantly on distributed registries and a registry information model that describes the functions of the APIs.

Members of the XML/edi Group took part in early attempts to define the direction of EDI, using the new XML technology. David Webber of the XML/edi Group, Robert Crowley of the X12 EDI standards committee, and Rik Drummond of CommerceNet formed an ad hoc task group in 1998 to define algorithms for generating XML elements from the X12 database tables. The task group wrote one of the first DTDs for a working EDI transaction (a purchase order), and provided some initial thoughts on the use of XML namespaces and repositories. The group also offered ideas on combining object-oriented technology with XML, a line of thinking that became much of the basis for ebXML.[4]

Another contribution of the XML/edi Group was its work on defining the role of repositories in business data exchanges using XML. In a 1999 white paper, Webber (with contributions from group members Betty Harvey, Denis Hill, Ron Schuldt, Martin Bryan, Dick Raman, and Gerard Freriks) spelled out the functions that repositories provide. Those functions include

- Identifying the data exchanged among trading partners
- Defining a standard structure and relationships of the data exchanged

- Providing connections to universal business or product identification databases such as UPC/EAN product numbers, or taxonomies such as the Universal Data Element Framework (UDEF) to encourage interoperability
- Determining authorized parties to the transactions
- Providing common mapping, scripting, workflow, or processing tools
- Offering standard forms and screen displays for human interaction

These repositories would therefore contain all of the objects companies needed to exchange data with each other, using an open, standards-based approach. They would include the business process designs, expressed as XML scripts and linked to the XML message structures.

Trading partners would interact with repositories using a software routine called an *application program interface* (*API*) that would allow either automated or human access methods. Companies would probably need to access several repositories; thus, the structure and API would need to be standardized. The paper recommended that industry organizations or agencies responsible for government procurement host these repositories.[5] The ebXML technical architecture relies significantly on distributed registries and a registry information model that describes the functions of the APIs, a model similar to the one outlined by the XML/edi Group.

The XML/edi Group's work on repositories inspired early research and development on an XML/EDI repository at the University of Denver's Daniels College of Business. René Kasan, a graduate student at the Daniels College, developed a prototype repository that stored business objects for exchange between trading partners. She enlisted the help of faculty member Don McCubbrey, as well as local EDI practitioners Ron Schuldt and Will Thayer, and relied to a large extent on the groundwork started by the XML/edi Group.

The work of the group, particularly through the efforts of European founders Martin Bryan and Benoît Marchal, had a major impact on the development of XML for business data exchange in Europe. The *European Committee for Standardization* (which uses the French acronym *CEN*) started a workshop under its *Information Society Standardization System* (*CEN/ISSS*). The workshop defined several DTDs for generalized transactions as well as those specific to the healthcare industry.[6]

As the XML/edi Group sought to structure and define the vision, the traditional EDI organizations struggled to understand the impact XML would have for them.

EDI: Still Important After All These Years

Chapter 1, "There's No Business Like E-Business," describes *Electronic Data Interchange* (*EDI*) and focuses on its accomplishments and drawbacks, especially for smaller businesses. EDI offers valuable lessons in its 30 years of experience, despite EDI's mixed record with smaller businesses, from which emerging frameworks like ebXML should learn.[7] This section examines these lessons in detail to see how they're being absorbed into the ebXML approach. Understanding the entrenched EDI systems is important in clarifying and distinguishing how ebXML is moving beyond the rigid limitations it encompasses to a new, more powerful model.

Basic Message Structure

The EDI standards, such as ASC X12 in North America and UN/EDIFACT elsewhere in the world, show the value of creating a basic message structure applicable across industries. For example, a variety of industries have adopted the standard X12 invoice (transaction set number 810), advance ship notice (856), purchase order (850), and purchase order acknowledgment (855) transactions. Having a common message structure defined in advance makes it

Having a common message structure defined in advance makes it possible for software vendors to develop packages that can address multiple industries, and thus spread their development costs over a wider pool of customers.

possible for software vendors to develop packages that can address multiple industries, and thus spread their development costs over a wider pool of customers. The basic structure of these transactions provides a template for building common solutions, thus making the job at least somewhat easier. And having a basic transaction structure helps make it possible for companies in various industries to agree on a common message structure (although using the implementations of those messages is rare outside the specific industry).

Paradoxically, the success of this approach is also one of its problems. Attempting to shoehorn everyone's business transactions into one fixed set limits the scope and breadth of what can be achieved. Moving beyond these limitations is the key to success for ebXML and also the lynchpin of the approach of the technical architecture for ebXML.

Interchangeable Components

A further aspect of EDI is the use of interchangeable components in business messages, which can be reused across many industries. As mentioned earlier, different industries can use the same basic transaction set (invoice, advance shipping notice, and so on). Each transaction set in turn has three sections called *tables*: heading, detail, and summary. The *heading* has data that applies to the message as a whole, such as identification of sender and receiver, and transaction tracking number. The *detail* area, as the name implies, contains the substance of the message, such as line items on a purchase order or shipping dates and times. The *summary* table holds data showing totals, such as total number of line items or total monetary amounts in the transaction. The summary can also contain hash totals for quality assurance, in which trading partners can sum the totals in the detail table and compare them to the hash totals.[8]

Each table in turn is composed of *data segments*, which are functionally related collections of data elements. Chapter 1 presents a data segment that represents dates and times, certainly a piece of information applicable to a wide range of business uses. Data segments then break down into *data elements*, both simple and composite. The vast majority of the data segments and elements are reusable components, which makes it easier to take advantage of previous EDI development work, as well as to ensure compatibility with modern software development practices. The goal of the ebXML core components group is to create an extensible mechanism for managing reusable groups of information. The traditional EDI view of data segments and elements has been replaced with an XML-based model of parent-and-child groupings of information representing core (common and consistent) pieces of business information and associated process semantics.

Business Semantics

The vast majority of data segments and elements are reusable components, which makes it easier to take advantage of previous EDI development work, as well as to ensure compatibility with modern software development practices.

A significant contribution of EDI to business data exchange overall and ebXML in particular is the accumulated experience of defining the semantics for the thousands of companies now exchanging EDI transactions or messages, which are tested over time and designed to meet real-life business needs. The industries and companies using EDI today have thought through the business scenarios, needs of trading partners, and external constraints (such as legal requirements), and brought forward a set of messages and data elements that companies send to each other in high volumes every day. The future development of business data exchange using XML needs to make use of this rich base of practical experience with e-business.[9] The ebXML core component work is designed to allow the reuse of this existing knowledge base.

Business Procedures

In developing a technology for EDI, the standards committees also established good business practices, which in some cases became part of the standards themselves. Early on, trading partners sending and receiving EDI transactions discovered—to no one's surprise—that doing business electronically required a formal set of business procedures. We share a selection of those best practices in this section.

Ground Rules Established in Advance

Business trading partners need to establish agreements in advance stating the ground rules for these exchanges. These agreements correlate in the EDI world to the *trading partner agreement* (*TPA*). These agreements spell out the business process with its associated electronic transaction sets to be exchanged, responsibilities of senders and receivers, versions of the standards used, and exception procedures (what to do in case of problems). They also offer agreed-upon legal stipulations that apply to all transactions—often called *boilerplate* for a particular industry domain and implementation. In EDI messages, trading partners can simply refer to the TPA rather than spelling out its provisions each time. One whole part of the ebXML specifications deals exclusively with the steps required to assemble such electronic collaboration protocol agreements (CPAs), and particularly how to create your own collaboration protocol profile (CPP) to allow your business to participate with others using the ebXML specifications.[10]

Unique Identification

The next important aspect is that every message sent and received needs a unique identification number. Unique identifiers on the messages, companies exchanging EDI transactions could not distinguish one particular message from others in a business process sequence. Also, any auditing of message traffic requires unique identifiers on messages. In case of problems, auditors need to establish an electronic audit trail[11] to determine responsibility for actions. Unique identifiers help avoid processing duplicate messages as well. ebXML embraces this principle and supports multiple classification schemes for unique identifiers.

The parties in the transactions also need unique identification. Paper forms can capture company name and address locations, which is all a reader needs to tell one party from another. With electronic transactions, however, sending and receiving systems need more reliable indicators of the parties involved in the transactions. As a result, some industries have established their own identification systems, the most well known being the company codes assigned by the Uniform Code Council for bar codes and retail transactions. The common *Universal Product Code (UPC)*[12] found on retail grocery labels has a one-digit UCC prefix that identifies the particular numbering system, such as regular product identifiers or store coupons. A five-digit company code assigned by UCC follows the prefix. When combined with the UCC prefix, the resulting identifier is guaranteed to be unique.[13]

Many companies already have a D-U-N-S number for credit reporting; thus, using it for electronic transactions adds little burden to the respective trading partners.

Other industries have chosen to use identifiers assigned by a third party, such as Data Universal Numbering System (D-U-N-S) codes, a nine-digit string assigned by Dun and Bradstreet (D&B). Companies doing business with the U.S. government, for example, now need a D-U-N-S number for federal agencies to accept their transactions. Many companies already have a D-U-N-S number for credit reporting; thus, using it for electronic transactions adds little burden to the respective trading partners.[14]

Meanwhile, the need for unique identification extends to products documented in EDI transactions. The use of manufacturer product numbers across the supply chain is a practice started in the grocery industry, and is now ubiquitous. The bar code scanners in retail stores capture the same identifiers applied to the product label by the manufacturer. Wholesalers or distributors in the chain also use that number. As a result, all parties in the transactions have the same product identifiers, which simplifies the transactions and reduces uncertainties.[15]

Transmit Variable Data

We described earlier how trading partner agreements let companies establish the legal ground rules for transactions and also provide a document that they can reference in their messages without repeating the information each time. That same principle applies more generally to data sent in EDI transactions, namely that trading partners send only variable data—new or changed information—not data that the companies already have in their information systems. For example, a shipping notice sent by a seller of goods to a buyer can reference the purchase order number that authorized the shipment in the EDI transaction, rather than repeating all of the details in the order. As a result, the electronic ship notice does not need to supply the delivery date requested by the buyer; the buyer already has that information in the purchase order.

Functional Acknowledgment

Nearly all EDI transactions trigger an acknowledgment from the receiving party. The purpose of this acknowledgment is to verify to the sender that the receiving system not only got the transaction but was also able to process and interpret the business information without any problems. Any problems are reported back to the sender accordingly. The transaction used for this purpose most often in X12 is called the *functional acknowledgment* (transaction set number 997 in the X12 standard), which provides for a verification of receipt as well as a review of the X12 syntax in the EDI file.[16]

Companies exchanging messages need to be aware of the limitations of standard functional acknowledgments, however. While the functional acknowledgment transaction can document receipt of the original message by the receiving system, it doesn't indicate when the receiving company used the data to update its files or engaged in any action that the message requested. The EDI standards include separate transactions to report on these business activities. For example, the purchase order transaction set in the X12 standard has a matching purchase order acknowledgment transaction, as well as related order change and change acknowledgments. And while the functional acknowledgment can test the X12 syntax in the original message, it doesn't check the business content. If an electronic purchase order has incorrect product identifiers or part numbers, for example, only the trading partners' internal systems can catch these errors.

The ebXML Transport Packing and Routing specifications provide extended mechanisms that completely address these needs and provide new systems for today's web services and electronic marketplaces that EDI never supported.

Describing Business Processes with the Unified Modeling Language (UML)

Electronic business needs an architecture that can work independently of hardware platforms, operating systems, software packages, network services, and even markup languages. To get complex systems in different companies and even different industries to talk to each other, as well as building a capability to handle future business coming from platforms as yet undetermined, means defining this overall structure in a whole new way. Also, e-business needs a way to connect business practices and processes directly to their representative technology.

The tool used by many participants in the ebXML initiative and many other e-business efforts to achieve these objectives is the *Unified Modeling Language (UML)*. This language—actually more of a way to graphically define business processes for software system design and development—defines the components in the business processes as *objects*. This object orientation makes the business processes the rationale and reference point for the design of e-business data exchanges.

Objects are the software building blocks of object technology, designed to run on any system, without regard to the software or equipment platform used to create the object.

UML was created as a software designer's shorthand notation tool, thus providing a level of abstraction useful for classifying software objects and processes. UML is weaker as an overall business process definition because it lacks the enforced ability to capture and track roles, responsibilities, and relationships critical to documenting human business interactions. Theoretical work in the field of business-process representation continues, such as Zachman Frameworks (www.zifa.com) and *Dynamic Systems Definition Methodology* or *DSDM* (www.dsdm.org).

In some instances, UML can have too much functionality or too little. For simple systems, it may complicate and obscure otherwise trivial needs. For large-scale, complex systems, other tools may be needed to capture the full breadth of the process sequences involved. This inability to build models for large, complex systems particularly applies to self-referencing or self-modifying systems.

UML takes a top-down approach to modeling, which has value in many circumstances. However, where the focus is more on the activity of the individual components, UML can bring the wrong set of tools to the job. Consider for instance applying UML to the game of chess, where the model would begin with defining all use cases—that is, all possible sequences of piece moves—rather than analyzing the set of moves undertaken by the 16 different pieces. Clearly, applying UML itself to a problem has to be evaluated on scope and needs. Often, the simple information-modeling capabilities of XML syntax alone can be sufficient.

Object Technology and Business Processes

We need to provide a little background on object technology here. Tech Encyclopedia defines an *object* as "a self-contained module of data and its associated processing." Objects are the software building blocks of object technology, designed to run on any system, without regard to the software or equipment platform used to create the object.[17]

The idea of modular system design is hardly new. However, as Harry Featherstone notes, object technology brings something new to the table, namely the ability to create models of business processes, and to decompose those processes down to the technology level, while staying true to the business process. The idea is to have the technology better represent the business process, rather than bending the processes to fit the needs of the technology.

By defining business processes with these modeling techniques, designers can separate technology requirements from business semantics or content, which increases the likelihood of communicating successfully among various physical implementations.

Business process models represent the internal business processes and data in a standard format, by providing the following features:[18]

- A consistent way of capturing user requirements and clarifying business semantics
- Better communications among parties, by introducing more objectivity in the communications process
- More traceability and documentation of customer requirements
- A way to apply improvements to existing processes

UML uses a visual graphical metaphor to achieve these objectives. While written initially for software development, its use has expanded to the design of inter-enterprise applications that reflect the object-oriented approach. UML doesn't require any particular solution, but it does encourage an approach based on use cases, centering around a neutral technical architecture, with an iterative and incremental process.[19]

Architectural Views

UML enables business analysts and systems designers to organize the knowledge and relationships generated in the development of models in various ways, to meet a set of problems and solutions, called an *architectural focus*. The set of elements from a model that address the architectural focus is call an *architectural view*, including the following types:

- The *user model view* encompasses a problem and solution as understood by those individuals whose problem the solution addresses. This view is also known as the *use case* or *scenario view*.

- The *structural model view* covers the structural dimension of a problem and solution. This view is also known as the *static* or *logical view*.

- The *behavioral model view* includes the behavioral dimension of a problem and solution. This view is also known as the *dynamic, process, concurrent,* or *collaborative view*.

- The *implementation model view* encompasses the structural and behavioral dimensions of the solution's realization. This view is also known as the *component* or *development view*.

- The *environment model view* covers the structural and behavioral dimensions of the domain in which the solution is realized. This view is also known as the *deployment* or *physical view*.[20]

For example, financial settlements covering the process of invoicing through funds transfers may define an architectural focus. The different collection of elements defined in a model of the financial settlements process would comprise one or more architectural views.

UML offers nine types of diagrams for modeling systems (see the following for an example of use cases and Chapter 8 for examples of most of the other diagrams):[21]

- *Use case diagrams* model business processes.

- *Sequence diagrams* model time dependencies and events.

- *Collaboration diagrams* model interactions within a system.

- *State diagrams* model the behavior of system objects.

- *Activity diagrams* model the behavior of use cases, objects, and operations.

- *Class diagrams* model the static structure of a system, particularly the entities that exist within the problem context, their internal structure, and their relationships to other entities. Class diagrams aid in recognizing business information objects, the basic elements of electronic business documents.

- *Object diagrams* model the static structure of an instance or detailed state of a system at a given point in time.
- *Component diagrams* model the structural or behavioral dimensions for developing a solution.
- *Deployment diagrams* model productive implementation of a system in its domain.

Use Cases

The proponents of UML claim that the technical diagrams it uses are accessible by businesspeople who can therefore take part in use case analysis and understand the resulting diagrams. Use cases describe the performance of systems, showing the actors, actions, and sequences (including variations), that result in value to the actors. Because they're relatively easy to build and understand, and require only limited special technical expertise, use cases often are the first step in the analytical exercise. They also help provide a sound base for communications between business and technical staff.[22]

Edward Kenworthy describes these steps for conducting a use case analysis:[23]

1. Identify who will use the system directly, called the *actors*.

2. Pick one of those actors.

3. Define what that actor wants to do with the system. You will need to develop a use case for each of these things that the actor wants to do with the system.

4. For each of the use cases, select the course that best describes what normally happens when that actor uses the system. This is called the *basic course*.

5. Describe that basic course in the description for the use case. Use the dialogue of "actor does X and system does Y." Keep the dialogue at a high level. Describe as well the things that an actor would need to know, and what the actor does that the system needs to know.

6. Once the basic course is described, then go on to alternative courses to the basic course. Each of the alternatives becomes an extension to the basic course.

7. Review each of the use case descriptions. Those descriptions with a high degree of overlap are called the *common use cases*. The common use cases essentially describe a single process.

8. Repeat steps 2–7 for each actor.

Use case diagrams illustrate the processes described in the use case scenarios. They often identify the actors with stick figures and have ovals with text enclosed, describing the processes. The order of the ovals indicates the sequence. Figure 5.1 shows a sample use case diagram from the running store example in Chapter 3, "ebXML at Work."

Figure 5.1

Use case scenario diagram.

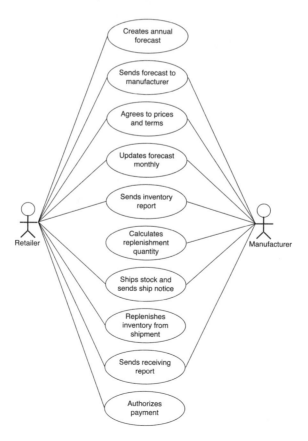

Further analysis with sequence, class, or activity diagrams normally requires technical specialists. However, starting with use case scenarios locks in the basic business requirements of a system or interactions among systems; thus, the use case stage is one in which business rather than technical expertise is required.

The major problem with this approach occurs when the actors cannot be neatly categorized and therefore have to be artificially prescribed in order to make the method work. Furthermore, business problems can often be more accurately described in terms of what is *not* allowed, as well as what the designers envision as permitted.

In systems analysis, tools and terminology may change, but the fundamental principles often stay the same. Thus, many of the good ideas in UML had been identified and formalized earlier and in other ways. While the object-oriented software community gave us the term *use case* and gave it a formal role in UML, the process follows the same basic approach to needs and workflow analysis practiced by systems professionals for 20 years.

Other analytical methods, such as the *Dynamic Systems Definition Methodology (DSDM)*, also prescribe a sequence of steps to capture and document abstract concepts of systems design. Like ebXML, DSDM does not impose a specific modeling technology, but lets practitioners select their own tools to identify and document components of business systems.

The ebXML approach is similar to the DSDM approach in that, rather than attempting to prescribe a particular modeling technology, an XML business process layer allows implementers to select their own preferred tools, and then ultimately derive and populate the business process XML content that ebXML requires as the end product.

Use Case Scenario

We can give an example of a use case with one of the scenarios from Chapter 3, namely the running store's vendor-managed inventory. For simplicity, we'll stick with the basic course in this example. The actors are Marathoner (the store) and the shoe manufacturer.

The following table shows the setup for Marathoner:

Actions	Actor Needs to Know
Creates annual sales forecast	Previous year sales, scheduled events, promotion plans, special conditions
Sends forecast to manufacturer	Manufacturer capabilities and limits
Agrees to prices and terms with manufacturer	Manufacturer capabilities and limits
Updates forecast monthly, shared with manufacturer	
Sends inventory status report to manufacturer	
Receives shipment and ship notice from manufacturer	
Replenishes inventory from shipment	
Sends receiving report to manufacturer	
Authorizes payment	

The following table shows the setup for the shoe manufacturer:

Actions	Actor Needs to Know
Receives annual forecast from Marathoner	Store's capabilities and limits
Agrees to prices and terms with Marathoner	Store's capabilities and limits
Receives monthly forecast update	Store's annual forecast
Receives periodic inventory report	
Calculates replenishment quantity	Store's annual forecast and updates
Ships replenishment stock, sends ship notice	
Gets receiving report from Marathoner	

Refer to Figure 5.1 for the diagram for this scenario, showing the interactions with both actors and the sequence of actions.

UML and UN/EDIFACT

UML provides useful tools for understanding and documenting business processes in ebXML, but UML is not required to use ebXML technology.

The e-business standards community sees significant relevance to the object-oriented approach. The X12 and UN/EDIFACT committees joined forces in 1998 to explore the use of UML to build the next generation of EDI standards. In 1999, X12 combined with American Express and Visa in a demonstration project of UML techniques applied to procurement transactions involving a corporate purchasing card. The UN/CEFACT organization has a Techniques and Methodologies Work Group (TMWG) that has spearheaded the work on object-oriented technologies for the UN/EDIFACT side of this partnership.[24] (See the later discussion of UN/CEFACT in the section "ebXML Founding Organizations and Process.")

In October 2000, X12 voted to begin creating accredited cross-industry XML standards based on ebXML. This work, coordinated with UN/EDIFACT's counterpart workgroup, includes defining business processes and core business objects.[25]

An entire discussion of UML is well beyond the scope of this book. Further information on UML can be found at the web site of the Object Management Group (www.omg.org), the organization that standardized UML and promotes its development. The site has introductory papers and tutorials. The site of software developer Rational (www.rational.com) also has good introductory materials on UML.

As we have noted, UML provides useful tools for understanding and documenting business processes in ebXML, but UML is not required to use ebXML technology. The ebXML architecture uses production rules to translate models written in UML (or other modeling languages) at their finest degree of granularity to XML. Work is underway through initiatives such as the *XML Metadata Interchange* (*XMI*) to translate directly from UML models to XML syntax.[26]

RosettaNet: XML for the Supply Chain, with an Emphasis on Business Process

So far, this chapter has discussed the work done in EDI and UML that contributed significantly to the development of ebXML, as well as the contributions of the XML/edi Group. The *Rosetta Net Consortium* is an initiative that put many of these ideas into practice well before ebXML and shared that useful experience during the development of ebXML.

RosettaNet combined an early industry XML vocabulary with business process analysis and supply-chain integration. This consortium, nurtured initially by IBM and Ingram Micros, works in the computer technology industry and has become a metric for other industries. As a result, its influence is felt well beyond its original industry boundaries.

RosettaNet, begun in 1998, has some 350 members in the information technology industry, broadly defined to include computer manufacturers, chip and circuit manufacturers, software developers, and distributors of products in the industry. The consortium seeks to develop a common language, thus taking its name from the "Rosetta Stone" written in 196 BC and discovered in Egypt in 1799 that helped comprehend for the first time the hieroglyphics of ancient Egypt.

RosettaNet's use of business process analysis separates it from most other vertical industry vocabularies. Rather than jumping immediately into defining XML messages, the early sponsors, utilizing resources provided by IBM, chose to first define business processes in considerable detail. This provision for a top-down business process methodology can also be implemented using the ebXML specifications. The inventories of processes undertaken by RosettaNet can serve as a reference point for other industries using ebXML.

In April 1999, less than a year after its founding, RosettaNet released its first *Partner Interface Processes (PIPs)*, which are specifications for business process alignment. RosettaNet carried out extensive process modeling to find out how companies in the supply chain interacted with each other to perform their normal business activities.[27]

RosettaNet breaks down the PIPs into eight categories, with one reserved for RosettaNet administrative functions. The seven categories covering industry business processes are described in the following sections. We present the descriptions of clusters here in some detail to illustrate the need for industries to define processes both comprehensively and in detail, to reflect the realities of doing business in that industry.

Cluster 1: Partner, Product, and Service Review

The first cluster provides for the collection and distribution of information for creation of trading partner profiles and subscriptions for information about products. One segment in this cluster contains PIPs for automated support for setting up a trading partner account, and for maintaining important trading partner information, such as shipping and billing locations. Another PIP in this cluster defines the process for establishing subscriptions for the exchange of product information among trading partners, as well as changes, cancellations, and confirmations of these subscriptions.[28]

Cluster 2: Product Information

The second cluster of PIPs covers the distribution of sales catalogs and related technical data, and the obtaining of extended specifications beyond the basic data. A separate segment handles updates, such as change notices, for these pieces. The first group of these PIPs includes the original distribution of product information, and a series of queries—products, marketing information, sales promotions/rebates, technical specifications, and product lifecycle and discontinuance. Other PIPs handle electronic commerce queries, distribution of product numbers (known as *stock-keeping units* or *SKUs*), and change notices for various marketing and product announcements.[29]

Cluster 3: Order Management

This cluster covers many of the basic supply-chain functions, with separate segments for quote and order entry, transportation and distribution, financial interactions, and custom configurations. The quote and order-entry series covers processes including requests for quotes, prices, and availability; quick transfers of shopping cart contents; purchase order management; and queries on order status and work in progress. The transportation segment includes PIPs projections, ship notices, delivery management, claims, and changes. The financial segment covers invoicing, remittances, product returns, and reconciliations. The product configuration segment has a series of PIPs covering the complex processes for developing and managing custom-engineered products for customers.[30]

Cluster 4: Inventory Management

The fourth PIP cluster covers processes for forecasting, inventory allocation and reports, sales reports, replenishment, and price protection. The forecasting segment includes processes for collaborative sales and order forecasts, forecast submissions, notifications, and confirmations. The allocation segment concerns allocation of scarce inventory to buyers. The inventory-reporting segment covers inventory reports, reconciliations, errors, and reconciliation discrepancies. The sales-reporting segment includes PIPs for several types of sales reports and error notifications. The price-protection segment covers processes for price-protection announcements, requests, claims, and provisions, as well as new order price changes.[31]

Cluster 5: Marketing Information Management

This cluster offers PIPs for exchange of marketing leads, campaign plans, design registrations, and ship-from-stock and debit transactions. The first segment in this cluster covers processes for exchanging data on sales opportunities, including management, queries, and notifications of leads. The second segment includes PIPs for distribution of marketing activity information such as incentive programs, claims, and rebates. The third segment covers processes for electronic component design registrations. The fourth segment also applies to electronic components and covers ship-from-stock and debit authorization processes.[32]

Cluster 6: Service and Support

The sixth cluster provides PIPs for technical support after the sale, service warrantees, and asset management. The first segment covers warranties and has one PIP for service registration. Another segment has PIPs for technical support and service management, including requests for service events, transfers of service-event ownership, notification of solutions, and service status queries. A third segment scheduled for asset management is covered under the warranty segment.[33]

Cluster 7: Manufacturing

As of December 2000, this cluster had not yet defined its processes, but will include PIPs for the exchange of messages for supporting a virtual manufacturing enterprise, covering design, configuration, process, quality, and other data needed on the shop floor.[34]

RosettaNet Implementation Framework

RosettaNet has defined guidelines for exchanging messages based on PIPs, called its *implementation framework*. It begins with an overall business model that spells out how companies interact within the PIPs and with each other. The business model has five parts:

- Creation of PIP guidelines that provide detailed specifications to supply-chain partners
- Distribution of those specifications to supply-chain partners
- Validation of the message content exchanged among trading partners

- Extensions of guidelines for special trading-partner implementations (but they cannot override original RosettaNet specifications)
- Exchange of extended guidelines to allow for validation of these special messages[35]

The RosettaNet technical architecture matches up to the seven-layer ISO open systems interconnect reference model, with most of its interactions contained in the highest or application layer of the ISO reference model. The one exception is RosettaNet's security layer that corresponds to the session layer in the ISO model.

The RosettaNet architecture focuses on four application layers, each with a set of protocols and messages:[36]

1. *Action layer*—the main business actions that contain or accompany the primary message content

2. *Transaction layer*—monitors the sequence of action messages that perform the work

3. *Process layer*—contains the choreography of transactions for executing the PIPs

4. *Service layer*—provides resources to perform network and related business functions

RosettaNet business messages consist of a header and message body with the content. Each message is contained in a Multipurpose Internet Mail Extensions (MIME) package used in email and many other file transfers. The message header and body themselves are encoded in XML.[37] The ebXML messaging specifications also use a combination of MIME and XML headers.

The *headers* include a preamble that includes the version, date and time, authority code, and usage code that indicates a test or production message. These elements appear in all messages. The *service header* identifies the parties in the exchange, the processes covered by the exchange, and the transactions and business actions in the message. Each of these parts has a separate sub-header. The *service content* is the business section of the message.

RosettaNet defines separate protocols for the exchange of request and response messages overall, as well as special protocols for web browsers using HTML and common gateway interface codings. The specifications also define protocols for HTTP and Secure Socket Layer (SSL) exchanges.[38]

Unlike some other early XML business vocabularies, RosettaNet defines its security specifications in some detail, rather than leaving the function to implementers. These specifications include a digital signature and an authentication model using both SSL and digital signatures.[39] The specifications define what it means to be in technical compliance with RosettaNet specifications (PIPs, protocol messages, server-to-server transfers, and security). The document also gives detailed definitions of RosettaNet-compliant organizations, including users, initiating organizations, servicing organizations, third-party agents, and technology solution providers.[40]

RosettaNet Dictionaries

Definitions for the semantics of RosettaNet messages are found in their dictionaries. The group offers three main types of dictionaries, each consisting of lists of individual data items:

- *Business dictionary*, including business properties and business data entities, as well as a separate list of fundamental business data entities
- *Electronic component technical dictionary*
- *Information technology technical dictionary*

The business dictionaries provide the elements for the business action messages defined throughout the specifications. Both the electronic component and information technology dictionaries are used to define products. As of December 2000, the electronic component dictionary was in beta testing.[41]

The momentum that RosettaNet generated in the use of XML in a traditional supply-chain arena acted as a catalyst for the existing EDI establishment to step across the bridge and embrace XML as a central plank for the future of business transaction standards.

Klaus-Dieter Naujok in the summer of 1999 put in motion events that led to the formation of the ebXML initiative itself, broadly based on the vision of openEDI and XML/edi that had been discussed in a white paper published earlier that year.[42]

ebXML Founding Organizations and Process

During its 18-month development phase, November 1999 to May 2001, the ebXML initiative operated under a joint agreement of the *Organization for the Advancement of Structured Information Standards* (*OASIS*) and the *United Nations Centre for Trade Facilitation and Electronic Business* (*UN/CEFACT*).

OASIS is a membership consortium of businesses, mainly software vendors, for the development of specifications based on public standards for structured documents, such as SGML and XML. It organizes working groups on these specifications, which have developed conformance test suites and a registry of XML vocabularies, known as `XML.org`. OASIS also hosts the XML-DEV listserv, the developer of SAX (see Chapter 4), as well as the comprehensive *XML Cover Pages*, an exhaustive resource of developments involving XML.[43]

UN/CEFACT is the UN's agency for developing worldwide policies to encourage trade, especially in the context of emerging economies. Given their mandate, electronic business has always been a special focus, as access to world markets is key to development. Officially, UN/CEFACT falls under the Economic Commission for Europe, but its scope cuts across regions, and more than 1,500 public and private sector experts take part in its work. UN/CEFACT focuses much of its efforts on increasing the participation of smaller businesses in global trade and reducing bureaucratic barriers to trade, by standardizing documents and data formats. Among UN/CEFACT's working groups is one responsible for maintaining the UN/EDIFACT traditional EDI standard, as well as a business process group that has researched the potential of object-oriented development technologies.[44]

UN/CEFACT is a recognized international standards organization. It is one of the signatories to a March 2000 memorandum of understanding with the *International Electrotechnical Commission (IEC)*, the *International Organization for Standardization* (French acronym *ISO*), and the *International Telecommunication Union (ITU)*. This memorandum divides responsibilities for standards development and gives UN/CEFACT responsibility for those standards related to e-business.[45]

During its development phase, the ebXML initiative kept its bureaucracy to a bare minimum. It had no permanent staff and relied almost entirely on volunteers. A chair, vice chair, and two other executive committee members comprised the official leadership, with two members of the leadership from OASIS and two from UN/CEFACT. The following project teams, led and staffed by volunteers, performed all of the work:

- ebXML Requirements
- Business Process Methodology
- Technical Architecture
- Core Components
- Transport/Routing and Packaging
- Security
- Registry and Repository
- Quality Review
- Proof of Concept
- Trading Partners Profiles
- Marketing, Awareness and Education

The initiative made it easy to take part in ebXML. It imposed neither membership fees nor requirements to attend meetings or take part in conference calls. Enrolling required completion of a simple online form and selection of the project teams in which to participate.

The ebXML teams and leadership met quarterly. The quarterly meetings began in July 1999 and finished in May 2001, taking place in North America, Europe, and Asia. Participation at the meetings, like the listservs, was open to anyone, although meeting organizers collected a nominal meeting fee to help defray expenses.

The teams developed the specifications and technical reports in the quarterly meetings, as well as through telephone conference calls and the listservs established for each team. Once the teams felt they had enough of the issues resolved to open for public comments, the draft specifications were posted on the ebXML web site for review.

Anyone could download and comment on the draft specifications and technical reports; commentators weren't required to be ebXML participants. A quality-review team maintained consistency among the various documents. Specifications went through at least two iterations of public review, while technical reports had one public review. Specifications contained the official ebXML rules, called *normative documents*. Technical reports contained advisory and preliminary information, such as guidelines or examples of output. ebXML published the work on core components as technical reports rather than full specifications, since it had not had enough time to complete its detailed development.

Since the end of the development phase in May 2001, OASIS and UN/CEFACT divided the continuation of the ebXML work, with OASIS taking the infrastructure project teams and UN/CEFACT keeping those teams working on business content. The infrastructure teams operating under OASIS include transport-routing-packaging, registry/repository, trading partners, and security. It also took the proof-of-concept team that will work on conformance testing and implementation assistance. The UN/CEFACT teams include business process and core components. A joint management group will provide coordination, as well as carry on the work of the technical architecture and marketing teams.

Endnotes

[1] Bruce Peat and Richard Light, "XML/EDI: Advantages of including Electronic Data Interchange (EDI) entities with eXtensible Markup Language (XML)," 1 June 1997, www.xmledi-group.org/xmledigroup/bp01.htm.

[2] Bruce Peat and David Webber, "Introducing XML/EDI, the e-business framework," XML/edi Group, August 1997, www.xmledi-group.org/xmledigroup/start.htm.

[3] Martin Bryan et al., "Guidelines for using XML for Electronic Data Interchange," Version 0.05, 25 January 1998, XML/edi Group, www.xmledi-group.org/xmledi-group/guide.htm.

[4] "Preliminary Findings and Recommendations on the Representation of X12 Data Elements and Structures in XML," X12C Ad Hoc Task Group on the use of XML with X12 EDI, version 1.0, 31 August 1998.

[5] David Webber et al., "White Paper on Global XML Repositories for XML/EDI," February 1999, XML/edi Group, www.xmledi-group.org/xmledigroup/repository/RepWPv1.PDF.

[6] "Interim Report for CEN/ISSS XML/EDI Pilot Project," CEN/ISSS Electronic Commerce Workshop, 1999, www.cenorm.be/isss/workshop/ec/xmledi/Documents_99/xml001_99.htm.

[7] Alan Kotok, "XML and EDI: Lessons Learned and Baggage to Leave Behind," XML.com, 4 August 1999, www.xml.com/pub/a/1999/08/edi/index.html.

[8] "EDI Standards," EDI Tutorial, National Institute of Standards and Technology, 27 February 1996, www.nist.gov/itl/div896/ipsg/eval_guide/subsection3_5_5.html.

[9] Kevin Kail, DISA annual conference keynote address, 7 March 2001.

[10] Because of the legal implications of TPAs, these documents should be reviewed by an appropriately qualified legal council. The American Bar Association has a manual on TPAs that includes a model agreement. See www.abanet.org/buslaw/catalog/5070258.html.

[11] IBM Corporation has donated more than two years of work and intellectual property on TPA to the ebXML initiative. See www.ebXML.org for more details.

[12] Retail bar codes are called *UPC* in North America and *EAN* (for European Article Number) in the rest of the world.

[13] "UCC-12 (U.P.C.) Guidelines Section 1.2," Uniform Code Council, undated, www.uc-council.org/ reflib/00810/01-TOC/01-01.html.

[14] "Why Do I Need a D&B D-U-N-S Number?" Dun & Bradstreet, undated, www.dnb.com/duns_update_US/ 0,1310,0-223-1012-0,00.html.

[15] "Getting Started with ID Numbers and Bar Codes," Uniform Code Council (undated), www.uc-council.org/ id_numbers/id_getting_started_with_id_num.html.

[16] "Functional Acknowledgment," EDIDEV (undated), www.edidev.com/FunctionalAcknowledgement.htm.

[17] See www.techweb.com/encyclopedia/ defineterm?term=object.

[18] Harry Featherstone, "Object Oriented Approach for Open-edi Standards Development," ENIX Newsletter, Spring 1999, http://enix.epa.gov.tw/enixnews/ 1999spring/FA_OOEDI.htm.

[19] Sinan Si Alhir, "Applying the Unified Modeling Language (UML)," 1 August 1998, http:// home.earthlink.net/~salhir/applyingtheuml.html.

[20] Sinan Si Alhir, "The Foundation of the Unified Modeling Language," 7 August 1998, http:// home.earthlink.net/~salhir/ thefoundationoftheuml.html.

[21] Luis X. B. Mourão, "Topic of the Week for June 1st, Unified Modeling Language," LAN Times, 1 June 1998, www.lantimes.com/ltparts/discuss/discuss59.htm.

[22] Craig Dewalt, "Business Process Modeling with UML," 7 December 1999, Johns Hopkins University.

[23] Edward Kenworthy, "Use Case Modeling: Capturing User Requirements," The Object Practitioner's Guides, 2 December 1997, www.zoo.co.uk/~z0001039/PracGuides/ pg_use_cases.htm.

[24] "ASC X12 Explores Object Oriented E-Business Standards Development," Data Interchange Standards Association, 1 November 1999.

25 "EDI Standards Communities Agree to Jointly Develop Business XML," Data Interchange Standards Association, 25 October 2000, `www.disa.org/apps/pr/prdoc.cfm?Name=489`.

26 XMI 1.1 RTF Main revised document, Object Management Group, 2 October 1999, `www.omg.org/cgi-bin/doc?ad/99-10-02`.

27 "$700 Billion IT Industry Set to Embrace RosettaNet Global Business Standards Aimed at Aligning IT Supply Chain to Leverage Internet and e-Commerce." RosettaNet press release, 12 April 1999, `www.rosettanet.org/`.

28 "Cluster 1: Partner, Product and Service Review," *Cluster, Segments, and PIPs*, RosettaNet, 12 September 2000, p. 2.

29 "Cluster 2: Product Information," *Cluster, Segments, and PIPs*, RosettaNet, 12 September 2000, pp. 3–5.

30 "Cluster 3: Order Management," *Cluster, Segments, and PIPs*, RosettaNet, 12 September 2000, pp. 5–10.

31 "Cluster 4: Inventory Management," *Cluster, Segments, and PIPs*, RosettaNet, 12 September 2000, pp. 10–13.

32 "Cluster 5: Marketing Information Management," *Cluster, Segments, and PIPs*, RosettaNet, 12 September 2000, pp. 13–16.

33 "Cluster 6: Service and Support," *Cluster, Segments, and PIPs*, RosettaNet, 12 September 2000, pp. 17–18.

34 "Cluster 7: Manufacturing," RosettaNet, `www.rosettanet.org`.

35 RosettaNet Implementation Framework Specification, version 1.1, 8 November 1999, pp. 15–16.

36 RosettaNet Implementation Framework Specification, version 1.1, 8 November 1999, pp. 18–20.

37 RosettaNet Implementation Framework Specification, version 1.1, 8 November 1999, p. 21.

38 RosettaNet Implementation Framework Specification, version 1.1, 8 November 1999, pp. 26–35.

39 RosettaNet Implementation Framework Specification, version 1.1, 8 November 1999, pp. 42, 45.

40 RosettaNet Implementation Framework Specification, version 1.1, 8 November 1999, p. 49.

[41] "Dictionaries," RosettaNet, www.rosettanet.org.

[42] See www.xmledi-group.org/xmledigroup/action.htm. Select item 8 from the menu.

[43] For more information about OASIS, see www.oasis-open.org.

[44] "Knowledge of UN/CEFACT," www.unece.org/cefact/knowlg/knowlg.htm.

[45] "Standardization in the Field of Electronic Business," www.unece.org/ebi.htm.

Chapter 6

Business Requirements for ebXML

The ebXML initiative set for itself a series of objectives in business terms that establish baselines for the performance of ebXML (the product), and in effect define its standards for success. At its third meeting in May 2000, the initiative approved *Electronic Business XML (ebXML) Requirements Specification Version 1.0* as its first completed document.[1] This chapter describes ebXML's requirements and discusses its relationships with other XML business frameworks.

The requirements document had as its official purpose to provide functional specifications for the design of the technical architecture, but the importance of the ebXML requirements extends beyond the guidelines for the people writing the ebXML specifications. First, the requirements must reflect the needs of conducting business in the 21st century. The important decisions on whether to use ebXML will rest with the top executives of companies, and the requirements provide benchmarks for executives to judge the relevance of ebXML to their operations.

Second, the requirements offer designers and developers of e-business systems a set of real-world guidelines for their work. The ebXML technical documents provide specific targets for the performance of e-business services and, in some cases, instructions for the physical content details exchanged in messages. However, the companies developing e-business solutions or the end-user companies themselves will actually build the systems that create these services and exchange the messages. They will find the overall ebXML requirements to be a helpful reality check during the course of doing their work.

Basic Goals and Scope

The ultimate technical goal of ebXML is stated as "[providing] an XML-based open technical framework to enable XML to be utilized in a consistent and uniform manner for the exchange of electronic business data in application-to-application, application-to-human, and human-to-application environments—thus creating a single global market™."2

This goal statement includes several important elements, as discussed in the following sections.

Role of XML

Facsimile (fax) machines don't care what goes on the page sent to or from other fax machines; the fax is simply a digital representation of a visual image. With ebXML, however, the content of the message itself is vital.

The ebXML specifications deal with electronic business services based on XML. While the systems built on ebXML may incorporate other technologies, be written in various programming languages, access any number of different databases, and work on a diverse set of operating systems, XML is the glue that allows these different systems to work together. A key factor in making ebXML happen is utilization of the World Wide Web Consortium's (W3C's) collection of technical specifications on XML and related technologies.

While its implementation focuses on using XML as the format for message exchanges, ebXML draws on other standards and specifications as well. The requirements document identified several of the standards organizations from which it drew guidance, including the Internet Engineering Task Force (IETF), International Organization for Standardization (ISO), Institute of Electrical and Electronics Engineers (IEEE), International Electrotechnical Commission (IEC), and the Object Management Group (OMG), as well as the founding organizations of ebXML, UN/CEFACT and OASIS.

Open Technical Framework

Anyone wanting to use the ebXML specifications can utilize the documents, without fees or preconditions. None of the specifications involve proprietary systems or software. The process used to develop the specifications is also open, with anyone wanting to take part included in the development process. At no time did ebXML require membership fees or organizational endorsements to take part in the development teams.

Consistency and Uniformity

Standards provide a bedrock of consistency and uniformity that assures builders of systems that they can successfully exchange data with other systems built on the same set of standards. This idea didn't begin with ebXML, of course, but the involvement of so many standards organizations helped make it a central principle. As a result, companies with ebXML-compliant systems should be able to exchange ebXML messages, as easily as facsimile machines can exchange fax messages anywhere in the world. The ebXML sponsors also intend to submit its end product documents to become an international standard accredited by a suitable international standards body.

Electronic Business Data

Facsimile (fax) machines don't care what goes on the page sent to or from other fax machines; the fax is simply a digital representation of a visual image. With ebXML, however, the content of the message itself is vital. The e-business messages and services governed by ebXML are tied to business processes and contain core components that detail the information interchange (using a vocabulary that establishes a consensus among industries, or between trading partners). The ebXML message format can contain any form of payload, of course, but the key difference is that, unlike with faxes, the recipient is able to deploy machine processes to automatically recognize, interpret, and utilize the content.

Application-to-Application, Application-to-Human, and Human-to-Application Environments

The specifications recognize that people and systems need to interact with each other to conduct e-business, and thus the specifications must address all of the contingencies and nuances that this entails. With existing EDI transactions, e-business messages are sent from one trading partner mailbox to another, and EDI explicitly does not address either the resulting integration with internal business systems or the need for human interactions to complete the service delivery. Unlike EDI, ebXML seeks to address the integration and human elements directly.

Creating a Single Global Market

ebXML should enable any company of any size in any industry to interact with any other company of any size in any other industry

The key word in this part of the goal statement is *global*,[3] which has a double meaning. First, as you might expect with any document related to the work of the United Nations, the specifications must work anywhere that can support the basic technical infrastructure, and work in any written human language. XML itself provides the ability to utilize any written language using a technique called the *Unicode double-byte encoding system*. Second, ebXML cuts across industry and business function boundaries. It needs to be accessible to trading partners in any kind of industry or line of business, and for all business processes. Thus, ebXML is not an accounting or procurement or logistics specification, but a technical framework that covers all of those processes and beyond.

The scope of the ebXML initiative covers all business sectors, from the largest multinational enterprise to medium-size and small companies that seek to engage in commerce with other businesses or with consumers. Also, systems based on ebXML need to be fully interoperable *across* industry boundaries. As a result, ebXML should enable any company of any size in any industry to interact with any other company of any size in any other industry.[4]

The requirements also carefully delineate the business-to-business and business-to-consumer scope of the specifications. Currently ebXML puts first priority on meeting the needs of businesses for interactions among businesses and between businesses and consumers. However, the specifications cover only the business end of business-to-consumer exchanges, with the consumer side of the equation beyond its scope.

The requirements note that companies can also apply ebXML technology to interactions among applications within an enterprise. But the requirements give first priority to transactions among businesses or between businesses and consumers, over internal interactions between applications within a company.[5]

Meeting the needs of a global marketplace of course requires more than technical specifications. Companies need to meet a myriad of legal and cultural issues, as well as varying business practices within industries. We expect industry groups and trade-promotion agencies to address these issues, which extend beyond the scope of the ebXML specifications.

General Principles and Business Requirements

The initiative elaborated on the technical goal statement with several principles to guide its development work. Under those principles, the ebXML specifications should do all of the following:

- Make electronic business simple, easy, and ubiquitous.
- Use XML to the fullest extent possible.
- Offer an open standard that enables business transactions across industry boundaries for both business-to-business and business-to-consumer commerce.
- Bring together the structure and content of various XML business vocabularies into a single specification.

- Offer a migration path from current EDI standards, as well as XML vocabularies.
- Encourage industry efforts with immediate or short-term objectives to come together under a common long-term goal.
- Avoid solutions requiring end users to invest in proprietary software or impose constraints requiring specialized systems to conduct e-business with ebXML.
- Keep adoption costs to a minimum.
- Support multiple written languages and accommodate common rules of national and international trade.
- Apply the business requirements of the Ad Hoc Working Group on SIMPL-EDI, Forms, and Web-based EDI (SIMAC) whenever possible.[6]

The SIMAC group proposed SIMPL-EDI (the spelling is intentional) as a way of making EDI easier and less expensive for smaller businesses. The group suggested that if business processes were simplified, EDI itself could be made simpler. SIMAC also proposed messages or transactions consisting of only a core set of data, rather than defining every piece of data exchanged between trading partners. SIMPL-EDI assumes that application-to-application exchanges can occur without human intervention. It also assumes that trading partners can reference common databases, such as product numbers and descriptions, rather than exchanging the data themselves.[7]

In addition to these principles, the requirements provide a list of general specifications for business solutions that ebXML should address. They include many of the principles listed earlier, as well as other important features:

- A process for determining compliance with ebXML, with design rules for developing messages compliant with ebXML specifications and W3C requirements for XML.

- Support for vertical solutions—those based on specific industries or companies—as well as solutions that address business functions that cut across industry or company boundaries.
- Ability to implement simple, low-cost solutions for smaller businesses, but still enable full-featured solutions if needed by larger enterprises.
- Allow for a range of implementations, from a subset of core features in ad hoc exchanges to highly structured interactions.
- Provide a consistent business process modeling language and methodology, including a *meta-model*—literally, a model of models—that allows for the development of individual business process models.
- Support current business processes and practices, yet still allow for new business processes developed through modeling methodologies.
- Enable a series of core components in a neutral syntax, to allow for mapping to previous messages and technologies.
- Support industry XML schemas with elements and tags that support the industry's business processes, as well as capturing the full semantics of an industry's vocabulary.
- Offer fully interoperable messages with specifications for packaging, transport, and routing.
- Meet security needs of businesses, especially confidentiality.

The requirements include a special note on the need to reduce costs, not only as a company's bottom-line strategy but to help gain competitive advantage. The cost of e-business adoption that a company can incur include everything from the initial development of e-business systems, through installation and integration with other business systems, as well as ongoing operations and support. One of the key objectives of XML is lowering the cost of exchanging business data, and clearly success will be measured on how well ebXML can deliver on this promise.[8]

Interoperability

A key issue for ebXML is interoperability—called "the primary requirement of the ebXML initiative"—and the specifications spell out the meaning of that concept. The specifications identify four focus points of interoperability:

- The ebXML architecture itself
- Messaging
- Extensibility
- Taking advantage of existing technology

For ebXML, the idea of interoperability goes well beyond most dictionary definitions of the term. We now consider each of these aspects in turn.

Architecture

The ebXML architecture provides a picture of the technology for making the exchange of business data happen. The specifications list the features of the architecture that make it possible for companies to exchange data seamlessly. They also point out that incorporating these features can help meet other requirements, such as the ability to operate across various computing platforms.

But the specifications recognize that meeting all of these requirements may not be immediately achievable. Where all parties are not at the same level of maturity in using ebXML, one or more of the companies exchanging the data may need to create special-process steps, including mapping or conversion routines, which can bridge the gaps but add time and cost to the exercise.

These architectural features identified by the specifications include common understandings of certain issues:

- **Business processes.** The companies exchanging data must be involved in the same transaction, as part of the same business process. For a company to send a shipping notice to another company as part of an order/delivery process, for example, both companies need to have their systems prepared for that particular exchange. If the receiving party is unable to interpret or adequately process the message it receives, this can lead to failure of that part of the business process. A company may inadvertently send such a message to a trading partner, and therefore remedial actions will be required at that point in the process.

■ **Meanings of terms.** When companies exchange data, they need to use common semantics for the data exchange. For example, in the printing industry the term *signature* has a specific meaning that's much different from that of most of the rest of the business world. Thus, when doing business with a printing company, a trading partner has to make certain that the word *signature* used in the financial context is distinguished from the printing industry's special meaning.

■ **Character encoding.** For data exchanges in the standard ASCII character set used for Roman alphabets, representing the data rarely presents a problem. For non-Roman character sets, however, that representation can become a problem. Fortunately, the Unicode standard and ISO standard 10646 already provide a common way of representing characters.

■ **XML representation.** For data expressed in XML, all of the parties to the exchange need to have common element tags and attributes, as well as a similar XML document structure for the data to be meaningful. In other words, the messages exchanged among the parties should reference the same XML layout and structure; technically this is achieved by using a document-type definition (DTD) or schema.

■ **Security implementation.** All of the parties in an exchange of data need to be on the same level of security and have the same privileges with the data. If one party encrypts a message, for example, and another party cannot decrypt the data, the exchange of data does no good.[9]

Messaging

The ebXML specifications give the interoperability requirements for the transport, routing, and packaging of messages, so that trading partners can reliably send and receive their business data. In addition, the guidelines for message exchanges are designed to be applicable independently of the physical systems developed for sending and receiving the data. This approach acts as insurance against obsolescence as newer interchange technologies come along.

- **Network and data-transfer protocols.** All of the parties need to operate under the same basic technical procedures for transferring the data. For example, if one party uses email to send the data but the other parties are anticipating web-based messages such as those using the Simple Object Access Protocol (SOAP), the exchange will require a transfer system that can link their messaging delivery together. Clearly, the more compatible individual systems are, the better the reliability that will be achieved in message transfers.

- **Reliable message delivery.** In ebXML, reliable messaging is defined as the delivery of a message no more than once, which means only one delivery or no delivery at all. In some cases, *not* receiving a message can be better for a company than receiving multiple messages. For example, if a company received multiple invoices, it might respond with multiple payments, but no invoice triggers no action in response.

- **Neutral syntax.** If industries have special requirements for message transport, packaging, or routing, they need to store those requirements in a neutral syntax so that trading partners can retrieve those policies with systems running under any computing platform.

- **Message configuration.** The specifications require ebXML to give details of the message format and structure, showing the configuration of the envelopes, headers, and payloads. These details make up most of the ebXML messaging specifications.

- **Queries to servers.** The requirements call
  for ebXML servers to respond to queries
  about the services that they support. While
  ebXML included this function in its specifications, it became an activity of the registry
  functionality of ebXML rather than message-
  delivery servers.[10]

Extensibility

The specifications note the need for businesses to put
more than the basic ebXML functions into a system.
For example, systems built or packaged to support
ebXML will sometimes support internal business
processes, such as exchanging messages among organizational units or reporting company financial data
on an intranet. Therefore, ebXML systems need to
accommodate these extensions, while at the same
time preserving the basic standard functions.[11]

Taking Advantage of Existing Technology

Requirements for ebXML's interoperability include
the ability to relate to previous methods for electronic data exchange, as well as migrating from new
technologies to ebXML. Some of the first ebXML
applications will likely take place in companies
already using EDI or other XML vocabularies. These
companies will certainly want to integrate their
investment in these systems with ebXML, and thus
any definition of interoperability needs to include
this vital aspect.

An important part of the connection between current data exchange technologies and ebXML is the
common data items in the current exchanges and
ebXML messages. While these data items may be
expressed in a different syntax, they still represent the
same ideas, particularly when they don't change
across contexts.

Internally, ebXML calls these common items *core
components*, and they can be reused both within and
across messages. Business processes using the core
components then provide the precise meaning of
these items by providing the context for the
definition.

Time data items, for example, are vital for business and used in many ways and in many different messages. Time is expressed in many EDI and XML transactions using the ISO standard 8601 as hh:mm:ss in 24-hour notation. Thus, a physical time defined as 17:52:00 has a precise meaning and can be used interchangeably in many different messages and applications. But while the meaning is precise, it's also limited. It needs a context to make it useful for business understanding. If the time data in a message sent by an airline to a travel agent reads 17:52:00 ETA (where *ETA* stands for *estimated time of arrival*), it has more business meaning and utility than simply the time value itself.

The ebXML specifications include a requirement to express core components in a neutral syntax, which makes them deployable among both XML vocabularies and EDI transactions. This syntax neutrality also must extend to spoken languages as well as markup languages, to help make the core components more applicable across business processes and contexts, as well as support ebXML's other requirements for globalization. The specifications consider this requirement so important that if the ebXML working groups cannot find a methodology to generate core components, they recommend that ebXML build its own.

The specifications cite the importance to businesses of providing a migration path to ebXML from their current EDI transactions based on accredited standards and previous XML vocabularies. Providing a migration strategy or methods is considered beyond the scope of the initiative. Nonetheless, the specifications encourage the developers of the technology to keep an eye on this migration issue.[12]

Legal and Security Requirements

The issue of security in e-business has gone from an arcane technical concern to a basic issue in exchanging data among companies and individuals. In 1999, many online businesses adopted a voluntary set of guidelines and best practices called the *Standard for*

Internet Commerce (`www.gii.com/standard/`) that includes several provisions for addressing these concerns. The driving motivation for developing this standard was the continued viability of electronic business over the Internet. The standard meets five basic needs:[13]

- Increase consumer satisfaction and confidence in doing business on the Internet.
- Establish merchant credibility and trustworthiness for customers.
- Help merchants provide a world-class customer experience, innovate rapidly, and lower their costs.
- Support and enhance self-regulation of Internet commerce.
- Help merchants and customers deal with a proliferation of guidelines and symbols.

Because many potential customers have had to overcome security fears before making online purchases, individual businesses have also taken the issue seriously and built in the necessary precautions. A November 2000 survey by ePublicEye, a rating service for online businesses, found the proportion of Internet merchants that use secure transaction processing rose from 85% in 1999 to 93% in 2000, and about 9 in 10 online companies also reported having privacy policies published on their sites.[14]

The need for security in the exchange of data will range from one business scenario to another. In some cases, such as quick lookups of public information, will have little or no security attached to the process. But in most instances, even for the most routine exchanges of data, trading partners will want to protect the transactions.

The messaging services specifications noted the need for ebXML to support security for individual electronic business documents, as well as continuous network sessions, where a number of interactions can occur. The use of session-based security is important for scenarios in which trading partners may have many interactions over a limited period of time. The session-based security model also supports business relationships in which one party monitors in real time the systems of another, such as vendor-managed inventories.

The requirements discuss several individual aspects of security that ebXML needs to address. While these requirements apply to business systems in general, business needs will dictate the extent to which these requirements are implemented from one business system to another.

- **Confidentiality.** Trading partners need to conduct their interactions with the assurance that the information remains known only to the parties sharing this information. Adequate confidentiality limits the possibility of eaves-dropping.

- **Authentication of sender and receiver.** As e-business becomes more voluminous, more global, more intermittent, and more impersonal, the numbers of potential trading partners will increase from all over the globe, and their interactions become less frequent and more irregular. Companies exchanging data need to have confidence that all parties engaged in the transactions are really whom they claim to be and not imposters seeking to engage in fraud. This concern raises the need to identify and credential the parties involved in the business transaction.

- **Integrity.** Companies engaged in e-business need assurance that the data items received by one party are the same as the data items sent by the originating party. Trading partners need to limit the possibility of distortion of the message by non-malicious intent, such as network errors, or by deliberate attempts to falsify or otherwise manipulate messages.

- **Non-repudiation of origin and receipt.** Parties engaged in e-business need to provide a record that the transaction actually took place, and that it could not have been a

forgery. Electronic transactions need to have
the same level of commitment as a signed
paper document to hold parties accountable to
that commitment.

■ **Archiving.** Companies need the capability to
reconstruct the meaning and intent of one or
more transactions several years after the transactions themselves took place. The specifications note that in some instances companies
may need to archive their business documents—both physical and electronic—for
up to 30 years to meet records-retention
requirements.

The specifications indicate that companies can
rely on trusted third parties to provide authentication and non-repudiation services.
Archiving is one area in which many companies have used third-party services for some
time.[15]

Digital Signatures

The specifications include a separate section on
digital signatures and note their legal and security
implications for identifying the parties in electronic
business interactions, and thus their impact on
ebXML's authentication requirements discussed earlier. UN/CEFACT, one of the sponsors of ebXML,
identified the need for authentication of trade documents through means other than the traditional
physical signature as early as 1979.[16]

Digital signatures have now been enacted in law in
North America, Europe, and Asia, so as to have the
same legal standing as the traditional pen-and-ink
variety, and the specifications cite a 1999 California
statute (1999 CA SB 1124) that provides an extended
definition of a digital signature:[17]

> *"Digital signature," for the purposes of this section,
> means an electronic identifier, created by a computer,
> that is intended by the party using it to have the
> same force and effect as the use of a manual physical
> signature. The use of a digital signature shall have
> the same force or effect as a manual signature if it
> embodies all of the following attributes:*

It is unique to the person using it.

It is capable of verification.

It is under the sole control of the person using it.

It is linked to data in a manner that if the data is changed, the digital signature is invalidated.

> While we can expect to see more software that fully integrates data from businesses into end-user applications, we will have plenty of human hands entering data as well.

Digital signatures have since become part of U.S. federal law. On 30 June 2000, the U.S. Congress passed and President Clinton signed into law the Millennium Digital Commerce Act (Public Law No. 106-229). Title I of the act affirms the validity of electronic signatures and prohibits their denial of legal standing in many business interactions. Title II directs the Department of Commerce to promote the acceptance and use of digital signatures in interstate and foreign trade, as well as to study the potential barriers to their acceptance within and outside the United States. Title III amends the Securities and Exchange Act of 1934 to reflect this law, but still require manual signatures if needed to deter fraud.[18]

Legal Requirements

The specifications identified a few other legal requirements related to security and digital issues. These requirements include full audit capability, a mechanism to ensure completeness of a transaction, versioning control to help reconstruct the full semantic meaning of transactions, and compliance with the 1979 UN/CEFACT recommendations that identified the need for authentication methods other than traditional signatures.[19]

Accommodating the Human Element

As indicated in the general principles, ebXML needs to work in a range of trading partner environments and business processes. One of the key variables, and a factor that separates ebXML from traditional EDI, is the extent of human involvement in the exchanges among companies. EDI transactions assume that the messages go from one system to another—either directly or through a mailbox—with no human intervention at either end. Systems based on EDI-style exchanges often have high volumes and predictable formats that allow for mapping directly out of or into the trading partner business systems.

While ebXML messages need to support these kinds of interactions, they also need to manage those with direct human involvement and intermediation. Some companies may not have the volume to support a fully integrated system that automatically generates or captures and transforms data from trading partners. In other cases, the applications may require human review, such as patient healthcare records or simple email-based message interchanges. As indicated in the general requirements, ebXML also needs to support business-to-consumer interactions, and while we can expect to see more software that fully integrates data from businesses into end-user applications, we will have plenty of human hands entering data as well.[20]

Businesses will also capture data from paper forms or need to generate paper forms according to pre-defined formats, and ebXML-compliant systems need to accommodate these contingencies. Trading partners may specify their own output formats, or industries may have their own standard formats, such as for descriptions of hazardous materials. In 1981, the United Nations defined a common format for paperwork used in international commerce, called the *United Nations Layout Key for Trade Documents*. The layouts are specifically mentioned in the ebXML requirements as an example of a standardized style sheet for paper forms that act as input for or output of business systems.[21]

Globalization

The need for global e-business solutions, defined in this case as the ability to operate anywhere in the world, is an important issue for ebXML, due in no small part to its United Nations sponsorship. The specifications note that the requirements already cite the need to simplify current methods of data exchange and harmonize the large number of options available. These steps will help build an overall business metamodel and foster the use of core components in a neutral syntax. These are two key ebXML sections that make the specifications more readily available to diverse national and multinational enterprises.

Also, as cited in its own general requirements, ebXML makes full use of existing standards and specifications, especially those that support business activities that cross national boundaries. The standards cited include the use of XML 1.0 (described in more detail in Chapter 4, "The Promise of XML"). However, the requirements list other standards that encourage multinational business.

Unicode allows for encoding most of the world's known character sets, including scientific and mathematics symbols. Exchanging data in major language groups such as Arabic, Mandarin Chinese, and Kanji (a Japanese character set) becomes feasible with Unicode.

An important standard in this group is *Unicode*, a specification that enables systems to represent non–Roman character sets, which is also supported by XML 1.0. The latest version of Unicode (3.0) matches up to the international standard for character sets, ISO/IEC 10646-1:2000. It uses two bytes or 16 bits per character, and provides codes for more than 65,000 characters.

As a result, Unicode allows for encoding most of the world's known character sets, including scientific and mathematics symbols. Exchanging data in major language groups such as Arabic, Mandarin Chinese, and Kanji (a Japanese character set) becomes feasible with Unicode. It also allows for the encoding of private character sets and reserves some 8,000 code points for further expansion.[22]

Unicode builds on the work done earlier by an International Organization of Standards committee on computer representation of character sets that resulted in ISO standard 10646 in 1993. The *Universal Multiple-Octet Coded Character Set*, as it is called officially (abbreviated *UCS*), enables the internal computer representation of these characters as well as their exchange between systems. It provides for the coding of the characters, not their complete representation as human-readable text. Unicode closely follows the ISO 10646 characters and contributes to the further development of that standard.[23]

The UN Economic Commission for Europe, the official parent organization for UN/CEFACT, recommended in 1978 to adopt ISO 4217 for representing currencies in international trade transactions.[24] With the rapid growth of international transactions over the web, more and more commercial sites are not assuming the use of one currency over another and specifying the currency in which the transactions take place. ISO 4217 provides standard currency codes for trade transactions.

Another ISO standard, ISO 3166, offers standard country names in French and English, as well as two-character codes. The idea of standard country names and codes sounds simple enough, but consider the changes in country names just in the period of 1990 to 2000, with the end of the Cold War and turmoil in Africa and Asia. Because of the quick and sometimes drastic changes, ISO established a maintenance agency for the names and codes that issues periodic updates in between the normal five-year standards cycle.[25]

ISO also has standard codes for language names, represented in its standard 639. The standard provides for both two- and three-character codes for each known human language ranging from Afar to Zuni.[26] The Internet Engineering Task Force has designated the two-character ISO 639 codes for language tags in Internet technical standards, such as Multipurpose Internet Mail Extensions (MIME), used in ebXML messaging envelopes.[27]

In keeping with its United Nations roots, ebXML uses English as the standard language for its deliberations and documents, but will provide translations into other languages at a later point.[28]

Openness

ebXML established its own development processes to be as open as possible, by not charging membership fees to take part in the development of the specifications and allowing open public comments on all draft specifications. In the specifications themselves, the requirements focus on the openness of operations of registries and their associated repositories, two key elements in the ebXML architecture. In this case, openness means being available and accessible to do business, not just democratic.

Registries list the business process models, message formats, industry schemas and vocabularies, core components, trading partner profiles, and other objects needed by trading partners to conduct electronic business. Repositories store the actual business artifacts themselves whose definitions the registry provides. The registry acts as the access point and index to the repositories, both for human-readable lookups and automated data transfer. The design of ebXML anticipates that companies will likely have many interactions with registries in the course of learning about an industry's requirements for e-business, listing their companies' characteristics and needs, and discovering the capabilities of trading partners.

In this case, openness means being available and accessible to do business, not just democratic.

Registries will be maintained by industry groups or standards organizations, or as for-profit enterprises if the business opportunities arise. But their availability needs to be assured, if ebXML is going to work globally.

Like the web itself, ebXML registries and repositories need to be distributed rather than centralized into one or a few centers. A centralized approach simply could not handle the anticipated high volume of traffic. Likewise, many companies will need to access several registries to conduct business electronically. For example, an industry registry would likely provide most of any company's vertical business processes and schemas, but the company will likely do business with banking, accounting, or transportation companies, which may mean accessing those registries as well. The need for a distributed series of registries clearly supports the ebXML openness and availability requirements.[29]

From Requirements to Specifications

This chapter provides an overview of the requirements of the major architectural components of ebXML and how they contribute to its overall mission. (Chapter 8 discusses the orchestration of these components in the overall ebXML architecture.) The next chapter looks at related web services specifications and their relationship to ebXML.

Endnotes

[1] Michael C. Rawlins of Rawlins EDI Consulting led the requirements project team. Mark Crawford of Logistics Management Institute served as editor of the requirements document.

[2] Electronic Business XML (ebXML), Requirements Specification Version 1.06, May 8, 2001, p. 7.

[3] The phrase "creating a single global market" is a registered trademark of the ebXML Working Group.

[4] Electronic Business XML (ebXML), Requirements Specification Version 1.06, May 8, 2001, pp. 8–9.

[5] Electronic Business XML (ebXML), Requirements Specification Version 1.06, May 8, 2001, p. 11.

[6] Electronic Business XML (ebXML), Requirements Specification Version 1.06, May 8, 2001, pp. 9–10.

[7] "Electronic Data Interchange (EDI)," Giga Transaction Services, 6 July 2000, www.telin.nl/NetworkedBusiness/ GigaTSsotac2/Sota_v1_Electronic_Data_Interchange _EDI.htm.

[8] Electronic Business XML (ebXML), Requirements Specification Version 1.06, May 8, 2001, pp. 12–13.

[9] Electronic Business XML (ebXML), Requirements Specification Version 1.06, May 8, 2001, p. 15.

[10] Electronic Business XML (ebXML), Requirements Specification Version 1.06, May 8, 2001, p. 16.

[11] Electronic Business XML (ebXML), Requirements Specification Version 1.06, May 8, 2001, p. 16.

[12] Electronic Business XML (ebXML), Requirements Specification Version 1.06, May 8, 2001, pp. 17–18.

[13] "About Us, The Standard for Internet Commerce," Global Information Infrastructure, http:// 167.216.203.34/standard/about.html.

[14] "New Survey Suggests That Small to Mid-Sized E-Businesses Are More Prepared for This Year's Holiday Shoppers," ePublicEye, 15 November 2000, www.epubliceye.com/pr29.htm.

[15] Electronic Business XML (ebXML), Requirements Specification Version 1.06, May 8, 2001, p. 18.

[16] "Authentication of Trade Documents by Means Other than Signature, second edition," UN/ECE Trade Facilitation Recommendation No. 14, March 1979, www.unece.org/cefact/rec/rec14en.htm.

[17] Electronic Business XML (ebXML), Requirements Specification Version 1.06, May 8, 2001, pp. 19–20.

[18] "S.761, Bill Summary & Status for the 106th Congress," Congressional Research Service, http://thomas.loc.gov/cgi-bin/bdquery/z?d106:SN00761:@@@D&summ2=m&.

[19] Electronic Business XML (ebXML), Requirements Specification Version 1.06, May 8, 2001, p. 19.

[20] Electronic Business XML (ebXML), Requirements Specification Version 1.06, May 8, 2001, p. 11.

[21] "United Nations Layout Key for Trade Documents," Recommendation No. 1, second edition, UN/ECE, March 1981, www.unece.org/cefact/rec/rec01en.htm.

[22] "The Unicode Standard: A Technical Introduction," Unicode, Inc., December 2000, www.unicode.org/unicode/standard/principles.html.

[23] Olle Järnefors, "A short overview of ISO/IEC 10646 and Unicode," Royal Institute of Technology (KTH), Stockholm, Sweden, 26 February 1996, www.nada.kth.se/i18n/ucs/unicode-iso10646-oview.html.

[24] "Alphabetic Code for the Representation of Currencies," UN/ECE, 13 July 1998, www.unece.org/cefact/rec/rec09en.htm.

[25] "ISO 3166 Maintenance Agency (ISO 3166/MA)," 12 June 2001, www.din.de/gremien/nas/nabd/iso3166ma/.

[26] "Codes for the Representation of Names of Languages," U.S. Library of Congress, June 2001, www.loc.gov/standards/iso639-2/bibcodes.html.

[27] Harald.T.Alvestrand, "Tags for the Identification of Languages," Internet Engineering Task Force RFC 1766, March 1995, www.ietf.org/rfc/rfc1766.txt?number=1766.

[28] Electronic Business XML (ebXML), Requirements Specification Version 1.06, May 8, 2001, p. 11.

[29] Electronic Business XML (ebXML), Requirements Specification Version 1.06, May 8, 2001, p. 12.

Chapter 7

ebXML and Similar Web Services Specifications

With the growth of electronic business, a number of initiatives have started that offer some of the same features as ebXML. Chapter 5, "The Road Toward ebXML," discusses the groundbreaking work of RosettaNet and the XML/edi Group that provided some of the important ideas for the development of ebXML. This chapter discusses other ongoing specifications and services for e-business messaging, discovery, integration, and interoperability that are especially relevant to the way ebXML content will be delivered and orchestrated:

- Simple Object Access Protocol (SOAP)
- Universal Description, Discovery and Integration (UDDI)
- Web Services Description Language (WSDL)
- BizTalk™[1]

Simple Object Access Protocol (SOAP)

Simple Object Access Protocol (SOAP) offers an XML-based language for the exchange of messages over decentralized and distributed environments such as the web. Its authors, from Microsoft Corp.; IBM and its Lotus Development subsidiary,

Now that ebXML has also adopted SOAP as the foundation for its messaging transfer (and by extension the W3C's emerging XML protocol standard, in which SOAP plays a major role), using SOAP provides alignment and interoperable message handling with a broad range of emerging related standards, systems, and tools.

DevelopMentor; and Userland Software, submitted version 1.1 of SOAP to the W3C as a Note in May 2000.[2] Since then, the W3C has put in place the XML Protocol Working Group, whose purpose is to formalize the earlier SOAP work as a robust W3C specification for exchange of XML transactions between application programs via the Internet. The whole focus is to develop a simple and easily implemented application-to-application layer that can be used with scripting languages. (The W3C is scheduled to deliver the specifications as a formal recommendation in September of 2001.)[3]

In March 2001, ebXML adopted a variation of SOAP called *SOAP Messages with Attachments*, a specification that, as the name implies, allows for adding binary attachments to the basic SOAP message.[4] The extension to add support for binary content is required to allow secure exchanges using digital certificates, as well as business messages with binary content, such as pictures and illustrations. This chapter discusses only the basic SOAP specification. Chapter 8, "ebXML Technical Architecture," goes into some detail in explaining how ebXML applies the SOAP Messages with Attachments specification to its messaging functions.

As the name implies, SOAP 1.1 aims to provide a simple and lightweight method for exchanging structured data in peer-to-peer relationships. It defines the message package, offers encoding guidelines for data used in applications connected by these messages, and provides rules for representing *remote procedure calls* (*RPCs*), a type of online interaction in a distributed environment. The authors defined SOAP as a series of building blocks to maintain its simplicity for most potential users.[5]

SOAP's importance extends beyond its offer of an XML-based message protocol. The other specifications described in this chapter all use SOAP for its messaging functions and, as a result, it helped generate these several new e-business initiatives. Now that ebXML has also adopted SOAP as the foundation for its messaging transfer (and by extension the W3C's emerging XML Protocol standard, in which SOAP plays a major role), using SOAP provides alignment and interoperable message handling with a broad range of emerging related standards, systems, and tools.

SOAP Messages

SOAP *messages* are XML documents (textual documents) defined inside an outer SOAP *envelope*. SOAP messages must have this envelope to meet the specifications. Within the envelope is a SOAP header and body. SOAP messages must have a body, but the header is not required in all instances. The XML grammar rules for envelopes are found in an XML *namespace* (`http://schemas.xmlsoap.org/soap/ envelope/`). The use of namespaces is a syntax device in XML to avoid name clashes, hence the term "namespace." Particularly when you exchange XML, you need a simple way to denote the markup tag names you're using from other potential fragments of XML elsewhere in the exchanged XML. For instance, `<address>` may occur in the SOAP header for Internet delivery, and also in the payload `<address>` as the postal delivery, but these two things clearly need to be handled separately. See Chapter 4, "The Promise of XML," for more discussion of XML namespaces.

The SOAP envelope serves as the first element in the document and thus identifies it as a SOAP message. The SOAP *body* contains the information transmitted to the receiver. Each message must have a body, so there cannot be an empty SOAP message. If the message has a SOAP *header*, it appears as the first child element in the envelope, and before the body.[6]

The SOAP header allows the sender to add management or control information in the message, important for routing, security, or proper handling by the recipient. This element has very few rules of its own, but relies on XML namespaces identified by the sender for its semantics. However, the specification identifies two attributes that can appear in a SOAP header:

- actor—Senders may want to route SOAP
  messages through intermediaries, or designate
  parts of the message for certain recipients.
  SOAP headers are designated only for the
  recipients of the messages and cannot be for-
  warded to other recipients, but recipients can
  insert a new header for the next recipient. The
  actor attribute uses Uniform Resource
  Identifiers (URIs)—Internet resources or locations such as web addresses—as values, and
  indicates the recipient of the header. Without
  the actor attribute, the recipient must assume
  that it is the only and ultimate destination for
  the message.

- mustUnderstand[7]—This attribute tells the
  recipient whether the header entries made by
  the sender are required to be processed or can
  be ignored, and has values of 0 (No) and 1
  (Yes). Absence of this attribute is the same as a
  value of 0. For example, a header may have a
  security key and encryption that the receiver
  needs to process and correctly decrypt the
  resulting message body.

If a SOAP message has only a SOAP body element
and no SOAP header, it has the same meaning as a
message identifying the default actor and a
mustUnderstand attribute with a value of 0 (No).[8]

The SOAP body is a mandatory part of the SOAP
message. The first level of sub-elements under the
body are called *body entries*, and consist of the default
XML namespace reference for the body. Further levels down in the SOAP body may use the combination of more namespaces and local names, but this
isn't mandatory.[9]

The only content for a SOAP body specifically
defined in the specification is the Fault element used
to provide status or error information. The Fault element consists of four sub-elements:

- faultcode—required in each Fault element,
  and must contain one of the specified codes in
  the specification definition provided by the
  implementer.

- faultstring—an explanation of the faultcode, required in a Fault element.[10]
- faultactor—provides information on the party that caused the fault, using the actor attribute discussed earlier.
- detail—for application-specific information related to the SOAP body content, required if the receiver could not process the SOAP body contents.

First-level sub-elements are called *detail entries*, and are identified by a combination of namespace URI and local name. However, the fault report cannot contain information about errors in SOAP header entries, which must be transferred in the SOAP header. The absence of a detail indicates that the fault lies somewhere else other than the processing of the SOAP body.[11]

SOAP uses the existing long-established HTTP and remote procedure calls (RPC) standards of the IETF as the underlying middleware plumbing to physically move the XML content across the web between web servers.[12] This means that any existing web server or HTTP-compatible middleware component can also handle SOAP messaging.

SOAP Coding

SOAP allows senders to identify the kinds of data exchanged in SOAP messages. This ability is exploited in ebXML, with the header explicitly allowing the receiver to quickly analyze the header information to determine the business action required. For instance, what type of transaction is being received, and from whom? Security crosschecks can deduce whether this is permitted, and then the correct business processing can be started automatically for that body content.

While XML offers many ways to express structured data in documents, the demands of application-to-application exchanges require tighter synchronization, and that meant tightening the rules for business exchanges. With SOAP, these various types of exchanged data can range from simple discrete values to complex compound entities, such as entire control verbs, interchange command parameters, and value sets. Both the sending and receiving systems must exactly match on these critical control items to ensure that the correct actions result. SOAP borrows liberally from the XML Schema specification, and makes a distinction between simple and compound types. *Simple types* are values (names, measurements, enumerations) with no further subdivisions or parts. *Compound types* are collections of values that have some relationship to each other. For example, a typical North American street address consists of three simple types: a street number, street name, and apartment or suite number, related as parts of the same street-address entity.

Each compound value has a function called an *accessor*, which can be the name of its role in the message or an ordinal number that serves as an identifier or descriptor of the data. For example, in a purchase order or invoice, the party to whom the invoice is sent is called the *Bill-To party*. In a SOAP message, a compound data type would include the accessor Bill-To (it identifies the role of the data in the invoice), as well as the value for the element, such as a DUNS number.

If the application requires it, the accessor can make the compound type unique. The uniqueness can refer to the type of data within the application, by using a unique name (such as date/time stamp) as the accessor. By using a URI, by definition a unique data string, you can also create a universally unique type as the accessor.

For simple types, SOAP adopts the types defined in part 2 of the XML Schema specification.[13] This list is rather lengthy, but the SOAP specification discusses those more likely to be used in SOAP messages such as strings and enumerations (lists of specific selections) in more detail. For compound types, SOAP defines structs and arrays, two concepts borrowed from software design. *Structs* are compound values distinguished by the accessor name, as in the invoice

SOAP's simple design, ability to support data types, and close compatibility with RPC have made it a popular set of tools for providing messaging functions.

Bill-To example just described. An *array* is a compound value in which its position in the collection (for example, cell, row, or column numbers in a spreadsheet) distinguishes it from all the others in the collection.[14]

Because of its development from remote procedure calls (RPCs), the SOAP specifications show the use of SOAP for RPC exchanges. The SOAP body carries an RPC's method call and response. Both the RPC call and the response are modeled as structs, as defined by the compound type rules noted earlier. Any faults returned use the SOAP `Fault` element. The SOAP header can contain any supporting information needed by the remote system to process the request, such as identifiers or authorization data. The RPC call and response parallel the HTTP or web transport protocol request and response architecture. The specifications show how SOAP can bind to HTTP.[15]

SOAP's simple design, ability to support data types, and close compatibility with RPC have made it a popular set of tools for providing messaging functions. The other specifications in this chapter also use SOAP, which acts as an endorsement of these features and abilities.

Universal Description, Discovery and Integration (UDDI)

The *Universal Description, Discovery and Integration (UDDI)* specification offers a way to help companies locate trading partners and discover their capabilities for conducting electronic business. A consortium led by Microsoft, IBM, and Ariba announced UDDI in September 2000.[16]

The basic laws of economics and business assume that suppliers and customers already know of each other's existence and abilities to meet the needs of the marketplace. One of the main reasons for companies engaging in electronic business is to open new markets and find new sources of supply more easily than before.

To achieve this desired state, however, companies need a common way of identifying potential trading partners and cataloging their e-business characteristics. Otherwise, they can miss entire communities of potential trading partners, only because they didn't show up on the searching company's radar screen.

The problem here is not with the trading partners, but (figuratively) with the type of radar used. UDDI proposes a specification for defining a registry to identify and describe e-business services, query other companies, and share information. In other words, it proposes a common radar for spotting and describing the trading partner communities in which companies operate.[17]

UDDI describes the *services* that companies offer over the web, defined as functions that companies offer to other businesses, using the Internet as connective tissue. This idea of services goes beyond the simple exchange of messages. For example, a company can offer the ability to look up and report its product line by UPC/EAN code (the number represented in retail bar codes) for use in purchase orders or other electronic documents. This kind of function helps trading partners interact with the company electronically but is not strictly speaking a form of message exchange. It does, however, represent the type of service that UDDI can describe.

UDDI proposes three ways of listing companies in a registry, using the familiar telephone directory as an analogy:

- White pages, or basic identification: name, address, and key points of contact
- Yellow pages, or classification by a standard index of business and industries
- Green pages, or technical capabilities and services related to the conduct of electronic business

Using a UDDI registry, companies can discover the existence of potential trading partners and basic information about them, find companies in specific classifications, and uncover the kinds of e-business services offered to interact with these companies.

Using a UDDI registry, companies can discover the existence of potential trading partners and basic information about them (white pages), find companies in specific classifications (yellow pages), and uncover the kinds of e-business services offered to interact with these companies (green pages).[18]

UDDI Information Types

UDDI relies on features of the XML Schema specification, because of its abilities to support many types of data (see a similar discussion of SOAP, earlier in this chapter, as evidence of this feature) and to construct data in many different structures and models. (See Chapter 4 for a description of these features of XML Schema.)

UDDI defines four types of information for providing the white/yellow/green pages functions just described. The basic business information such as company name and contacts (white page listings) is contained in an XML element called businessEntity. This element also contains identifiers, such as D-U-N-S numbers or UCC company codes, as well as classifications or categories under which the company falls, which correspond to the yellow-pages functions.

Two XML elements provide descriptions of services, or green-pages information: businessService and bindingTemplate. The businessService element describes collections of related activities and functions, somewhat like the business process models defined in ebXML, but specifically for enabling machine-to-machine connections and interactions. Included under businessService are web addresses and details of hosted services such as digital marketplaces. It also covers any other additional technical data, such as software settings, that the trading partner's system needs to connect and exchange data.

The bindingTemplate provides references to details about the data formats and requirements of the trading partners. A key part of the bindingTemplate is the tModel that acts as a reference to the specifications that contain the metadata (data about data) with these critical details.[19]

These various elements have a hierarchical relationship, in which each businessEntity can contain one or more businessServices, which in turn can have one or more bindingTemplates (one-to-many relationships). However, a tModel can have any number of bindingTemplates referencing any number of tModels (many-to-many relationship); thus they are not unique to bindingTemplates.

For example, a company (businessEntity in UDDI-speak) advertises that it can accept orders, shipping notices, and invoices electronically, and provide online inventory searches for regular customers. These various services (businessService) can support several protocols or specifications (XML vocabularies, EDI standards, and so on), each having a separate bindingTemplate. The bindingTemplate can reference each specification or protocol with a tModel.

Each element has a key with a unique identifier, with the names businessKey, serviceKey, bindingKey, and tModelKey. Each of these items is represented as an attribute of its respective element in the schema. The uniquely identified keys are vital for UDDI to offer global registries of these e-business services.[20]

Programmer's API

The UDDI documents include specifications for an *application programming interface* (*API*) for automated interactions with a UDDI-registered site. All of these interactions use a request-response model, in which each message requesting service from the site generates some kind of response, even if nothing more than a simple acknowledgment. The specifications define two types of exchanges with UDDI-registered sites: inquiries and publishing.

Inquiries, as the name implies, enable parties to find businesses, services, or *bindings* (technical characteristics) meeting certain criteria. The party can then get the corresponding businessEntity, businessService, or bindingTemplate information matching the search factors. The inquiries support three kinds of query patterns: browse, drill-down, and invocation.

The *browse* and *drill-down* patterns work together and are common database access functions. The searcher uses broad criteria to find the entities, services, or technical characteristics meeting general requirements and then drills down to find the more specific features.

The *invocation* pattern returns new `bindingTemplate` information, and is used particularly when these technical details may change because of failure of the operator site or changes in the site's configuration. Normally, the requestor will store the `bindingTemplate` data and use the details for routine accesses. If for any reason those normal exchanges don't work, the requestor needs to query the target site for an updated `bindingTemplate`. The invocation method performs this specific query and returns the new information.

UDDI sites use the publishing functions to manage the information provided to requestors. These operations give the site operators power to delete the current data and provide updates as needed. Of course, these functions require prior authentication. UDDI doesn't specify authentication procedures, but leaves them up to the operator site. An appendix to the document spells out the publishing security requirements in more detail.[21]

Web Services Description Language

Soon after the announcement of UDDI came the *Web Services Description Language (WSDL)*, a companion to UDDI, authored by Microsoft, IBM, and Ariba, the same companies that developed UDDI. WSDL offers an XML protocol for describing network services based on XML. WSDL is now also submitted to the W3C as a Note and steps are underway to work formally on WSDL (`www.w3.org/TR/wsdl`) in the context of related work within the W3C. An extended version of WSDL is a vital component to the delivery of the next generation of web services, and also to orchestrating business processes via the Internet itself. From the ebXML user's perspective, WSDL could make it possible in the future to process the ebXML Business Process Specification Schema.

WSDL builds on earlier XML vocabularies that define network protocols such as Information and Content Exchange[22] and Web Distributed Data Exchange.[23] Like UDDI, WSDL uses SOAP for its messaging functions to exchange data among remote applications, but can also use MIME and native HTTP transport protocols.[24]

WSDL Elements

The services defined in WSDL have five major elements:

- Ports—the network addresses of the message senders and receivers, called *end-points*.
- portType—the kind of operations supported by the senders and receivers.
- Binding—the protocol and data format specifications defined by the portType.
- Message—the data exchanged between end-points.
- Types—data types defined in the messages exchanged between end-points.

WSDL doesn't develop a large-scale new vocabulary, but relies mainly on the XML Schema specification for defining much of its content. The data types defined in the Types element in WSDL recommend XML Schema by name as preferred resource. WSDL messages also make use of XML Schema by defining component elements with qualified names (QNames) data types as specified in XML Schema.

Each portType is defined in terms of the operations it supports. WSDL identifies four basic kinds of operations:

- **Notification.** The end-point sends a message.
- **One-way.** The end-point receives a message.
- **Solicit-response.** The end-point sends a message and receives a related message (acknowledgment).
- **Request-response.** The end-point receives a message and sends a related message.

The bindings define the details of the message format
and protocol for each operation identified for each
portType. Each binding is given a unique name,
with corresponding input, output, and fault for each
operation.

At many points in the specification, WSDL allows for
references to outside resources, called *Extensibility
Elements*. These external resources allow services
defined with WSDL to call up any number of other
service definitions for their message formats and protocols. However, WSDL requires extensibility elements to use XML namespaces different from
WSDL, a sensible requirement to prevent potential
duplication in naming conventions.[25]

BizTalk

Microsoft Corporation started BizTalk as a way to
help break down the significant obstacles faced by
companies of integrating applications, both within
their organizations and among their trading partners.
Companies' internal systems, such as enterprise
resource planning, accounting, and marketing support
(for example, sales tracking) are often developed
independently of each other. As a result, a company's
information technology staff often finds itself
strapped trying to get these systems to work together.

The problem is compounded when trying to get one
company's systems to interact with those of suppliers,
customers, financial services, and government services. The same integration problems faced internally
are now magnified when transacting business across
organizational boundaries.

As this book discusses at length elsewhere, XML
helps overcome some of the challenges. Because of its
status as a respected W3C technical specification,
XML provides a way to devise a common vocabulary
that can help companies define common messages
and bridge this gap. Microsoft offers BizTalk to provide a common business message framework, as well
as a community to encourage solutions that offer
greater interoperability.[26]

BizTalk includes a framework specification and a repository of schemas called Biztalk.org complying with this specification. The Biztalk.org site also functions as a self-help community for BizTalk users. Microsoft offers a BizTalk server that supports the framework specification. In December 2000, Microsoft announced its release for licensing and general availability. According to the announcement, some 50 companies are already using the BizTalk server in some production capacity.[27]

The following sections discuss the BizTalk framework specification and the related Biztalk.org repository. It should be noted that as of mid 2001 the Microsoft BizTalk server system does not have a native capability to interact with ebXML-compatible systems. However, since it does support SOAP-based messaging exchanges, there appear to be no large technical barriers for the BizTalk server to physically transfer ebXML-compatible content as simple payloads.

BizTalk Framework

The BizTalk Framework, now in version 2.0, provides specifications for the exchange of XML documents and messages. The specifications give detailed instructions for constructing these messages and for their transfer using standard Internet protocols. They identify four sets of requirements that any solution needs to address:

- A language with the capability to specify and exchange structured or unstructured information across organizations and applications
- Support for transformation rules to allow for the conversion of formats across organizational and application boundaries
- Communication protocols at the application level to enable message transfers across computing platforms, as well as organizations and applications
- Ability to secure messages for integrity, privacy, and non-repudiation

The document notes that XML addresses some of these concerns, but with the proliferation of business vocabularies defined in XML, the need for a common framework to provide interoperability also increases. And while systems and software for translating among these different vocabularies, called *middleware*, are coming onto the market, none of them meet all of the requirements for interoperability.

BizTalk is based largely on XML, with support for both Microsoft's own XML Data Reduced (XDR) and the W3C Schema syntax, but also incorporates other Internet standards such as Hypertext Transfer Protocol (HTTP), Multipurpose Internet Mail Extensions (MIME), and other XML vocabularies such as the Simple Object Access Protocol (SOAP). It doesn't deal with issues such as trading partner agreements or business process specifications. BizTalk 2.0 builds on the first version by adding more features compliant with SOAP, as well as more transport-related features, MIME, and the emerging XML-Schema specifications from the W3C.[28]

Logical Layering

The BizTalk framework addresses three basic layers in the interactions among companies:

- *Transport*—the delivery mechanism over the Internet, using protocols such as HTTP (web) or SMTP (email)
- *BFC Server*—functions provided by a server compliant with the BizTalk framework
- *Application*—responsible for generating and processing business documents

Most of the BizTalk framework specifications focus on the BizTalk Framework Compliant (BFC) Server, although they also define the bindings, connections, and interfaces to the transport protocols and business applications.[29]

BizTalk Document Header

The message structure for BizTalk documents uses the Simple Object Access Protocol (SOAP) that includes an outer envelope layer, as well as header and body sections. The header describes the message's routing, provides identification, indicates the services required, and offers a listing of the message contents. The SOAP header in BizTalk requires the mustUnderstand attribute with a value of 1, which means that the recipient of the message must process the header entries.

For these functions, the header has a series of elements:

- endpoints
- properties
- services
- manifest
- process

The endpoints element, mandatory in a BizTalk message, identifies the message and destination, using sub-elements labeled to and from. BizTalk allows either use of technical locations, such as web addresses, or business-defined identifiers, such as D-U-N-S numbers or tax IDs. If business identifiers are used, the transport protocols in the outer layers need to provide the delivery location in order to have the message delivered. Also, the syntax of the delivery location may depend on the software running respective servers.[30]

The properties element, also mandatory, provides identification for the message. The identifiers include a machine-generated unique string using a protocol such as the Universal Unique Identifier (UUID), as defined by The Open Group.[31] The identifiers also include sent-at and expires-at elements defining the lifetime of the document for business action.

The properties element has a sub-element giving the topic or general subject matter of the message. BizTalk recommends using a consistent way to name the topic, such as web address or URI, so that the receiving system can accurately interpret the contents.[32]

The services element refers to delivery services, and provides directions for reliable delivery of the BizTalk message, as well as an indicator of the intended recipient. A `deliveryReceiptRequest` sub-element indicates the desire for a delivery acknowledgment from the receiver. A `commitmentReceiptRequest` indicates the need for a business acknowledgment (as opposed to technical delivery) of the message's substance. Both the delivery and commitment sub-elements give addresses to which the recipient should return these acknowledgments, as well as deadlines for their receipt.[33]

The `manifest` element gives a catalog of the message contents. This catalog not only lets the receiver know the contents of the message body, but indicates the presence of attachments or references to external documents that serve the same function as attachments. BizTalk allows for MIME format when messages need to carry both XML and non–XML data. The manifest indicates the presence of an attachment, and thus the presence of a compound document using the MIME format. The recipient can use the manifest to double-check that all attachments arrived intact.

The manifest element consists of one or more `reference` sub-elements that identify either an attached document or an external reference that acts as an attachment. For example, an external reference may consist of a web address pointing to a large graphics file that the recipient can download separately if needed.[34]

The `process` element describes the business process context of the BizTalk document. A `type` sub-element identifies a business process already agreed upon by the trading partners for understanding the substance of the message. For example, an invoice message may be part of a larger payments process that the message could reference in this part of the header. To further identify the process, the element has an `instance` sub-element to identify a specific document that describes the process and that the recipient can reference. The process element has an additional `detail` sub-element that provides for further references or a location to report exceptions.[35]

BizTalk Document Body

The BizTalk body uses the SOAP body structure. The body of a BizTalk document references an XML namespace that defines the application governing the business content. If the body of the message contains multiple documents—for example, an invoice and separate payment instructions—BizTalk uses a feature of SOAP that specifies whether subsequent parts of the body are considered sub-elements or separate elements.[36]

BizTalk doesn't specify the business content of the message body beyond data types derived from the XML Schema specification. The document identifies three data types from XML Schema:

- timeInstant—a date/time stamp meeting the format requirements of ISO standard 8601 (representations of dates and times)
- uriReference—an Internet resource, such as a web address, which can be an absolute address (complete syntax), or relative address pointing to another location on a referenced site
- complexType—an element with more than one kind of content related to each other; for example, a text string and decimal number combined as a street address

BizTalk also specifies the xsi:type attribute from the XML Schema document for elements to identify their specific data types.[37]

Reliable Delivery of BizTalk Messages

BizTalk provides for two kinds of services to help ensure that trading partners receive and act on the messages exchanged, as well as prevent duplication of messages that can cause duplicated actions. The specifications define two types of receipts: delivery and commitment receipts (discussed earlier).

BizTalk recommends a set of actions for message senders and receivers, called endpoints in the specifications. Senders should maintain copies of messages in durable storage for any needed recovery in case of failure. Senders should also request delivery receipts and correlate those receipts with the original message identifiers. Retries should continue until a receipt for the message is returned, the deadline in the delivery receipt expires, or the maximum retry count is exceeded.

Receivers of BizTalk messages should also process and return delivery receipts, as well as develop procedures ensuring that the message is delivered and processed only once. The specifications recommend maintaining durable storage of all accepted BizTalk documents until the expiration date in the header. Receivers of messages may be able to log only the identities of the documents rather than the documents themselves, since they are required to use a unique identifier.[38]

Securing BizTalk Messages

BizTalk provides for three kinds of security for its messages: enveloping (encryption), signing, or a combination of enveloping and signing. Since the combination of message header, body, and attachments may require different levels of security within the same message (for example, encrypted attachment only), the specifications provide detailed instructions and references to the original S/MIME documentation.[39]

BizTalk.Org Repository

Microsoft offers BizTalk users a registry for the schemas (www.biztalk.org) that users develop according to the BizTalk specifications. BizTalk.org stores the schemas in a web-based repository that makes the schemas available to the public at large. Companies or organizations developing schemas can also register them privately so only the trading partners can access them.

The BizTalk.org repository allows registered users to access the repository of schemas. All of the public schemas are categorized by industry category with the North American Industry Classification System (NAICS).[40] The site lets visitors browse, view, or download the schemas, as well as sample code and documentation about each schema.

Early in its development, BizTalk required its schemas to use a special flavor of XML called *XML Data-Reduced (XDR)*, a subset of XML-Data, which was a predecessor of XML-Schema.[41] As a result, all of the 454 schemas registered with BizTalk.org as of mid-February 2001 use the XDR format. On 31 January 2001, Microsoft announced that BizTalk.org started accepting schemas in the XML Schema format.[42]

Companies or organizations can register their schemas with BizTalk.org without physically storing them in the repository. The registration captures the following information about each schema:

- Object name, the name displayed for the schema
- Summary, a brief description
- File name when stored with BizTalk.org
- Keywords to help visitors search the schemas
- Schema location in BizTalk.org or on another server
- Schema sample location, a sample document validated against the schema
- Documentation, giving contact details, error handling instructions, and any other special conditions[43]

BizTalk.org also connects to BizTalk newsgroups to help build a community of users, as well as help and background files.

Endnotes

1 BizTalk is a registered trademark of Microsoft Corporation.

2 W3C Notes are technical documents on topics related to the work of W3C and submitted to the organization for discussion. Acceptance as a Note by the W3C implies no endorsement, nor does the W3C claim any editorial responsibility for its contents.

3 XML Protocol Activity Statement, World Wide Web Consortium, 4 April 2001, www.w3.org/2000/xp/Activity.

4 SOAP Messages with Attachments, W3C Note, 11 December 2000, World Wide Web Consortium, www.w3.org/TR/SOAP-attachments.

5 "Introduction," Simple Object Access Protocol (SOAP) 1.1, World Wide Web Consortium, 8 May 2000, www.w3.org/TR/2000/NOTE-SOAP-20000508.

6 "SOAP Envelope," Simple Object Access Protocol (SOAP) 1.1, World Wide Web Consortium, 8 May 2000, www.w3.org/TR/2000/NOTE-SOAP-20000508.

7 This is not a typo. One of the less endearing features of technical documents in information technology is "camel case" notation that not only strings together words but capitalizes in the middle of the string, ostensibly to see where one concatenated word ends and the next begins. While camel case is common for engineers, it contributes to the well-founded but still unfortunate dread that normal people have of technical writing.

8 "SOAP Header," Simple Object Access Protocol (SOAP) 1.1, World Wide Web Consortium, 8 May 2000, www.w3.org/TR/2000/NOTE-SOAP-20000508.

9 "SOAP Body," Simple Object Access Protocol (SOAP) 1.1, World Wide Web Consortium, 8 May 2000, www.w3.org/TR/2000/NOTE-SOAP-20000508.

10 To the credit of the SOAP authors, the specifications say that this sub-element should also "provide at least some information explaining the nature of the fault."

11 "SOAP Fault," Simple Object Access Protocol (SOAP) 1.1, World Wide Web Consortium, 8 May 2000, www.w3.org/TR/2000/NOTE-SOAP-20000508.

12 R. Srinivasan, "RPC: Remote Procedure Call Protocol Specification Version 2," Internet Engineering Task Force, Request For Comments (RFC): 1831, August 1995, www.ietf.org/rfc/rfc1831.txt.

13 "XML Schema Part 2: Datatypes," W3C Candidate Recommendation, 24 October 2000, www.w3.org/TR/2000/CR-xmlschema-2-20001024/datatypes.html.

14 "SOAP Encoding," Simple Object Access Protocol (SOAP) 1.1, World Wide Web Consortium, 8 May 2000, www.w3.org/TR/2000/NOTE-SOAP-20000508.

15 "Using SOAP for RPC," Simple Object Access Protocol (SOAP) 1.1, World Wide Web Consortium, 8 May 2000, www.w3.org/TR/2000/NOTE-SOAP-20000508. Note, however, that using SOAP for RPC is not limited to the HTTP protocol binding.

16 Industry Leaders Join to Accelerate Business Integration and Commerce on the Internet, 6 September 2000, www.uddi.org/uddipr09062000.html.

17 UDDI Executive White Paper, 6 September 2000, pp. 2–3.

18 UDDI Technical White Paper, 6 September 2000, p. 2.

19 UDDI Technical White Paper, 6 September 2000, pp. 6–8.

20 "Core structure reference," UDDI Data Structure Reference V1.0., UDDI Open Draft Specification, 30 September 2000, pp. 5–6.

21 UDDI Programmer's API Specification, Version 1.0, 6 September 2000.

22 Information and Content Exchange, World Wide Web Consortium, 26 October 1998, www.w3.org/TR/NOTE-ice.

23 The Web Distributed Data Exchange, www.openwddx.org/.

24 Uche Ogbuji, "Using WSDL in SOAP applications," IBM Developer Works, Web Services Library, November 2000, www-106.ibm.com/developerworks/library/ws-soap/index.html?dwzone=webservices.

25 Web Services Description Language (WSDL) 1.1, IBM Developer Works, Web Services Library, 21 March 2001, www.w3.org/TR/wsdl.

26 See www.biztalk.org/home/framework.asp.

27 "'Signed, Sealed and Delivered'—BizTalk Server 2000 Released to Manufacturing; Pricing and Licensing Detailed," 12 December 2000, `www.microsoft.com/ presspass/press/2000/Dec00/ManfReleasePR.asp`.

28 "Introduction, Specification Scope and Evolution," BizTalk Framework 2.0: Document and Message Specification, December 2000, pp. 2–6.

29 "Logical Layering," BizTalk Framework 2.0: Document and Message Specification, 12 December 2000, p. 9.

30 "BizTalk Document Header Entries," BizTalk Framework 2.0: Document and Message Specification, 12 December 2000, pp. 13–14.

31 Universal Unique Identifier, The Open Group, 1997, `www.opengroup.org/onlinepubs/9629399/apdxa.htm`.

32 "Document Identification and Properties," BizTalk Framework 2.0: Document and Message Specification, 12 December 2000, pp. 14–15.

33 "Delivery Services," BizTalk Framework 2.0: Document and Message Specification, 12 December 2000, pp. 16–17.

34 "Document Catalog," BizTalk Framework 2.0: Document and Message Specification, 12 December 2000, pp. 18–20.

35 "Process Management," BizTalk Framework 2.0: Document and Message Specification, 12 December 2000, pp. 20–21.

36 "The BizTalk Document Body," BizTalk Framework 2.0: Document and Message Specification, 12 December 2000, pp. 11–12.

37 "Use of XML Schema Data Types," BizTalk Framework 2.0: Document and Message Specification, 12 December 2000, pp.6–7.

38 "Reliable Delivery of BizTalk Documents," BizTalk Framework 2.0: Document and Message Specification, 12 December 2000, pp. 22–28.

39 "Securing BizTalk Documents and Messages," BizTalk Framework 2.0: Document and Message Specification, 12 December 2000, pp. 34–38.

40 See `www.census.gov/epcd/www/naics.html` for details.

[41] Timothy Dyck, "XML Messaging Framework," eWeek, 12 March 2001, www.zdnet.com/eweek/stories/general/0,11011,2694009,00,html.

[42] "BizTalk.org Web Site Upgraded," 31 January 2001, www.biztalk.org/news/biztalk_org_upgrade.asp.

[43] BizTalk Help, undated, www.biztalk.org/Help/help.asp.

Chapter 8

ebXML Technical Architecture

The combination of real-world business needs, previous experience with EDI, and availability of new web technologies offered the ebXML initiative an opportunity to craft a new technology for conducting electronic business. This chapter discusses ebXML's technology in more detail, in order for companies to evaluate its potential to support their business goals. This additional level of detail should also help technical managers and specialists get a head start on implementation and making transition plans to ebXML.

However, this chapter is not a substitute for the ebXML specifications or technical reports themselves. While rich in detail, the chapter doesn't provide the kind of concrete guidance that systems developers need to write new systems supporting ebXML. Only the ebXML specifications themselves can provide those kinds of details, and we encourage technical developers to download the documents (available free of charge) from the ebXML web site (www.ebxml.org). Another good techical resource is the ebXML Developers List; see www.ebxml.org/participate.htm for more details and to sign up.

The chapter describes the various parts of the ebXML technical architecture and related issues:

- Business process specifications as used in ebXML

- Registries and repositories that store the data objects used in ebXML messages and list potential trading partners
- Technical aspects of the trading partner relationship, called *collaboration protocol agreements* (*CPAs*), for establishing the rules of the road
- Messaging services that specify the packaging of ebXML messages, as well as their transport and routing
- Core components that provide the ability to exchange messages between industries
- Steps for getting a company operational with ebXML

Business Process Specifications

Standards provide an independent roadmap for developing systems, not just independent of specific vendor products, but also of the underlying technologies. One of the key objectives of ebXML is to capture trading partners' business practices and interactions systematically, and represent them accurately and independently of any specific ways of implementing those transactions.

One of the key objectives of ebXML is to capture trading partners' business practices and interactions systematically, and represent them accurately and independently of any specific ways of implementing those transactions.

In ebXML, the business process specifications also provide the connection between business practices and their technical implementation. The specifications define the ways in which trading partners engage each other, to the point of configuring their respective systems to actually do business, at what technicians call *runtime*. ebXML expresses these business process specifications as XML *document type definitions* (*DTDs*), and later as XML schemas, or in the Unified Modeling Language (UML).[1]

Chapter 4, "The Promise of XML," discusses XML and UML in some detail, but we can provide a little background in UML here as well. A number of good modeling methods exist. Many ebXML participants recommend the approach adopted by UN/CEFACT, one of the sponsoring organizations of ebXML. This approach, called the *UN/CEFACT Modeling Methodology*, relies heavily on UML that represents business processes graphically and at various levels of detail. The UN/CEFACT approach, in turn, is based on the Open-EDI Reference Model, as defined in ISO standard 14662.[2]

ISO standard 14662 establishes a reference model, which means a framework for further standards work. In this case, the reference model outlines a different approach to EDI, based on business scenarios rather than the traditional EDI concept of individual transaction sets or messages. The basic scenarios cover much of the interactions between companies and, as a result, the extended period and lengthy development cycle needed to establish an e-business relationship can be reduced significantly.

One particular value of UML is its ability to represent the interactions of objects in different ways, which at a high level it calls *views*. ISO 14662 defines two ways of looking at the interactions among companies: a *business operational view* (*BOV*), and a *functional service view* (*FSV*). The BOV captures the business relationships among companies, while the FSV concentrates on the information technology aspects of the relationship—service capabilities, interfaces, and protocols.[3]

The BOV focuses on high-level interactions among companies and related requirements. It covers the semantics of business data (the terminology used in an industry), as well as accepted conventions and agreements. For example, a common practice in an industry may require the manufacturer to pay for transportation; thus, a price quotation would need to include a separate line item for transportation.

An important characteristic of the BOV, at least as far as ebXML is concerned, is the collection of specific interactions into overall scenarios or processes. A scenario would cover delivery of related services or interactions to meet specific objectives, and thus would include a series of related transactions among trading partners. A purchasing scenario or process, for example, would account for the series of interactions beginning with the price quotation, and continuing through purchase order, purchase order change, and purchase order acceptance.

The functional service view addresses system interactions and requirements. It includes issues such as message syntax, naming conventions, and communications protocols. While the FSV is not unimportant in the reference model, clearly the intention of the standard is to have the BOV requirements drive the implementations expressed in the FSV.[4]

Businesspeople may legitimately ask whether the business process specifications are really necessary, especially where industries already have defined their processes and developed messages in EDI or XML vocabularies. Remember that the ebXML specifications are designed as modules. If an industry has already defined its processes, messages, and core components, businesses may be able to skip this step. However, if the industry is in a state of rapid change or needs to work with other industries with different processes, it may find the business process methods and models useful.

Modeling Requirements and Analyzing Processes

The BOV begins with the knowledge and experience companies bring to interacting with each other. In some cases, the trading partners can capture that knowledge and experience in a set of business requirements. UML employs use case descriptions and diagrams for documenting and visually representing these requirements.

Use cases describe the activities of one or more actors that engage the system in question, to return some value to the actors as a result of that system. *Use case diagrams* are visual representations of a set of business scenarios showing the relationships and interactions among the actors.[5] See Chapter 5, "The Road Toward ebXML," for more discussion and examples of use cases and use case diagrams.

Companies wanting to do business with each other rarely need to start from scratch in defining their relationships, but more often than not can rely on a base of experience already established by years of interactions, sometimes electronic (with EDI) and

Individual companies probably will not need to perform the kinds of analyses that generate the business models stored in ebXML repositories. Most of these tasks will be undertaken by industry associations or consortia that can devote the resources required.

sometimes in hardcopy form. In some cases, experience can be drawn from multiple industries; for example, accounting or transportation practices adopted by most businesses.

In ebXML, this store of basic knowledge on business collaboration is captured in a core library that connects a specific industry's terminology to more generic business models. This core library includes industry terminology, data and process definitions, established relationships, and cross-references to commonly accepted industry classifications or *taxonomies*. Where industries have already defined core libraries, companies will likely use them. If industries don't have this core library defined, they'll need to establish one and register it for use with ebXML.[6]

For example, in the paper industry (at least outside North America), both producers and consumers use ISO-defined standard sizes for office and printing plant paper stock. This industry-defined scheme is used throughout the business for ordering and production management, and is reflected in machinery and systems using cut-size paper, such as that for computer printers and copying machines. The paper industry will likely register these standard paper sizes for ebXML-compliant exchanges among paper companies, printing plants, and copy machine and computer printer manufacturers.

Individual companies probably will not need to perform the kinds of analyses that generate the business models stored in ebXML repositories. Most of these tasks will be undertaken by industry associations or consortia that can devote the resources required. In this chapter, however, we outline the steps in the process to show the nature of the thinking behind the ebXML specifications, and perhaps give a small head start for those in the business world who want to get involved in these industry-wide efforts. Also, when industries cannot agree on common definitions of processes or semantics, companies may need to develop their own process models.

Please note that the examples and illustrations in the following discussions are only illustrative of the process and are not intended to serve as a complete tutorial. The references at the end of the book can give the reader more details about UML.

The analyses of business processes themselves will generate UML activity, sequence, and class diagrams. *Activity diagrams* show the flow of business-level events among the actors and system, and show both the actions taking place at a high level and their sequence.[7] Figure 8.1 shows an example of an activity diagram, illustrating part of the inventory-replenishment process from the Marathoner running store case study described in Chapter 3, and portrayed in a use case in Chapter 5.

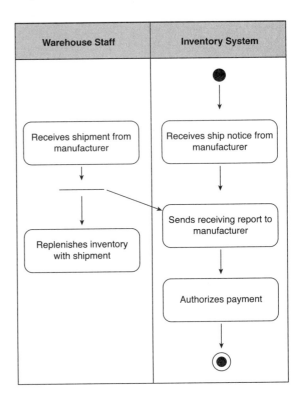

Figure 8.1
UML activity diagram
example.

Sequence diagrams illustrate the interactions taking place both among objects within a system and with parties outside the system. In a sequence diagram, the actors and objects are arrayed horizontally and the time sequence is represented vertically.[8] Figure 8.2 gives an example of a sequence diagram, again from the Marathoner running store case study.

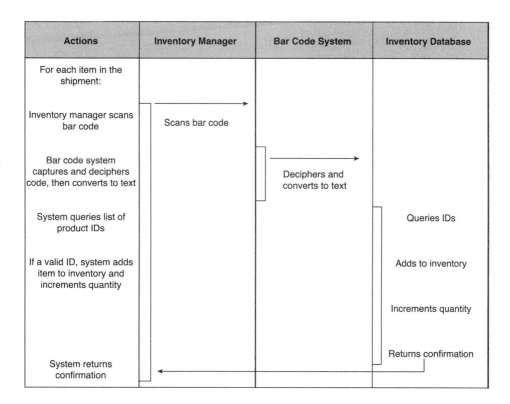

Actions	Inventory Manager	Bar Code System	Inventory Database
For each item in the shipment:			
Inventory manager scans bar code	Scans bar code		
Bar code system captures and deciphers code, then converts to text		Deciphers and converts to text	
System queries list of product IDs			Queries IDs
If a valid ID, system adds item to inventory and increments quantity			Adds to inventory
			Increments quantity
			Returns confirmation
System returns confirmation			

Design Tools for Business Messages and Services

With the scenarios identified, processes defined, and interactions documented, enough material is available to design the individual transactions and services used by the trading partners. A key product of this design phase is UML *class diagrams*, which show the different kinds (classes) of data objects and their relationships to each other. Classes include definitions of the data objects themselves, as well as operations or functions performed on those objects.

Figure 8.2
UML sequence diagram example.

Class diagrams also show the relationships among data objects, in what UML calls *associations*. Associations show the connections between objects, give a verbal description of the relationship, indicate whether the relationship is mandatory or optional, and specify whether the relationship allows for multiple objects.[9] Figure 8.3 gives an example of a UML class diagram, using a few items from the traveler database outlined in Chapter 3.

Class diagrams can start defining the messages exchanged between trading partners. They identify the individual pieces and collections of data that are needed by the trading partners to perform their business tasks. In Figure 8.3, for example, a travel agent would need the identity and location data from a customer to put together a traveler profile that the agent could then use for reservations, confirmation messages, and delivery of tickets.

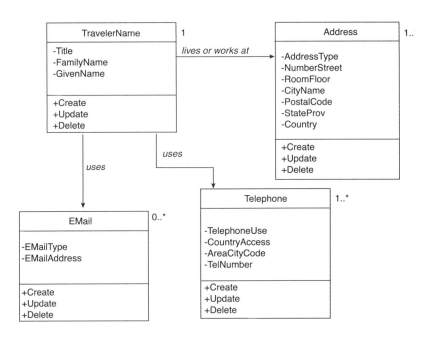

Figure 8.3
Example of UML class diagram.

Class diagrams provide another critical function for ebXML; namely, the ability to compare processes from different industries at the data-element level. Comparing similar kinds of business scenarios at this level of detail shows where industries have comparable processes and where the terms used by the different industries may be functionally identical.[10]

Other products of the design phase include collaboration and state diagrams. *Collaboration diagrams* are similar to the sequence diagrams just discussed, but they show the behavior of groups of objects (rather than individual pieces), as well as the links between them. As a result, collaboration diagrams do a better job of showing how the collections of objects interact with each other, and thus are useful in defining messages and services.[11]

Figure 8.4 shows an example of a collaboration diagram, using the same inventory-management scenario described in Figure 8.2.

Figure 8.4
Example of UML collaboration diagram.

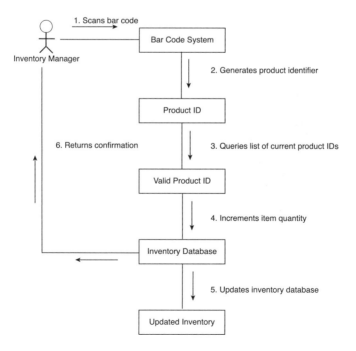

In Figure 8.4, the inventory system generates a confirmation message to the inventory manager. The confirmation tells the inventory manager that the inventory database now contains an item, represented by the product identifier, along with a quantity, and probably a text description (even the best inventory managers cannot commit all of their product codes and descriptions to human memory). You can imagine a class diagram (refer to Figure 8.3) for the confirmation message with those pieces of data.

Now imagine a similar kind of scenario, in which a supplier (manufacturer or distributor) receives an electronic message that the customer has unloaded the truck and entered a series of delivered items into inventory, or returned incorrect or damaged items. This kind of message, generated routinely and delivered automatically, can enable a supplier to manage the inventory of a business customer, delivering only the items that the customer needs to service its end users that day or week. The results are a more collaborative relationship between supplier and customer, with lower inventory costs, significantly reduced paperwork, and a greater level of customer service, without the supplier having to add significant new resources. This is what ebXML is all about.

State diagrams, also known as *statechart diagrams*, show the change in status of an object as a result of an action in which the object is involved. When an object receives an event it can do nothing and maintain its current state, or take actions of its own and change its state. In our inventory scenario, for example, a UML state diagram could show the change in state of the inventory database with the addition of new items to the inventory, as well as generating an action of its own, a confirmation message to the inventory manager.[12]

Companies use the meta-model to define business processes and subsequent schemas, patterns, elements, and core components. Users then can store these objects in registries, in either automated or human-readable form, for retrieval by current or potential trading partners.

Putting It All Together in a Metamodel

In ebXML, the specifications take the various tools offered by UML and others, and put them together in a package that allows industries or trading partners to document the interactions among companies doing business electronically. Note that ebXML calls this package the *eBusiness Process Meta Model*.

This *metamodel*—literally, a model of models—supports the requirements, analysis, and design phases described earlier, and results in a set of business processes, individual messages, and data items in those messages.

Each process includes the actors and choreographed series of transactions. The actors are the parties in the transactions, and the transactions themselves represent exchanges of electronic business documents. Business documents are composed of *business information objects*, which may be reusable in other processes or even in other industries. In turn, these business information objects are made up of core components, also reusable within or between objects, transactions, or industries. Business information objects may also, of course, have industry-specific business objects. For example, the paper industry computes the weight of paper using a measure called *basis weight*, which is unique to that industry.

The metamodel also provides a facility for putting a set of data items into messages on demand. This capability, called the *specification schema*, allows for definition of these collections either in UML or XML. The transactions may, if applicable, follow standard patterns of interactions for the industry. Also accompanying the specification schema is a set of common modeling elements to help populate the messages.

Translating from UML to XML requires production rules that specify the precise XML semantics for each UML object. For example, UML classes become XML elements and UML attributes are represented as XML attributes. Aggregate associations in UML become parent and child elements in XML.[13]

The documentation of these interactions through the specification schema becomes part of the *collaboration protocol agreements* (*CPAs*) between trading partners. The capabilities of companies to provide the messages or services described in the schema become part of the *collaboration protocol profiles* (*CPPs*), as they're known in ebXML.[14] Figure 8.5 shows the relationships among the metamodel and these components.

The ebXML specifications tell how the metamodel works in practice. Users such as industries or companies can use the metamodel to define their own business processes and the subsequent schemas, patterns, elements, and core components described earlier. Users then can store these objects in registries, in either automated or human-readable form, for retrieval by current or potential trading partners.

These business processes will define the roles of the trading partners and provide the sequence of message exchanges, called *choreographies*, among them. The processes will also provide the context for defining core components (described shortly), offer a framework for defining collaboration protocol agreements, and specify a responsible party for the process along with relevant contact information.[15]

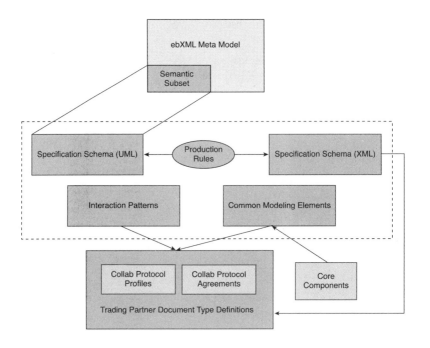

Figure 8.5
ebXML eBusiness Process
Meta Model.

Functional Service View

As mentioned earlier, the modeling methodology used by ebXML offers not only a business operational view that discusses business processes, but also a functional service view that describes e-business activities from the standpoint of the technology. The functional service view uses the same terms to describe ebXML components and services as the business process view, but it shows the relationships between the different systems, as well as the interfaces and protocols that need to be in place and operational. This view helps define the precise technical implementation of ebXML-compliant systems. Figure 8.6 provides a functional service view of the ebXML architecture.

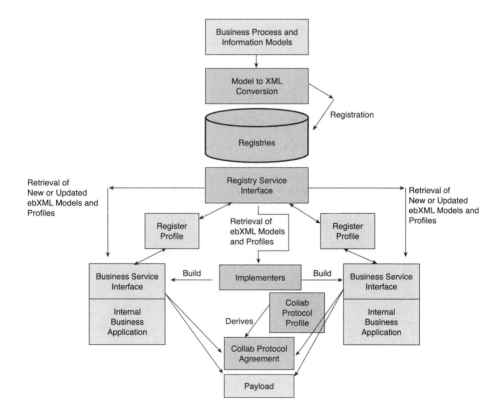

Figure 8.6
ebXML functional service view.

The functional service view shows the importance of the ebXML registries in the architecture. The registries store the business process models, either converted to XML syntax or in the native modeling language, most likely UML. The registries also list the profiles of companies with the capability to provide the messages and services registered in this repository.

Companies that want to register their capabilities at this site work through the registry interfaces. These interfaces also provide access to the other company profiles stored at this site, as well as the industry processes, schemas, and other data objects on deposit. The important functions of the registries are defined in more detail in the next part of this chapter.

Once trading partners complete the retrieval, registration, and discovery process, the business service interfaces of the company systems deal directly with each other, first to exchange the collaboration protocol agreements, and then to exchange the actual payloads with the business content.[16]

Registries and Repositories

Registries are the parts of the ebXML technology with which companies will probably have the most early contact, when searching for specifications and trading partners. As early as ebXML's third meeting in May 2000, Klaus-Dieter Naujok, the chair of ebXML, called the registries and repositories "the key to the whole initiative."[17] As a result, this part of the ebXML initiative has received more attention and scrutiny during its development than most other aspects of the project.

Readers will see in this chapter and throughout the book both the terms *registry* and *repository*, which need to be clarified. According to the ebXML registry services specification:[18]

> *The ebXML Registry provides a set of services that enable sharing of information between interested parties for the purpose of enabling business process integration between such parties based on the ebXML specifications. The shared information is maintained*

as objects in a repository and managed by the
ebXML Registry Services defined in the ebXML
Registry Services Specification.

Most of this part of the chapter, therefore, focuses on
the registries that perform these services, rather than
the repository that stores the objects.

Registry Functions and Locations

Registries perform several important functions
for ebXML, including, but not limited to the
following:[19]

- Submission of industry-wide schemas or document type definitions (DTDs) that define the
  industry messages and vocabularies
- Submission of industry business process
  models, from which are derived message
  choreographies, core components and their
  industry context, and industry-specific data
  items used in messages and data services
- Submission of company collaboration protocol
  profiles (CPPs) that identify the company and
  describe the supported capabilities and services
  related to the content indexed in that registry
- Discovery of trading partners, resulting from
  searches, either human or automated, for
  companies meeting certain criteria, or from
  manual browsing through lists of CPP entries

There are few precedents for these kinds of services,
but several suggestions have been made for their
operation. The specifications list potential hosts to
include public and private web sites, as well as application service providers, or virtual private network
services.[20] As of March 2001, organizations began to
announce their plans to develop or host ebXML
registries, including Data Interchange Standards
Association (DISA), which will include access to
the X12 EDI standards as well as XML industry
vocabularies supported by DISA.[21]

Registry Technical Architecture

Because many different kinds of companies and organizations will want to access ebXML registries, the technology proposed for them needs to be quite flexible. Registries will need to support access from normal web browsers, which don't have many built-in capabilities for accessing databases like those maintained by registries. As a result, the registries themselves will need to provide those capabilities as part of their host software.

At the same time, registries can expect some end-user software to have the capability to access the registries and work with the objects stored in the corresponding repositories. As ebXML begins to be implemented, some vertical market software or packages designed for registry management will likely appear on the market, with much more power than the routine web browser. These packages will have the registry interfaces built in, and registries will need to recognize their presence, such as through a logon script, and bypass these same interfaces provided at the host.

A third alternative implementation is through an automated interaction between the end-user's server and registry, where the company has made arrangements in advance to access the registry on demand for specific services. For example, a company needing frequent competitive bids for goods or services would be a candidate for this scenario.

Companies communicating with the registry use the same message formats as they would use for other ebXML messages. The section of this chapter on message services describes those formats in detail.

When companies use ebXML for exchanging messages, they first need to establish a trading partner agreement, called a *collaboration protocol agreement* (*CPA*) in ebXML parlance. Companies making their first or infrequent queries to a registry are not likely to first get a CPA established. As a result, ebXML recognizes an implicit CPA between companies and registries covering the six potential types of interactions with registries listed in the following sections.[22]

Registry Interfaces

The specifications define six types of interactions with registries. The first three cover connections directly with the registry:

- `RegistryService`. This is the service that permits access to the registry's two main functions, `ObjectManager` and `ObjectQueryManager`.
- `ObjectManager`. With this function, a company can submit data objects (CPPs, schemas), edit or modify the object characteristics, or remove objects.
- `ObjectQueryManager`. This function allows searches of the objects listed in the registry, performing browse, drill-down, or ad hoc queries.

The next three interactions cover connections directly with the end-user client software:[23]

- `RegistryClient`. This is the service that connects the end-user client to the services needed by the client to use the registry.
- `ObjectManagerClient`. This service calls back the client after submission of requests to the `ObjectManager` service, with notification of the results of that query.
- `ObjectQueryManagerClient`. This function also provides callback service, but for previously submitted requests to the `ObjectQueryManager` service.

Submitting and Managing Objects in a Registry

To enable content management, ebXML has specified the rules for listing objects—XML schemas or DTDs, business process models, collaboration protocol profiles (CPPs)—in a registry, as well as managing those objects during the time of their registration. A registry object goes through four stages in its lifecycle: submission, approval, deprecation, and removal. The registry attaches XML attributes, called *metadata*, to the object that the registry uses to classify the object and manage it throughout its registration period.[24]

The two main types of metadata are called `ExtrinsicObject` and `IntrinsicObject` in the XML schema with the electronic registry rules. `ExtrinsicObject` applies to those items submitted from external sources to registries, such as schemas or CPPs, where the properties of the object are not automatically known or understood.

`ExtrinsicObject` metadata includes properties or characteristics such as external uniform resource identifiers (web or email addresses, for example) and MIME types. If the properties are encrypted or otherwise not readable, the registry can still accept them, but they are called *opaque*.

`IntrinsicObject` covers those properties and characteristics already defined by the registry, and are those normally attached to objects already registered.[25]

When submitted, an object becomes a `RegistryEntry`, and is associated with one item in the associated repository. Each entry in the registry has a number of properties or attributes, the most notable of which are described in the following list:

- `Association`. Defines the relationship between a registry entry and other objects, and can cover potentially complex many-to-many relationships. The registry information model has 15 predefined associations to describe these relationships.
- `AuditableEvent`. Provides the ability to generate an audit trail for the entry. This ability includes associating registered users as part of the audit trail.
- `Classification`, `ClassificationNode`. Defines ways of categorizing registry entries, and since the kinds of classifications can vary significantly from one industry to another, registries need the flexibility to use their own classification schemes. `ClassificationNode` is a branch in the tree structure making up that scheme, while a `Classification` associates the registry entry with the `ClassificationNode`.

- `ExternalIdentifier`. Offers an additional means of identifying the registered item, such as D-U-N-S or UCC/EAN company identifier.
- `ExternalLink`. Provides a way for an object to reference Internet-based resources outside the registry, for example a schema that calls other schemas or DTDs.
- `Organization`. Describes the entity submitting the entry to the registry, including references to parent organizations.
- `Package`. Provides a way of grouping entries together, and also allows for managing this group as a whole.

If the registry needs to add attributes to an entry, it can use the `Slot` capability. This property allows for dynamically adding characteristics (called *slots*, thus the name) for an entry.[26]

Upon submission and approval, the registry gives each entry a unique identifier, unless the end-user's software has that ability. The specifications require a 128-bit *Universal Unique Identifier* (*UUID*) that provides a statistically unique identifier across registries.[27] The UUID is a contribution of the Open Group, formerly the Open Software Foundation. It consists of a network address, considered by definition unique, current time, and place that the ID was generated.[28]

Objects are submitted in the form of an ebXML message, using a `Registry.dtd` for validation. A registry entry submission includes a `RegistryEntryList` with the objects for submission. The entries can also reference other objects already registered.[29]

Registries have a set of messages for approval of objects submitted to registries. Once approved, an object becomes part of the registry's content and is open for use in the establishment of trading partnership or development of ebXML-compliant messages or services.

Registries also have the ability to *deprecate* a registered object. Deprecating an object means scheduling it for obsolescence, and thus it cannot be enhanced further through associations, classifications, or external links. However, registries will continue to list the object and otherwise operate it normally.[30]

A protocol in the registry allows for the removal of objects. This protocol gives the registry some flexibility in deleting only the repository item, but keeping the registry entry, in order to keep references to registry entry valid. A registry can also remove the object from both the repository and entry. This facility works only if references—associations, classifications, external links—have also been removed.[31]

Searching and Retrieving Registry Entries

ebXML envisions registries as open resources that companies or individuals can access at any time and find the objects they need to conduct business electronically. To make the experience working with registries as uniform as possible, the specifications provide detailed requirements for the operation of registry search features. ebXML requires each registry to offer both browse/drill-down and filtered query capabilities. Structured Query Language (SQL) search mechanisms are allowed as options on ebXML registries.[32]

The browse/drill-down query capability supports the following interactions:

- Get Root ClassificationNodes Request. A ClassificationNode is a branch in the tree structure of the scheme used to classify the content of the registry. This request retrieves a list of root ClassificationNodes, defined as those without parents, or the topmost nodes in the tree.
- Get Classification Tree Request. Each ClassificationNode has a sub-tree attached that represents part of the classification scheme for the substance of the registry's content. This request returns the classifications listed under

this node. The request allows searchers to specify the number of layers to drill down in the tree structure; a value of 1, for example, returns the immediate children and no more.

- `Get Classified Objects Request`. With this request, the searcher specifies a precise list of classifications for the registry to query. This request returns the entries matching the `ClassificationNode`s in the list and those in descendant branches of the tree structure under those nodes.[33]

ebXML registries must also support *filtered queries*, which provide for more precise and complex searches. Filtered queries use the semantics and structure of the *Registry Information Model (RIM)* rather than the classification scheme of the subject matter used in browse and drill-down queries. Registries use the RIM structure mainly for submitting and managing objects, as discussed earlier. However, the metadata assigned to objects for these management functions can also be used for queries. The specifications require registries to provide a profile of queries of the metadata that the registry supports.[34]

Each query to the registry database seeks entries that meet the criteria spelled out in filters based on the RIM metadata. The semantic rules used in these `RegistryEntryQuery` messages vary from one set of metadata to another, since they use different structures:

- *Associations*, either as source or target relationships of the object, as well as the specific registry entries associated with the object.
- *Classifications*, with subsequent `ClassificationNode`s identified.
- *Organizations*, either as the organization that submitted the object or the group currently responsible for it. In both cases, the query can include the contact for the organization.
- *Auditable events*, which can include a user and organization associated with that event.
- *External links*, which have no child elements in their filters.

Each `RegistryEntryQuery` XML element has a `RegistryEntryFilter` element with the desired filtering given in subsequent child elements representing the different types of RIM metadata.[35]

Once these queries have identified specific registry entries or repository objects, searchers can then use a similar approach to retrieve the metadata associated with the entries or the objects themselves. The `ReturnRegistryEntry` command allows for adding the filtering arguments used to search for the specific entries. It returns the metadata for the registry entry identified. The `ReturnRepositoryItem` command has a comparable but not identical set of arguments, since repository items have a different storage protocol than registry entries.[36]

Registries for ebXML objects may also provide support for more complex SQL queries, although this is not required, as is the case for browse/drill-down and filtered queries. ebXML specifies the syntax of SQL found in a subset of ISO/IEC standard 9075:1992, Database Language SQL. An appendix of the ebXML registry specifications provides predefined routines in template form.[37]

Retrieving Registry and Repository Content

Searchers can retrieve specific content from a repository using the `GetContentRequest` command. This request lists the references to the objects, perhaps generated through the queries described earlier. A successful request message returns a corresponding `GetContentResponse` message with the specified object as payload. Since the response may include multiple payloads, each item is individually identified in the manifest of the ebXML header for the response message.[38]

Registry Security

Registries used with ebXML must meet requirements to protect the integrity of their contents, authenticate the identity of authorized users, and control access for predefined roles. To protect the integrity of submissions, content sent from registry client software must have a digital signature that ensures that no one has tampered with the content en route or within the registry. Also, the signature verifies that content is associated with the submitting organization.

The ebXML registry specifications require authentication of parties seeking access on a per-request basis. However, the document leaves open future support for session-based authentications. Registries must implement authentication mechanisms using credentials based on digital certificates and signatures. Message headers may have digital signatures provided by the sender's ebXML messaging service, but, absent a signed header, a signature in the payload will suffice.

The specifications define three roles with different levels of access:

- **Content owner.** Submits content to the registry from an organization and has access to all procedures in the registry dealing with that content.
- **Registry administrator.** The party responsible for the management and operation of the registry, and with access to all procedures on all registry objects.
- **Registry guest.** Unauthenticated visitors to the registry who are entitled to read-only access to the registry objects.

Registries must implement default access-control policies that reflect these roles and privileges.

The one familiar type of security not required for ebXML registries is confidentiality. As indicated earlier, ebXML considers registries public resources, and all content submitted to an ebXML registry may be discovered and read by any visitor. As a result, registries must make their content available unencrypted.

Parties exchanging messages with registries may need the capability to encrypt the messages or at least the payloads. The specifications encourage but don't require encryption for these exchanges. However, registries will need the capability to decrypt content provided in protected messages.[39]

Trading Partner Profiles and Agreements

Companies need to know their trading partners and the rules of engagement before embarking on the exchange of business messages. ebXML builds these capabilities into its specifications. ebXML also connects the company profiles and agreements, so the capabilities of trading partners to engage in e-business are reflected in the agreements between the enterprises.

Background and Definitions

Since the exchange of business messages began with EDI, companies found they needed to establish ground rules for their interactions in advance, before the exchange of data actually started. These agreements, called *trading partner agreements* (*TPAs*), captured details such as the precise documents exchanged, networks used, points of contact in case problems developed, and in many cases the underlying assumptions—often called *boilerplate*—that governed the interactions between the parties.

The American Bar Association published a model TPA for EDI purchase orders, but many users found it adaptable to other transactions. As one would expect from an ABA document, it had authoritative legal references and offered a handy checklist that companies could use to make sure they covered all the bases before starting the flow of transactions. The model ABA document consisted of two parts: a) EDI communication terms, and b) underlying trade terms and conditions.

But some companies found the process for negotiating a formal legal agreement difficult and time-consuming. To shorten the process, some companies resorted to *declarative letters*, in which the company sent a letter to its trading partner stating terms; if the other party didn't respond, the originating company assumed they had no arguments with the terms.[40]

An IBM team led by Martin Sachs discovered that at least some of the conditions often included in TPAs lent themselves to capture and exchange in automated form, and in January 2000 proposed an XML vocabulary for trading partner agreements. Soon thereafter, IBM donated this work to ebXML.[41] Much of the ebXML specifications on TPAs is drawn from this earlier work by IBM.

TPAs represent one important document needed by companies engaging in e-business. Another kind of information exchanged is the capability of companies to conduct e-business, called a *trading partner profile* (*TPP*), used in the process of finding suitable trading partners. Many of these details on capabilities are made available in the registries described earlier.

ebXML defines some but not all of the details found in both trading partner agreements and profiles, and as a result introduces two new terms—*collaboration protocol profile* (*CPP*) and *collaboration protocol agreement* (*CPA*)—that make up the details found in ebXML specifications.[42] The following sections describe the CPP and CPA specifications, but the reader needs to remember that full trading partner agreements and profiles can comprise a good deal more information.

Overview of CPP and CPA Interactions

ebXML uses the term *collaborative process* for the business process used to exchange messages or establish e-business services. The ways that parties can exchange data are captured in an XML document called a *collaboration protocol profile* (*CPP*). As described earlier, ebXML registries often list these CPPs, and they become very useful in the process of discovering other trading partners.

CPPs are derived in part from the business process specifications that define the interactions among companies in an industry or business domain. The business process specifications are in most cases first defined in a modeling language but then implemented and stored in registries as XML documents. CPPs use XML extensions such as *XLink* that reference the precise elements in XML documents representing the business processes. As a result, a CPP indicates specific capabilities supporting business processes, with exact references in ebXML business process models. Also as a result, CPPs are processible documents citing specific capabilities and supporting specific business processes. CPPs can also identify specific business processes with unique identifiers.[43]

In addition to providing a discovery function, CPPs form the basis for constructing a CPA. Because the CPPs list the capabilities of companies seeking to do business electronically, the intersection of those capabilities among potential trading partners enables the companies to discover, at least in the beginning, those areas where they have common ground. This first interaction provides a starting point from which the companies can negotiate a CPA.[44]

At this stage, the ebXML developers could offer guidance on negotiating a CPA, but nothing solid enough for a standard. These guidelines are included in an appendix to the specifications document.[45]

The CPA provides a set of concrete and tangible interactions between the trading partners, and as a result each side can enforce the conduct of those interactions.

The CPA provides a set of concrete and tangible interactions between the trading partners, and as a result each side can enforce the conduct of those interactions. The parties use the business process definitions in the CPAs to configure their e-business systems when exchanging messages. Since the contents of the CPA are based on the entries in each company's CPP and negotiated between the parties, each side has a stake in making certain that the contents of the CPPs and CPAs are accurate and current.

Figure 8.7 shows two companies forming a CPA based on processes defined in a common industry repository. The industry has defined a series of processes: quotations, purchasing, shipping-receiving, invoices, and remittances. Two of the four companies with registered CPPs, Acme Industries and Consolidated Products, agree to do business electronically. Acme's CPP says its systems can support all of the industry processes except remittances, while Consolidated's CPP says it can handle everything but quotations. The companies negotiate a CPA covering the processes they have in common: purchasing, shipping-receiving, and invoices.

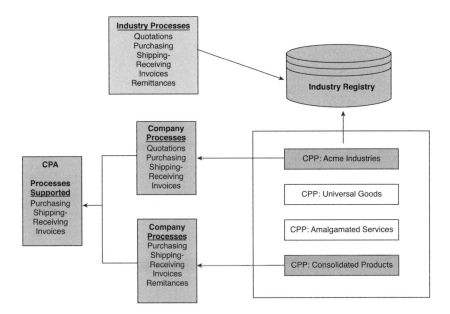

Figure 8.7 shows only the processes listed in the CPPs that contain other entries, such as message and transport protocols supported. Please note that while the registry lists the CPPs, the CPA is a document of interest and concern only to the two companies, and would not likely be indexed in an industry registry open to public view.

Companies will likely use software designed for conducting these interactions and set it up separately from the corporate databases. These kinds of software, known as *middleware*, will read the business processes, generate the appropriate messages, process incoming messages based on the contents of the CPAs, link to the company's back-end systems, and perform management services such as logging. Business processes, defined in a modeling language like UML but stored and processed in XML, contain references to a series of messages. These messages, in turn, contain the data elements needed by the parties and structured to conduct the business defined in the process.

Figure 8.7

Creating a CPA from CPPs in an industry registry.

A CPA can reference more than one business process, and therefore needs to clearly define where one process ends and the next process begins. The specifications recommend adding a way for the parties to request the start and end of these interchanges during the conversations.[46]

Collaboration Protocol Profiles

The collaboration protocol profile (CPP) describes three main functions of the company's e-business capability:

- **Process specifications.** Defines electronic business functions and services supported by the company.
- **Document exchange.** Specifies services provided to connect the process specifications to the transport functions for sending and receiving, including encryption and decryption, as well as addition of digital signatures.
- **Transport.** Identifies the services supported for sending and receiving e-business messages.

The document exchange and transport functions complement each other. For example, security features needed for e-business services can appear as part of the document exchange or transport functions, and will vary from one company to the next, depending on their implementation of these functions.

The CPP is an XML document, with the root element CollaborationProtocolProfile required in all instances. The root element references three XML namespaces for its content: the default ebXML tradePartner, XML Digital Signature from the World Wide Web Consortium (W3C), and XML Linking Language (XLink), also from the W3C.[47]

The root element has four immediate child elements. PartyInfo must appear at least once in the document. A Packaging element also must appear. An optional ds:Signature contains the digital signature. The fourth child element is Comments.

The `Packaging` element—with a number of sub-elements of its own—describes how the ebXML message headers and payloads are configured. It includes the document-level properties for security, including MIME capabilities.[48]

`PartyInfo` describes the company described in the CPP, which in turn has the following child elements, all of which are required in each CPP:[49] [50]

- `PartyId` identifies the company with a unique string and is accepted by both parties as an identifier. Examples are UCC/EAN assigned company codes or D-U-N-S numbers. Some identifiers may work only in specific industries, such as carrier codes assigned in air travel (IATA) or company codes in book publishing (SAN).

- `PartyRef` points to more data about the company, and uses XLink syntax. `PartyRef` can point to an ebXML or UDDI registry, or other resources such as the company's web site.

- `CollaborationRole` identifies the part the company plays in business process specifications. This element contains the data that describes the business processes supported by the company, as well as its role in those processes. We provide more information about this element shortly.

- `Certificate` identifies the digital certificates used for non-repudiation or authentication, including an identifier for each certificate and data that describe the certificate, as defined by the XML Digital Signature specification.

- `DeliveryChannel` describes the transport and message protocols the company supports, as described in the `Transport` and `DocExchange` protocols (described shortly). A delivery channel consists of one `Transport` and one `DocExchange`, and a `Characteristics` element providing security details.

- Transport defines details of the transport protocols (web, email, FTP, and so on) supported for message transmission. This element includes the protocols for sending and receiving, an end point that identifies the company's address for receiving messages, and security information for each specific means of transport.

- DocExchange describes the properties of the messaging services used by the companies for exchanging documents. The specifications describe the interfaces or bindings with ebXML messaging services, but allow for future expansion to allow for other kinds of messaging that ebXML may support. This element includes child elements for the following:

  - *Message encoding*, if a specific or special syntax is needed for messages sent to the company.

  - *Reliable messaging properties*, if more than "best effort" practices are required by the company, and including retries, retry interval, degree of reliable messaging (once and only once, or best effort), detection and discarding of duplicate messages, and time duration of persistent storage.

  - *Non-repudiation*, to prove the identity of the sender using an XML digital signature.

  - *Digital envelope*, to provide message encryption.

  - *Namespace*, detailing the namespace extensions required to implement the message services used by the company.

CollaborationRole

The `CollaborationRole` element contains the data describing the parts or functions played by the company in business processes supported by that company. Figure 8.8 shows the components making up this element. The main `CollaborationRole` element has an identifier attribute (ID) used for reference by other elements in the CPP. All of the other data come under the four child elements: `ProcessSpecification`, `Role`, `CertificateRef`, and `ServiceBinding`.

The `ProcessSpecification` element describes the processes that the company supports for the conduct of electronic business. The processes refer directly to the business process models defined by the industry or industries in which the company operates, and often found in ebXML registries as described earlier in this chapter.

Figure 8.8
`CollaborationRole` element and components.

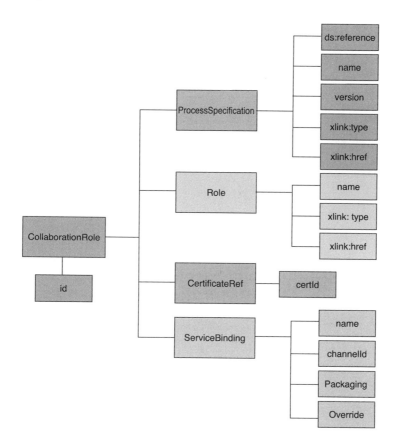

The element identifies the processes by name and version, using XML attributes. The element has two other attributes that use the XLink specification of XML to give XML documents direct access to other documents, in this case the business process models. One XLink attribute identifies its type, a locator, while the other gives the specific Internet address of the resource.

If the XML document with the business process model carries a digital signature, the ProcessSpecification element allows for a ds: reference child element to identify the digital signature and a separate attribute giving the Internet address for the signature. The ds:reference element cites rules defined by the XML Digital Signature specification with requirements and limitations that CPPs need to follow.

The Role element refers to the role played by parties in the business process models defined by the industries. In the CollaborationRole element, the role is described by a name attribute referring to the role name in the business process specification. This element also has the same two XLink attributes as ProcessSpecification, indicating locator type and Internet address for the part of the XML document with the role description.

The CertificateRef element carries an attribute, certId, that refers to the digital certificate in PartyInfo, and provides authorization to use the business process specification.

The ServiceBinding element names the delivery channels used for the messages sent to the company for this specific business process. This element has a name attribute that contains the name string to describe the specific services in ebXML message headers used as part of this business process. A channelId attribute identifies the default delivery channel for the messages in this business process.

The Override element, as the name implies, gives the company the ability to use a delivery channel different from the default channel identified for messages generated by this business process specification. The specifications note that the Override channel may not always be compatible with the capabilities of trading partners, and in those circumstances the parties need to resolve potential conflicts or revert to the default channels.[51]

Collaboration Protocol Agreements

Collaboration protocol agreements (*CPAs*) describe the agreement between two companies on technical characteristics that define the features, services, and processes in the electronic-business relationship between the two companies. As noted earlier, two companies create a CPA based on the capabilities in common in their respective CPPs, as well as any subsequent negotiations.

CPAs, like CPPs, are XML documents. The CollaborationProtocolAgreement element—the root element in the document—has a unique identifier (ID) attribute, assigned by one party but used by both. The specifications recommend that companies use a uniform resource identifier (Internet address, such as web or email address) for this identifier. This element also references four XML namespaces for ebXML trading partner specifications and business process models, as well as W3C specifications for digital signatures and XML Linking Language (XLink).[52]

The CPA has the following major child elements:

- Status is a required element indicating the state of progress in the development of the CPA, with choices of proposed, agreed, or signed. The signed option can take the form of a digital signature, as defined by the ds:Signature element (described shortly).
- Start and End elements, both required, indicate respectively the date and time the CPA goes into effect, and the date/time by which the parties need to renegotiate the CPA. The range of time between the Start and End values is called the *CPA lifetime*. The specifications give rules for handling conversations or transactions underway after the End date/time value, but it seems advisable that companies renew their CPAs well before the End value.

- **ConversationConstraints** is an optional element citing limits affecting the processing of messages exchanged between the two parties:
    - An *invocation limit* gives an upper limit on the number of units of activity covered by the CPA. With no invocation limit, the companies can conduct any number of activities until the End date/time.
    - A *concurrent conversations limit* puts an upper limit on the number of conversations between the parties processed at any one time, which can occur due to limitations in the capabilities of back-end systems.
- **PartyInfo** elements, one required for each company that is a party to the CPA. The **PartyInfo** element in the CPA is the same as the **PartyInfo** described earlier for the CPP. The actual business messages use the **PartyId** child element (also the same as described earlier) listed in the CPA in comparable entries as part of the ebXML headers.
- **ds:Signature**, at least one required, showing a digital signature. The specifications highly recommend meeting the requirements of the XML Digital Signature document. If the digital signature, itself an XML document, fails validation, the CPA is considered invalid. The specifications provide details for persistence of the digital signature, which apply to both the CPPs and CPAs.
- **Comment**, an optional element that gives added descriptive information in free-text form.[53]

> With MIME packaging, SOAP (and ebXML) can send non-XML binary payloads, such as digitized graphics files, making the format more usable for business purposes.

Message Services

The ebXML message services make it possible to exchange electronic business documents between trading partners, using any standard communications protocols, such as HTTP over the web or SMTP with Internet email. ebXML developed these transport, routing, and packaging functions earlier than the other parts of the technology, and as a result they are probably the most stable parts of the architecture. All of the ebXML proof-of-concept tests have demonstrated the draft messaging specifications, so they have gone through several iterations of testing.

The ebXML message format relies largely on the Simple Object Access Protocol (SOAP) specification. SOAP is an initiative started by four companies— Microsoft, IBM, DevelopMentor, and Userland Software—and later adopted by many more. It presents a simple XML-based message package, offers encoding guidelines for data used in applications connected by these messages, and provides rules for representing remote procedure calls (RPCs), a type of online interaction in a distributed environment. The authors submitted version 1.1 of SOAP to the W3C as a Note in May 2000.

At first, ebXML defined its own message format. When SOAP enhanced its specifications to include a version with attachments using a packaging scheme based on Multipurpose Internet Mail Extensions (MIME), a standard of the Internet Engineering Task Force, ebXML found it could use SOAP instead of its own format. With MIME packaging, SOAP (and ebXML) can send non-XML binary payloads, such as digitized graphics files, making the format more usable for business purposes.[54]

ebXML message services offer several key functions to exchange business messages between trading partners:

- **Message header processing.** Message headers provide the end-point address for the message, as well as routing information, a description of the contents, security information, and other important details about delivery. Creation of these headers by message senders draws data from the end-user application, collaboration protocol agreements (CPAs), and digital signatures, among other sources.
- **Message header parsing.** On the receiving end, the message service handler extracts or transforms the data in the headers for processing.

- **Security services.** These services include creation and interpretation of digital signatures, as well as authentication of the parties and authorization for further access.
- **Reliable messaging.** ebXML defines reliable delivery of messages with rules for persistence, retries, error messages, and acknowledgments.
- **Packaging.** This function includes the envelopes for the message as a whole, as well as dividing the message into containers for headers and payloads.
- **Error handling.** When the message service handler or user application encounters an error, this function reports the error to the parties.
- **Message service interface.** This function connects the user applications to the message service handler.[55]

Message Package

Business messages of any kind, whether postal mail, faxes, telegrams and telexes,[56] email, or over the web, have some characteristics in common. For example, they all have addresses formatted to enable accurate delivery of the message, routing instructions, and dates and times for logging or verification (for example, postmarks on postal mail). These data items, designed to help manage the flow of message traffic, are often grouped together at the top or head of the message (or on an outside envelope), and thus have the name *headers*. This separation of headers from the *body* or *payload* of the message—the business stuff—is a common feature of business messages, including SOAP and ebXML messages.

To cover the situation where a message has an attachment, particularly one in a different digitized format from the message itself, first ebXML and then SOAP adopted the Multipurpose Internet Mail Extensions (MIME) packaging for its messages. MIME was originally designed by the Internet Engineering Task Force to transmit non-text files via email. A specific flavor of MIME, called the Multipart/Related media type, allows for putting together multiple separate parts in a MIME package, which makes it applicable to the kinds of business messages envisioned for SOAP and ebXML.[57]

The basic SOAP message calls for an envelope with a header and a body enclosed. The enhancements to SOAP to allow for attachments wraps the SOAP envelope in one MIME part, and creates a separate MIME part for the message payload. Figure 8.9 shows the configuration of these pieces in an ebXML message.

As Figure 8.9 illustrates, ebXML configures the message as a series of layers. The communications protocol for the message, such as HTTP over the web or SMTP for email, provides the outermost envelope. Everything within this first layer includes the message specifications as defined by ebXML.

A MIME envelope encompassing the total SOAP with Attachments package provides the next layer in the structure. Within this total package layer comes a set of two MIME containers, each with its own envelope, one for the ebXML message headers and another for the payloads.

Figure 8.9
Message structure: envelopes, headers, and body.

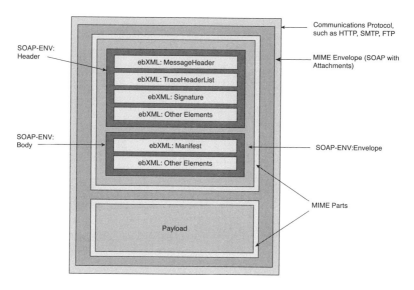

ebXML leaves the definition or selection of message payloads to the discretion of the sender. A message can carry multiple payloads if necessary. They can be any digitized content, from simple text messages (such as XML documents) to complex configurations of nested objects. However the message's manifest, part of the headers (see the next section), must list each payload in the message.

The contents of a SOAP envelope, defined as an XML file, includes the overall ebXML message headers but is itself a complete basic SOAP (version 1.1) document, and has two parts corresponding to a SOAP header and body. As in most structured business messages, the headers contain important addressing, security, and management details, which ebXML divides between the SOAP header and body segments.[58]

ebXML Message Headers

The ebXML message has two groups of headers, divided between the SOAP header and body. The first group contained in the SOAP header has five XML elements, described in the following sections.

MessageHeader

This element, required in each ebXML message, has data on the basic identity of the parties and references for the message. Its child elements and attributes include the following:

- From, To. As you might guess, these elements indicate the sender and receiver of the message and thus are required in each message. They each contain a PartyId element with a type of identifier (for example D-U-N-S or tax ID numbers) agreed upon by both parties. The type of identifiers is itself identified as an attribute to PartyId and the specifications strongly recommend using a standard Internet resource, such as a web address, as the source of the identifiers.

- `CPAId`. This required element references the appropriate documents or agreements that define the interactions between the parties, which can be an ebXML collaboration protocol agreement (CPA); see earlier discussions of CPAs.

- `ConversationId`. A *conversation* is a set of related messages, such as a paired invoice and remittance advice, and this required element makes it possible to locate the current message in the context of the overall business process.

- `Service`. This required element identifies the service within the receiving company that acts on the message. For example, the trading partners may agree to identify Accounts Payable as the service to process an invoice.

- `Action`. Also required, this element specifies the type of activity or processing desired for the message, and must be understood by the service identified in the headers (see the preceding bullet). An invoice, for example, could have Electronic Payment specified as an action.

- `MessageData`. This required element has a series of sub-elements providing for a unique message identifier, date/time stamp, reference to an earlier message (`RefToMessageId`, required in error and acknowledgment messages), and deadline by which the receiving party needs to receive and process the message.

- `QualityOfServiceInfo`. This element contains attributes for delivery semantics that indicate the need for reliable messaging (defined further below), request for a delivery receipt, and need to meet the precise order of delivery as specified by the sender.

- `SequenceNumber`. With this element, the receiving party can process the messages in a specified order, unique within a specific `ConversationId`. The specifications provide detailed rules for numbering messages and using sequence numbers when requiring reliable messaging.

- `Description`. This optional element provides a human-readable text explanation of the message's purpose or intent.
- `Version`. This required attribute of the `MessageHeader` element refers to the version of the ebXML message service specifications to which the message must conform (1.0 at the time of this writing). This version number can change as ebXML updates the specifications.
- `mustUnderstand`. This attribute of the `MessageHeader` element, provided by SOAP and required in ebXML messages, indicates that the receiving party must understand the contents of the `MessageHeader` element. In ebXML, this attribute must have a value of 1, meaning True or Yes.[59]

TraceHeaderList Element

If a message needs multiple hops to go from the sending to the receiving party, the `TraceHeaderList` gives the order of those hops from one message service handler to the next. Each hop has a `TraceHeader` child element that gives the Internet address for the sender and receiver, a date/time stamp, and a wild-card element for extensibility. The message can omit the `TraceHeaderList` if it has only one hop. The element has the version and `mustUnderstand` attributes discussed earlier.[60]

Via Element

The `Via` element conveys data from the sender of the message to the next ebXML message service handler to receive the message. Like the `TraceHeader`, the `Via` element services multi-hop message traffic, but this element is more applicable to scenarios where the data varies from one hop to another. Like the `TraceHeaderList`, the `Via` element has version and the SOAP `mustUnderstand` attributes. It also has a SOAP `actor` attribute, which requires the next SOAP-compliant recipient to process the message and not forward it without processing.

This element has the sub-elements CPAId, Service, and Action described earlier. In this case, CPAId applies only to the exchange of messages between the message service handler addresses, and not the trading partners. The Via element has an attribute for a synchronous reply that requires a response if the communication protocol supports two-way (Request/Response) conversations. The element also has attributes to indicate reliable messaging methods—ebXML's or from the transport protocol's method—and the type of acknowledgment required.[61]

ErrorList Element

Messages should use this element to report errors in the previous message if noted in the RefToMessageId in the MessageHeader element. As the name implies, this part of the header provides a list of errors, detailed in one or more Error sub-elements. The Error sub-element has a series of attributes describing various properties of the error:

- codeContext, giving a URI with the XML namespace or schema with the error codes.
- errorCode, a list of predefined codes referring to the MIME or XML headers or the delivery of the message itself. The codes *do not* apply to the business content or payloads, where any error messages are dependent on the user applications operating the payloads.
- severity, which indicates either a Warning or Error. Warnings mean that the problem is not so troublesome as to interrupt the flow of other messages in the conversation. An Error, on the other hand, indicates an unrecoverable problem, and no further messages will flow until resolved.
- location, which tells where in the message— except for the payload—the error occurred. If the message is a well-formed XML document, the attribute uses the XML Pointer Language (XPointer) syntax to identify the location. For MIME errors, location indicates the content-id of the MIME part containing the error.

- xml:lang, from the basic XML specifications, which gives the human language used for the text description of the error message.

The Error element can also give a text description of the error, although it's not required.[62]

Signature Element

Digital signatures verify the identity of the message senders and are an important factor in assuring the security of electronic business messages. While not required for ebXML messages, digital signatures are highly recommended. If the message header has more than one signature, the first signature must apply to the sender.

ebXML requires a namespace conforming to the XML Signature specification, a joint endeavor of the W3C and Internet Engineering Task Force. The specifications give detailed rules for the generation of signatures in ebXML messages.[63]

Manifest Element

The Manifest is the first element in the second part of the ebXML message headers contained in the SOAP body envelope (refer to Figure 8.9). This element describes the contents of the payloads, which makes it possible for the receivers to check the integrity of the contents, and can help the receivers extract the payload and determine whether they can process it before opening. ebXML requires a Manifest element if there is any data associated with the message but not in the header container. The most obvious data is found in the payload, but a Manifest is also required if the message references data elsewhere through an Internet address.

The key component in the Manifest is the Reference sub-element. Reference itself has sub-elements listing the schema from which the payload is defined, and a text description of the payload. The Schema sub-element gives the Internet address where it can be accessed and the version of the schema if needed. Reference also has an optional wildcard sub-element to provide extensibility.

Reference also has a series of attributes based on the XML Linking Language (XLink) that link the manifest to the Internet addresses of the payload object (required) and resources that describe the payload object.[64]

StatusResponse Element

This element, also among the second group of message headers, reports on the processing status of messages sent previously. It contains sub-elements with a reference to the previous message, a date/time stamp, and attributes for message status, as well as version and mustUnderstand attributes described earlier.

The messageStatus attribute indicates whether the target message service received the referenced message, or the message identifier was not recognized by the receiver. It can also tell if the status request is not authorized or accepted.[65]

DeliveryReceipt Element

Another element in the second group of headers tells the sender of a message that the target message service received the message. The MessageData element under MessageHeader has a RefToMessageId sub-element used for errors and acknowledgments, and in the case of acknowledgments identifies the previous message.

The DeliveryReceipt element has sub-elements indicating the sender of the acknowledgment and giving a date/time stamp. The element also has an attribute indicating the type of receipt, either a delivery receipt (the default) or an acknowledgment generated by a party other than the designated recipient. In this latter case, the acknowledgment gives an indication of processing by an intermediary or forwarder. The DeliveryReceipt also has an attribute noting whether it's digitally signed.[66]

The acknowledgment function provided by this element only tells the sender that the message got delivered to the receiving system. As in the case of EDI and other e-business messages, receipt implies neither an understanding of the message content nor a commitment to act on the message. One of the contributions of EDI is the pairing of action messages to provide a substantive business-level dialogue that goes well beyond simple acknowledgments. For example, as indicated in examples earlier in this book, ship notices can have corresponding receiving advice messages to show the shipper the items accepted into inventory by the recipient.

Message Handling Services

ebXML specifies two kinds of services to support business messaging: message status requests and message service handler pinging. Both sets of services use several of the header elements described earlier.

The message status requests and responses let a sender of a previous message know about the current state of the message. The status request message consists of the following:

- `MessageHeader` (required) with `From`, `To`, `RefToMessageId`, `Service`, and `Action` sub-elements. The `RefToMessageId` refers to the original message.
- `TraceHeaderList` element (optional).
- `Signature` element (optional).
- `StatusRequest` element (required).

The message status response has the following content:

- `MessageHeader` (required) with `From`, `To`, `RefToMessageId`, `Service`, and `Action` sub-elements. In this case, the `RefToMessageId` refers to the message status request.
- `TraceHeaderList` element (optional).
- `Acknowledgment` element (optional).
- `StatusRequest` element (required).
- `Signature` element (optional).

The message service handler ping service determines whether another comparable service is in operation. The ping message consists of the following:

- MessageHeader (required) with From, To, Service, and Action sub-elements. The Action in this case is Ping.
- TraceHeaderList element (optional).
- Signature element (optional).

The response to a message service handler ping is (of course) a pong that consists of the following:

- MessageHeader (required) with From, To, RefToMessageId, Service, and Action sub-elements. In this case, the RefToMessageId refers to the ping and the Action is Pong.
- TraceHeaderList element (optional).
- Acknowledgment element (optional).
- Signature element (optional).

Both sets of service messages have security implications. Recipients of status requests may ignore the request messages if they consider the senders unauthorized. Also, recipients of pings may ignore the messages if they believe the pings are a prelude to some kind of denial-of-service or comparable attack.[67]

Reliable Messaging

A key part of the message services as defined by ebXML is the concept of reliable messaging. One facet of ebXML reliable messaging is the storage of the message through its lifetime in a way that persists through any failure of system components. Another facet is delivery to the recipient once and only once.

The persistent storage requirement of reliable messaging recommends that parties configure their systems so the message data can survive a failure of any single equipment or software component. Also, in case of failure, messages still need to be processed as if the interruption never occurred. The specifications recommend that companies keep in persistent storage the complete message, as well as separate instances of the message identifiers and time of receipt. This maintenance of message data in persistent storage can reduce the occurrence of duplicate message receipts in case of interruption or failure.

Trading partners can choose to adopt reliable messaging as one of their protocols, either as part of the collaboration protocol agreement, or one message at a time. The `MessageHeader` element has a `QualityOfServiceInfo` sub-element with a `deliverySemantics` attribute. This attribute has values of `OnceAndOnlyOnce` or `BestEffort`. If set to `OnceAndOnlyOnce`, trading partners need to take steps guaranteeing that messages are re-sent in case of failure, and persistent storage is implemented to check against duplicate deliveries. If set to `BestEffort`, the trading partners can ignore these properties.

If the trading partners choose to implement reliable messaging, they need to take the following steps in their messaging systems. Senders need to do the following:

1. Create a message with a `TraceHeader` element identifying the sender and recipient Internet addresses.

2. Save the message in persistent storage.

3. Send the message to the recipient message service handler.

4. Wait for an acknowledgment from the recipient or take the appropriate action if none is returned.

Recipients of messages need to take these steps:

1. If the message is an acknowledgment, look for a message in persistent storage with the same identifier as in the `RefToMessageId` element and, if found, mark it as delivered.

2. If the message is not an acknowledgment, check whether it's a duplicate (a message identifier in persistent storage with the same value as the message).

3. If neither an acknowledgment nor a duplicate, then save the message identifier or entire message (if practical to do so) in persistent storage, compare the message identifier to the reference, mark the message as delivered, and send an acknowledgment.

4.   If the message is a duplicate, check for the
      first response to the received message in
      persistent storage and re-send the initial
      response.

The specifications give rules for acknowledgments.
Recipients of messages must send acknowledgments
if the `deliverySemantics` attribute is set to
`OnceAndOnlyOnce` or the `reliableMessagingMethod`
attribute is set to `ebXML`. The minimum requirement
for an acknowledgment is a `MessageData` element
with a `RefToMessageId` set to the same value as the
`MessageId` element in the message being
acknowledged.

If trading partners agree to reliable messaging and a
message fails to be delivered, the appropriate message
service handler (it can be either the sender or receiver) should generate a delivery failure notification
message. This message has an error code reflecting a
delivery failure.[68]

Security

The specifications recognize and list some of the risks
inherent in a business messaging service:

- Unauthorized access—Parties that are not
  allowed to gain access to resources or services
  trying to do so.
- Data-integrity attacks—Attempts to disrupt
  the contents of messages.
- Confidentiality attacks—Attempts to read the
  contents of messages.
- Denial of service (DoS) attacks—Attempts to
  overwhelm the ability of resources to cope
  with a flood of fake message traffic.
- Spoofing attacks—Similar to unauthorized
  access, but by groups of attackers rather than
  an individual.
- Bombing attacks—Similar to data-integrity
  attacks, but against an entire site or resource
  rather than individual records.

The messaging specifications recommend a series of countermeasures, beginning with due diligence by the managers of the message services and appropriate safeguards listed in the collaboration protocol agreement between the trading partners.

The document discusses a number of technical countermeasures either as requirements or recommendations. These steps include the use of digital signatures both on the original messages and receipts. Some of the steps discussed, however, are still in development, such as XML encryption and trusted date/time stamps.[69]

Core Components

An important goal of ebXML messages is interoperability, defined here as the ability of companies in different industries to exchange and understand data among different business domains and technologies. To help achieve interoperability, ebXML defines a series of common data items called *core components* that appear in different business messages yet still have common meanings. These common meanings enable companies using business terms in one industry to relate those terms to their counterparts in another industry. Businesses will (and should) use their own terminology to do business, but they will also want to interact with other industries with the same kind of ease and purpose. Core components help realize that goal.

As with business processes, the definition and management of core components will likely fall to industry organizations and standards bodies. Core components can get complex and political. The development of core components has lagged behind the rest of the ebXML initiative, and much of the hard work in this area remains. This section gives an overview of core components and samples of their use.

An example from different supply-chain scenarios illustrates this issue. From one industry to the next, a product manufacturer can be referred to as a *manufacturer, supplier, vendor,* or *factory.* A wholesaler of goods can be called *distributor, dealer,* or *merchant.* A retailer may be known as a *store* or *outlet.* The person buying the goods can be called a *customer, client,* or *end user.* Figure 8.10 illustrates the function of core components, to find common synonyms for these words, using these different supply-chain terms.

Figure 8.10 shows another feature of core components, namely the use of a neutral syntax to identify them. The chart calls the core components A, B, C, and D; in reality they have official dictionary names and unique identifiers. However, the use of a neutral syntax enables different industries to relate their particular business terms more easily to the core components. The neutral syntax also enables companies and industries to relate their existing EDI transactions and XML vocabularies to ebXML messages, by providing the same kind of common references used to relate different industries.

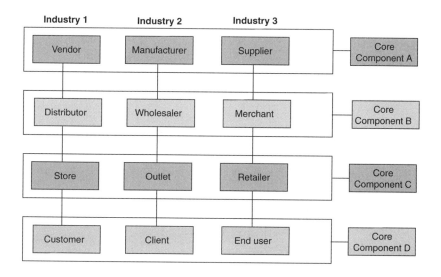

Figure 8.10
Core component examples.

The context for the terms provides still another important factor in determining core components. The context of a core component provides the specific business meaning of the data item, as determined by the business process and other variables, while the core component itself provides the basic interchangeable part.

The term *invoice*, for example, usually means a statement of charges levied by one company on another. However, one can also use the term in the context of international shipping, where a commercial invoice lists line items, quantities, prices, and deliveries of a shipment, and is used to compute duties or generate letters of credit. In this case, the business process context changes the meaning of the term *invoice*, and the ebXML core components need to reflect these process-defined variations.

ebXML provides a way of classifying the context of core components as one or a combination of the following categories:

- Business process
- Region (geopolitical)
- Industry
- Official constraints (such as regulatory)
- Product
- Role (buyer or seller, for example)[70]

Each of these categories can have different rules, called *context rules*, for modifying the core components, and the entries within the categories can also dictate different rules. For example, the process for making hotel reservations will vary depending on the type of customer. Individuals might call a telephone reservation number or log onto a web site, while businesses establishing corporate accounts go through an entirely different process. The process may also differ from one part of the world to another to reflect different legal constraints.[71] These sources of variation help explain why the definition of core components has been such a long and arduous process.

Simple or basic core components can also be grouped together to form aggregate core components. The basic core component has no further logical or semantic subdivisions, but may have an extendable list of valid code values. Aggregate core components consist of multiple basic components, and may have rules on the maximum number of times an embedded component is allowed or the order of the components in the aggregate object.[72]

Business messages in an industry will likely have data items unique to that industry, which in ebXML are called *domain components*, either *basic* or *complex*. If domain components find use outside the original industry, they can then become core components. Building a business document means assembling the collection of core and domain components, using the rules defined in the business process models for message structure, as well as other data items defined in the CPA and CPP documents.[73] ebXML provides a schema for assembling new electronic business documents, where the business process models may not have yet defined them.[74]

ebXML has developed a partial list of core components as of April 2001. Table 8.1 gives some examples, with aggregate and embedded components, and shows the reusability of some items.

Table 8.1 Sample Core Components[75]

Aggregate Entity	Embedded Entity	Component Reused	Definition (Aggregates)
party.details			Details on an individual, a group, or a body having a role in a business function
	party.type	identification.details	
	party.identification. details	party.identification.details	
	party.title.details	party.title.details	

continues

Table 8.1   Continued

Aggregate Entity	Embedded Entity	Component Reused	Definition (Aggregates
	postal.address	postal.address.details	
	location	location.details	
	communication.details	communication.details	
	party.nationality	identification.details	
	party.description.text		
	language	language.details	
	birth.date.and.time	date.and.time	
party.identification.details			Identification of a party by name and/or identifier
	party.identifier	identification.details	
	party.name.text		
	given.name.text		
	middle.name.text		
	surname.text		
	party.gender.code.details	code.details	

Starting a Company's ebXML Operations

A company needs to follow three phases to go from beginning to operational with ebXML. An *implementation phase* creates or acquires the basic ebXML-compliant systems. A *discovery-retrieval* phase learns the capabilities of trading partners. A *runtime phase* covers the exchange of ebXML messages. We expect that industry groups or enterprising companies will provide services to make some or all of these steps transparent to companies, but in one way or another they need to get done.

Implementation Phase

This first phase covers the initial startup of a company with ebXML, to build or acquire the applications for dealing with the ebXML specifications. In most cases, companies will be able to acquire stand-alone ebXML software, upgrade their current applications with off-the-shelf ebXML components, or use a web-based service, such as an application service provider. If the company needs to build its own systems, it will then need to acquire the official ebXML technical specifications.[76] These specifications, with supporting technical reports, are listed in Appendix B, "References," and downloadable free of charge from the ebXML web site (`www.ebxml.org`).

If the systems need to first reference an industry's business process specifications, a company can download the specifications from the appropriate registry. The business process specifications include process models in UML or a comparable language, or XML specifications in the form of a document type definition (DTD) or schema. These business processes either describe or provide the message sequences and data elements needed to do business with other companies in that industry.

The industry's specifications should identify which of the data elements in the messages are equivalent to the ebXML core components, and which are specific to the industry domain. Industry organizations that have defined EDI transactions should relate the items in these earlier EDI messages or transaction sets to the ebXML core components, in order to promote interoperability between EDI and ebXML. The work of X12 and the UN/EDIFACT Work Group to relate their EDI standards to the ebXML core components will help in this effort.[77]

Where an industry may not yet have developed industry-wide processes or messages, companies may need to develop their own processes and messages, and register them with the appropriate registries. Under these conditions, companies will need to work with individual company processes and messages rather than those defined for whole industries.[78]

If companies need to acquire these specifications, they will need software to access and interact with ebXML registries, which in turn will need the capability to generate and process ebXML messages.

Discovery and Retrieval Phase

Once the company has either acquired or developed a system with a business service interface as discussed earlier in this chapter (refer to Figure 8.6), it can begin interacting with ebXML registries to list its own readiness and find trading partners with the capabilities to do electronic business.

In this phase, companies register their own collaboration protocol profiles (CPPs) and download CPPs of potential trading partners from ebXML registries. These profiles provide the technical capabilities of trading partners, including the process and messages they support, and become the basis for collaboration protocol agreements (CPAs) between companies. As a result, companies need to keep their CPPs up to date in all of the registries where they are listed.[79]

Runtime Phase

This phase covers the exchange of messages or provision of web services through ebXML. In the first two phases, companies deal with ebXML registries, but in this phase they deal mainly with each other.

The first set of exchanges should establish a CPA between the companies, which will govern further interactions. The CPA is based in part on the CPPs, subject to further negotiations and agreement. Once the CPA is in place, companies can begin exchanging ebXML-compliant messages.[80]

Eventually, end-user software with easy point-and-click screens will handle many of the functions for getting started with ebXML, but at the time of this writing those sofware products were still in the experimental stage. ebXML pioneers will probably use general-purpose XML document editors or even plain-vanilla text editors to write their CPPs and CPAs.

The idea of "trading partner" here can mean more than individual companies. Companies implementing ebXML can include web-based application service providers, exchanges, or clearinghouses providing some of the functionality usually assigned to end-user software. These web-based service companies can make it possible for companies to use less sophisticated and thus less expensive software. For example, if a company doesn't plan to change trading partners frequently, it could use a third-party service to establish a CPA with a trading partner rather than pay for those functions in an end-user package.

Endnotes

[1] "Design Objectives," ebXML Business Process Specification Schema Version 1.01, 11 May 2001, p. 2.

[2] *Information technology—Open-edi reference model*, ISO/IEC 14662:1997, International Organization for Standardization, 1997.

[3] "Open-edi Reference Model," Electronic Data Interchange (EDI) Standards, Diffuse, February 2001, www.diffuse.org/edi.html.

[4] "Electronic Data Interchange: An Overview of EDI Standards for Libraries," IFLANET, International Federation of Library Associations and Institutions, 1993, www.ifla.org/VI/5/reports/rep4/44.htm.

[5] Kendall Scott, "Use Case," Unified Modeling Language Dictionary, Software Documentation Wizards, www.softdocwiz.com/UML.htm.

[6] "ebXML Business Operational View," ebXML Technical Architecture Specification v1.0.4, 16 February 2001, pp. 11–12.

[7] "Activity Diagram," An Introduction To The Unified Modeling Language (UML), CraG Systems, undated, www.cragsystems.co.uk/UMLIntro1_files/frame.htm.

[8] "Sequence Diagram," An Introduction To The Unified Modeling Language (UML), CraG Systems, undated, www.cragsystems.co.uk/UMLIntro1_files/frame.htm.

[9] "Class Diagram", An Introduction To The Unified Modeling Language (UML), CraG Systems, undated, www.cragsystems.co.uk/UMLIntro1_files/frame.htm.

[10] "ebXML Business Operational View," ebXML Technical Architecture Specification v1.0.4, 16 February 2001, pp. 11–12.

[11] "Collaboration Diagrams," An Introduction To The Unified Modeling Language (UML), CraG Systems, undated, www.cragsystems.co.uk/UMLIntro1_files/frame.htm.

[12] "Statechart Diagrams," An Introduction To The Unified Modeling Language (UML), CraG Systems, undated, www.cragsystems.co.uk/UMLIntro1_files/frame.htm.

[13] "Production Rules," ebXML Business Process Specification Schema Version 1.01, 11 May 2001, pp. 103–104.

[14] "Business Process and Information Modeling," ebXML Technical Architecture Specification v1.0.4, 16 February 2001, pp. 19–20.

[15] "Business Process and Information Modeling," ebXML Technical Architecture Specification v1.0.4, 16 February 2001, p. 21.

[16] "ebXML Functional Services View," ebXML Technical Architecture Specification v1.0.4, 16 February 2001, pp. 13–14.

[17] Alan Kotok, "ebXML Gathers Pace," XML.com, 24 May 2000, www.xml.com/pub/a/2000/05/24/ebXML/index.html.

[18] "System Overview," ebXML Registry Services Specification, Version 1, 10 May 2001, p. 9.

[19] "How the ebXML Registry Works," ebXML Registry Services Specification, Version 1.0, 10 May 2001, pp. 9–10.

[20] "Where the Registry Services May Be Implemented," ebXML Registry Services Specification, Version 1.0, 10 May 2001, p. 11.

[21] "DISA to Host ebXML-Compliant Registry and Repository for E-Business Standards," Data Interchange Standards Association, 19 March 2001, www.disa.org/pr_doc.cfm?Name=543.

[22] "Registry Architecture," ebXML Registry Services Specification, Version 1.0, 10 May 2001, pp. 12–14.

[23] "Interfaces Exposed by the Registry," ebXML Registry Services Specification, Version 1.0, 10 May 2001, pp. 15–20.

[24] "Life Cycle of a Registry Entry," ebXML Registry Services Specification, Version 1.0, 10 May 2001, p. 19.

[25] "RegistryObject Attributes," ebXML Registry Services Specification, Version 1.0, 10 May 2001, p. 20.

[26] "Registry Information Model: High Level Public View," ebXML Registry Information Model, Version 1.0, 8 May 2001, pp. 9–11.

[27] "Universally Unique ID Generation," ebXML Registry Services Specification, Version 1.0, 10 May 2001, p. 21.

[28] DCE Frequently Asked Questions, The Open Group, 23 October 1998, www.opengroup.org/dce/info/faq-mauney.html.

[29] "Sample SubmitObjectsRequest," ebXML Registry Services Specification, Version 1.0, 10 May 2001, pp. 22–24.

[30] "The Approve Objects Protocol, The Deprecate Objects Protocol," ebXML Registry Services Specification, Version 1.0, 10 May 2001, pp. 25–26.

[31] "The Remove Objects Protocol," ebXML Registry Services Specification, Version 1.0, 10 May 2001, pp. 26–27.

[32] "Object Query Management Service," ebXML Registry Services Specification, Version 1.0, 10 May 2001, pp. 27–28.

[33] "Browse and Drill Down Query Support," ebXML Registry Services Specification, Version 1.0, 10 May 2001, pp. 28–31.

[34] "Filter Query Support," ebXML Registry Services Specification, Version 1.0, 10 May 2001, p. 32.

[35] "RegistryEntryQuery," ebXML Registry Services Specification, Version 1.0, 10 May 2001, pp. 36–41.

[36] "ReturnRegistry Entry" and "ReturnRepositoryItem," ebXML Registry Services Specification, Version 1.0, 10 May 2001, pp. 53–60.

[37] "SQL Query Support," ebXML Registry Services Specification, Version 1.0, 10 May 2001, p. 69.

[38] "Content Retrieval," ebXML Registry Services Specification, Version 1.0, 10 May 2001, pp. 76–77.

[39] "Registry Security," ebXML Registry Services Specification, Version 1.0, 10 May 2001, pp. 78–81.

[40] Benjamin Wright, "V. Trading Partner Agreements, 7. EDI Implementation," *The Internet and Business: A Lawyer's Guide to the Emerging Legal Issues* (The Computer Law Association, 1996), www.cla.org/RuhBook/chp7.htm.

[41] Electronic Trading-Partner Agreement for E-Commerce (tpaML), Pre-submission Draft 1.0.3, IBM Corporation, 25 January 2000.

[42] "Introduction," Collaboration-Protocol Profile and Agreement, Specification, Version 1.0, 10 May 2001, p. 5.

[43] "System Overview," Collaboration-Protocol Profile and Agreement, Specification, Version 1.0, 10 May 2001, pp. 9–10.

[44] "Forming a CPA from Two CPPs," Collaboration-Protocol Profile and Agreement, Specification, Version 1.0, 10 May 2001, pp. 10–11.

[45] "Appendix F: Composing a CPA from Two CPPs (Non-Normative)," Collaboration-Protocol Profile and Agreement, Specification, Version 1.0, 10 May 2001, pp. 82–90.

[46] "How the CPA Works," Collaboration-Protocol Profile and Agreement, Specification, Version 1.0, 10 May 2001, pp. 13–14.

[47] "CPP Definition," Collaboration-Protocol Profile and Agreement, Specification, Version 1.0, 10 May 2001, p. 17.

[48] "Packaging Element," Collaboration-Protocol Profile and Agreement, Specification, Version 1.0, 10 May 2001, p. 42.

[49] "PartyInfo element," Collaboration-Protocol Profile and Agreement, Specification, Version 1.0, 10 May 2001, pp. 18–35.

[50] "DocExchange element," Collaboration-Protocol Profile and Agreement, Specification, Version 1.0, 10 May 2001, pp. 38–42.

[51] "CollaborationRole element," Collaboration-Protocol Profile and Agreement, Specification, Version 1.0, 10 May 2001, pp. 20–30.

[52] "CollaborationProtocolAgreement element," Collaboration-Protocol Profile and Agreement, Specification, Version 1.0, 10 May 2001, pp. 47–48.

[53] "CPA Definition," Collaboration-Protocol Profile and Agreement, Specification, Version 1.0, 10 May 2001, pp. 47–55.

[54] Alan Kotok, "ebXML Ropes in SOAP," XML.com, 4 April 2001, www.xml.com/pub/a/2001/04/04/ebxml.html.

[55] "Message Service Overview," Message Service Specification, ebXML Transport, Routing & Packaging, Version 1.0, 11 May 2001, p. 11.

[56] Some readers may need to ask their grandparents about telexes and telegrams, or visit the web site of the International Telecommunications Union at www.itu.int/home/ for the authoritative documents.

[57] E. Levinson, "The MIME Multipart/Related Content-type," Request For Comments: 2387, The Internet Society, August 1998, www.ietf.org/rfc/rfc2387.txt.

[58] "Packaging Specification," Message Service Specification, ebXML Transport, Routing & Packaging, Version 1.0, 11 May 2001, pp. 13–15.

[59] "MessageHeader element," Message Service Specification, ebXML Transport, Routing & Packaging, Version 1.0, 11 May 2001, pp. 19–25.

[60] "TraceHeaderList element," Message Service Specification, ebXML Transport, Routing & Packaging, Version 1.0, 11 May 2001, pp. 25–27.

[61] "Via element," Message Service Specification, ebXML Transport, Routing & Packaging, Version 1.0, 11 May 2001, pp. 30–32.

[62] "ErrorList element," Message Service Specification, ebXML Transport, Routing & Packaging, Version 1.0, 11 May 2001, pp. 32–33.

[63] "Signature element," Message Service Specification, ebXML Transport, Routing & Packaging, Version 1.0, 11 May 2001, pp. 34–35.

[64] "Manifest element," Message Service Specification, ebXML Transport, Routing & Packaging, Version 1.0, 11 May 2001, pp. 35–37.

[65] "StatusResponse element," Message Service Specification, ebXML Transport, Routing & Packaging, Version 1.0, 11 May 2001, pp. 37–38.

[66] "DeliveryReceipt element," Message Service Specification, ebXML Transport, Routing & Packaging, Version 1.0, 11 May 2001, p. 38.

[67] "Message Service Handler Services," Message Service Specification, ebXML Transport, Routing & Packaging, Version 1.0, 11 May 2001, pp. 40–42.

[68] "Reliable Messaging," Message Service Specification, ebXML Transport, Routing & Packaging, Version 1.0, 11 May 2001, pp. 43–49.

[69] "Security," Message Service Specification, ebXML Transport, Routing & Packaging, Version 1.0, 11 May 2001, pp. 52–54.

[70] "Context Classifications," Catalogue of Context Drivers, 10 May 2001, version 1.04, pp. 6–10.

[71] "Context Defined," Context and Re-Usability of Core Components, 10 May 2001, version 1.04, pp. 5–6.

[72] "Basic Information Entity, Aggregate Information Entity," Context and Re-Usability of Core Components, 10 May 2001, version 1.04, pp. 8–9.

[73] "Building Business Documents, Beyond Reuse," Context and Re-Usability of Core Components, 10 May 2001, version 1.04, pp. 10–11.

[74] ebXML Document Assembly & Context Rules, 10 May 2001, version 1.04.

[75] Excerpted from "Analysis of Submitted Aggregate Entities," Initial Core Components Catalogue, Ver 1.02, pp. 1–2.

[76] One more time, this book is *not* the official ebXML specifications.

[77] "X12 and UN/EDIFACT Craft ebXML-compliant Core Components," Data Interchange Standards Association press release, 27 February 2001, `http://xml.coverpages.org/ni2001-02-27-b.html`.

[78] "Implementation Phase," ebXML Technical Architecture Specification v1.0.4, 16 February 2001, p. 14.

[79] "Discovery and Retrieval Phase," ebXML Technical Architecture Specification v1.0.4, 16 February 2001, pp. 14–15.

[80] "Run Time Phase," ebXML Technical Architecture Specification v1.0.4, 16 February 2001, pp. 15–16.

Chapter 9

Moving from Theory to Practice

This chapter presents actual applications of ebXML principles to solve business requirements. The two applications presented here are available online as previews of anticipated ebXML-capable systems.

The first application distributes product catalog information to help small suppliers easily deploy their own online catalogs and then have an XML-enabled point of presence from which other ebXML-capable systems can directly query to retrieve stock availability and pricing information.

The second application offers a business semantic registry that relates to this catalog system. The registry is designed to provide metadata (descriptive data about the data) on the business information in the catalog. For instance, a list price of an item in the catalog is a decimal number, but what does that list price itself mean in business terms? Is it expressed in U.S. dollars? Is it a retail price, or a discounted price, is it tax paid or not? Querying the registry allows business partners to discover the answers to these questions and more.

The two applications are therefore coupled together to solve the overall business requirements and expressed as an ebXML-based solution. The U.S. Department of Defense (DoD) funded the original *CatXML* work (www.catxml.org) as part of an initiative called *EMall*, funded by the Defense Logistics Agency (DLA), and the follow-on registry implementation (http://nist.xmlglobal.com) was funded by the National Institute of Standards (NIST) as part of that agency's metadata registry inter-operability research (see www.nist.gov).

Of Catalogs and Suppliers

An old adage states that 25% of what MIS departments do relates to catalogs. The U.S. government similarly has an ongoing need to get reliable, accurate, and timely information from its suppliers. Because of laws ensuring open competition on federal procurements, agencies have a particular need to get data from their smaller supplies. DLA's EMall seeks to build an online marketplace for the DLA. The original idea behind online marketplaces, called *Netmarkets*, is to create an electronic environment in which nimble buyers and sellers can move in and out, effortlessly exchanging information, with the ultimate goal of growing their businesses.

Enterprises are now asking Netmarkets to provide features directly affecting catalog management, such as inter-exchange operability, robust collaboration, and demand forecasting. With the emerging adoption of ebXML as the standard for e-business, however, these demands may not be as daunting as they once seemed.

Obstacles arise from standardization and integration. Participants are faced with Netmarket vendors who rely on proprietary systems to ensure loyalty and adoption. If a business wants to participate in several Netmarkets, it needs to understand how to use its own business information each time. With Netmarkets, companies need to publish business information and data, dynamically update the content, and then integrate the data with various business flow applications. But when using more than one standard, joining the e-business train may seem like riding a roller-coaster. The government faces all these issues as it struggles to maintain a neutral and open front door for all its various and diverse suppliers, while at the same time reducing costs and increasing efficiency and ease of adoption.

In addition, catalog information is not just about marketing products, but also about marrying the data into specific back-office requirements, such as accounting and inventory management. Enterprises are now asking Netmarkets to provide features directly affecting catalog management, such as inter-exchange operability, robust collaboration, and demand forecasting. With the emerging adoption of ebXML as the standard for e-business, however, these demands may not be as daunting as they once seemed.

For developers working with XML and catalog management logic, the ultimate goal is to create a solution that helps manage multiple kinds of catalogs, encourages real-time information exchange, promotes end-to-end transaction integration over the Internet, and provides complete interoperability with all back-office systems. Of course, this is not a new idea; EDI and a variety of Enterprise Resource Planning (ERP) system vendor solutions have targeted these issues for years. Recently, the Open Applications Group (`www.oagis.org`) produced XML exchange formats, and its version 7.0 is now available. As a broad open standard, however, the OAG work is limited by its ERP's COBOL-esque heritage and backward compatibility needs.

The large Netmarket vendors have not been slow to address these areas. Corporations such as Ariba (cXML), Commerce One (xCBL), and others have developed their own proprietary XML-based vocabularies. These specific solutions may work in certain vertical industries served by a particular company. For cross-industry or inter-exchange communications, however, these unique vocabularies have limited interoperability. Therefore, DLA identified the need for this initial work to apply these concepts to produce an open, neutral XML catalog-exchange format, called CatXML™.

Uncle Sam Likes Small Businesses

DLA aimed its EMall requirements particularly at small businesses with minimal e-business resources, but who provide a significant level of support to the U.S. armed services. Specifically, the EMall project (www.emall.dla.mil) is designed to offer the four major military services—Army, Navy, Air Force, and Marines—a single requisition system for common parts and replenishable supplies.

The project created two proof-of-concept systems to demonstrate how small vendors can be quickly integrated into a larger central system, and to provide a distributed information grid to supply real-time catalog information without prohibitive performance overhead. From the original base syntax came an advanced version that supports completely scalable and dynamic information exchange for CatXML points-of-presence. A flexible "smorgasbord" approach allows trading partners to implement matching profiles quickly and effectively with both inbound and outbound information exchange, using the information server approach as its foundation. This approach is the ebXML idea in action, addressing real business issues.

An important goal for DLA is to provide a vendor-neutral specification founded in XML syntax that can be freely implemented. Since XML Global Technologies (www.xmlglobal.com), the system developer, and DLA are not vendors of proprietary catalog services or solutions, they have no particular axe to grind. As a result, catalog developers gain the advantage of using proven designs of components and methods, while at the same time being able to locally customize these components and methods to their specific industry base. The potential payoffs of CatXML come from its interoperability and cost savings across a broad spectrum of marketplaces. Figure 9.1 illustrates these items in the CatXML conceptual delivery architecture.

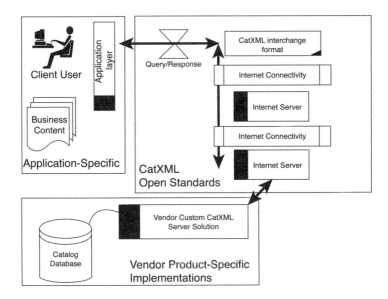

How Does the CatXML Approach Relate to ebXML?

Figure 9.1
CatXML conceptual delivery architecture.

The CatXML model aligns very well with ebXML. CatXML provides an open global system that allows a broad range of systems to interface with the CatXML server. The XML information contained in CatXML format should also allow querying or sending systems to consistently interpret the business information. By using the ebXML specifications, the original CatXML catalog XML formats have been upgraded to include the unique identifier (UID) referencing system that ebXML prescribes. By following the ebXML specifications, the associated ebXML registry can supply the precise business information and data formats to a company needing specific details that CatXML data records contain.

Another feature of ebXML is its ability to provide a single consistent transport layer, through its messaging specifications. Clearly, the CatXML server needs to speak to the world in a simple and open way so that a wide variety of systems can easily reach the information that the server provides. The ebXML specifications adopted the XML-based Simple Object

Access Protocol (SOAP) syntax for these messaging functions. Figure 9.2 shows the structure of the SOAP interchange header used by CatXML. This messaging example illustrates how the sender and receiver are identified, the quality of service levels used between them, and the message data type exchanged. SOAP is designed to be lightweight where appropriate and not overly burden the sender and receiver with technical requirements. Further examples of the message headers and other SOAP details can be downloaded from the CatXML web site (`www.catxml.org`), along with associated technical documentation.

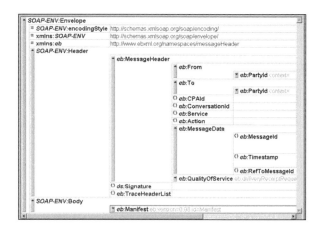

Figure 9.2

SOAP messaging envelope for referencing the CatXML server. (Screen shot provided by XML Spy, ver. 3.5.)

And Now for the XML in CatXML

Before looking at specifics of the underlying XML techniques, we need to examine some basics of organizing and structuring metadata. Too often we see metadata provided as an amorphous blob of elements and attributes with little regard to using parent/child structures to create groups of related elements—and thus easily accessible information blocks. The ebXML specifications refer to these accessible information blocks as *core components*— building blocks of business information that can be easily and consistently snapped together to create a coherent business information exchange (see Figure 9.3).

Once a well-defined group structure is established, a higher level of organization can then be created by separating the XML itself into physical components that are each included in a controlling parent template. This template approach allows trading partners to be flexible about the components they select, and the versions and sub-definitions they apply to the master templates. (All of these techniques can be found in the CatXML syntax examples. The value of good semantic models cannot be overemphasized here. Well-implemented XML should provide the foundation and stepping stones to emerging business applications.)

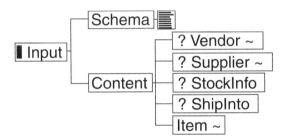

Figure 9.3
CatXML information hierarchy.

Next, CatXML seeks to address the problems of naming and semantics. Ultimately, ebXML registry systems based on reference unique identifiers (UIDs) will be the implementation of choice as they become available later in 2001. The NIST prototype is a precursor of these industry-enabling commercial registries. The UID linkage references provide neutral data identifiers called *Bizcodes* that allow collaborating businesses to synchronize their business semantics by labeling each piece of information exchanged. Therefore, the context and meaning of data sent by one trading partner can be readily matched to similar uses by the receiving business systems.

Similarly, the transport of CatXML messages uses an access/content input/response output model supported by the ebXML messaging services specifications and the SOAP messaging protocols. Figure 9.4 shows the actual structure of CatXML payloads delivered by ebXML message envelopes.

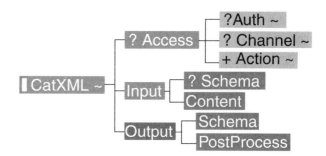

Figure 9.4
CatXML interchange
hierarchy.

The ebXML work has developed similar transport formats for registry interchanges, and these SOAP-based transactions are used in registry prototypes to show how metadata attached to catalog information can be queried, retrieved, and used by a web browser. Rounding out this section, Listing 9.1 provides a sample and more details of the actual CatXML syntax. Examples of the CatXML DTD and XML documents can be downloaded from the CatXML web site, along with documentation.

Listing 9.1   CatXML Controlling a Parent DTD Template Fragment

```
<!— CatXML base DTD.                                        —>
<!— Version 0.21 August 2000                                —>
<!— Conforms to ebXML core component specifications         —>
<!—                                                         —>
<!— To provide maximum flexibility in deploying             —>
<!— customized versions, the following business             —>
<!— functional information blocks are included as           —>
<!— five related DTD fragments. This allows just pieces     —>
<!— of the overall structure to be redefined selectively    —>
<!—                                                         —>
<!— Address information                                     —>
<!— Contact information                                     —>
<!— Shipping information                                    —>
<!— USGov product information                               —>
<!— Warehouse stock information                             —>
<!—

************************************************************************
*  Main definition of CatXML content schema structure  Version 1.1    *
*                                                                      *
************************************************************************
—>
<!ELEMENT Input (Schema, Content)>
<!ELEMENT Schema (#PCDATA)>
<!ELEMENT Content (Vendor?, Supplier?, StockInfo?, ShipInfo?, Item)>
<!— Establish link to UID reference location —>
<!ATTLIST Content
    UIDref CDATA #FIXED "http://www.catxml.org/UID/datatypes.xml"
>
```

```
<!ELEMENT Vendor (CompanyID, Name?, Address?, Contact?)>
<!ATTLIST Vendor
    vendorID ID #IMPLIED
>
<!ELEMENT CompanyID (#PCDATA)>
<!ATTLIST CompanyID
    context (Vendor | Supplier | Manufacturer | Other) "Vendor"
    idType (DUNS | Local | USDoD | EIN | TaxID | Other) "DUNS"
>
<!ELEMENT Name (#PCDATA)>
<!ENTITY % addressInfo SYSTEM "CatXML-address-V1.dtd">
<!ENTITY % contactInfo SYSTEM "CatXML-contact-V1.dtd">
<!ENTITY % shippingInfo SYSTEM "CatXML-shipping-V1.dtd">
<!ENTITY % usgovDoDInfo SYSTEM "CatXML-usgovDoD-V1.dtd">
<!ENTITY % stockInfo SYSTEM "CatXML-warehouse-V1.dtd">
%addressInfo; %contactInfo; %shippingInfo; %usgovDoDInfo; %stockInfo;
<!ELEMENT Supplier (CompanyID, Name?, Address?, Contact?)>
<!ATTLIST Supplier
    supplierID ID #IMPLIED
>
<!ELEMENT Item (supplierItemNo, (partName | prodName), barcode?,
➡ ((unitPrice, pricingType?) | priceRecord+), (MFGPartNo | MFGProdNo)?,
➡ MFGName?, itemCategory?, DoDcontent?, productOptions?, ordering,
➡ description?, productImage?, punchoutURL?, CatalogID?, remarks?,
➡ sampleInfo?)>
<!ATTLIST Item
    ItemID ID #IMPLIED
    UID CDATA #FIXED "CAT10501"
>
<!ELEMENT supplierItemNo (#PCDATA)>
<!ATTLIST supplierItemNo
    UID CDATA #FIXED "CAT10510"
>
<!ELEMENT barcode (#PCDATA)>
<!ATTLIST barcode
    codeType (UPC | EAN) "UPC"
    UID CDATA #FIXED "CAT10502"
>
<!ELEMENT unitPrice (#PCDATA)>
<!ATTLIST unitPrice
    currencyID %isoCurrencyCode; "1001"
    pricingType (retail | wholesale | export | any) "any"
    alternateAmount %number; #IMPLIED
    alternateCurrency %isoCurrencyCode; #IMPLIED
    alternateType (retail | wholesale | export | any) "any"
    expiryDate %datetime; #IMPLIED

    UID CDATA #FIXED "CAT10503">
```

The next section completes this technical review by
considering broader deployment needs.

Columbus, Registries, and Helping Discover the World

Setting off on a voyage of discovery into the unknown worked well in the 15th century as a business model. However, today we need consistent, repeatable, and secure processes. The ebXML registry is designed to allow trading partners to retrieve relevant business information quickly and easily about the physical information exchanged. In this case, the information exchanged is catalog data. Companies need to share that information globally so that trading partners can replicate the results and follow the path laid out for using catalog data.

The information structure in Listing 9.1 (see the preceding section) has also been used as the data structure underpinning a Korean Netmarket implementation. Looking at the syntax fragment in Listing 9.1, the `unitPrice` item has a number of attributes associated with it, and the UID reference `"CAT10503"`. In the NIST registry, this approach is used with a dashboard control-panel interface that allows the user to easily look up the business information associated with a particular UID reference. Then, as each piece of information is retrieved, the web page display is updated to reflect the new information that's now available to the business system.

The design in Figure 9.5 was developed to allow users to interact with the registry server and retrieve selected pieces of information, and then watch as the visual display of the form changes to reflect the new metadata made available about each business item. The XML content in the lower-left window updates with new XML content for each definition query you invoke, and the form display in the lower-right corner similarly adapts for each new piece of information rule returned.

Readers can try a demonstration of this system online to see how business information systems using an ebXML registry are able to selectively adapt to user requests. (Links to the live implementations can be found from this book's associated web site: `www.ebxmlbooks.com`.)

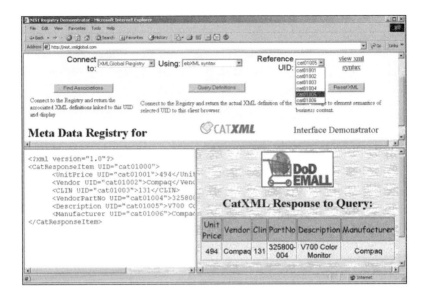

In a live application system, developers can pre-load these rule lookups for the ebXML application system. The business information processing can therefore take advantage of each of these consistent information packets returned by the registry.

Figure 9.5
NIST prototype of online registry interface.

Deployment Considerations and Benefits

Using ebXML as a model, CatXML allows for different levels of support for trading partners of different sizes and sophistication. The CatXML design can support any legacy information structure, while simultaneously providing completely dynamic output. In addition, because the CatXML architecture supports a distributed query information model, it avoids performance bottlenecks, thereby giving small trading partners the ability to take part in a broad selection of online Internet marketplaces.

The simplest CatXML-compliant implementation is a low-cost *point-of-presence* solution. The most obvious feature of the approach is that any computer system, anywhere, can access the catalog anytime. As a business model, this is well suited to many small suppliers who simply want to enlarge their market presence.

More sophisticated operations, however, are required to restrict and manage trading partner relations, and companies may want to define access channels and profiles for each of their trading partners.

The next level up the sophistication ladder is the *interchange server model*, which allows two or more trading partners to share information with each other in a closed model, using locally defined custom information formats. A typical interchange server application would be a supplier with three partners, each using different line-of-business systems that export information into fixed formats individually mapped to a CatXML-compliant format. To deliver these enhanced functions, the CatXML specification provides full interchange semantics. This enhanced performance includes a scheduler to acquire information automatically from remote suppliers. Typically, this acquisition would be a daily or weekly event, timed to coincide with catalog updates from the vendors' business systems. These updates are then consolidated into the existing catalog information. CatXML also supports the use of customized channels within information folders, so only content that matches a partner's retrieval profile will be returned to a remote system.

The highest level of sophistication is the *service provider model*, in which individual partners contract with a central service, allowing them to manage and control their catalog data distribution. Performance is a major concern in this model, as is support for real-time information access on items such as price and quantity on hand. The CatXML syntax provides a flexible model that supports real-time information querying on an as-needed basis. The CatXML information grid then follows on as an extension by linking a combination of the other CatXML models. Large organizations such as the U.S. government EMall system require these kinds of business capabilities.

The CatXML initiative reflects ebXML in several other ways. It uses XML content in a truly native fashion, without having to require participants to alter the format of their own local XML content.

Additionally, it exploits the capabilities of ebXML syntax to provide a high degree of maintainability and extensibility in line with the original design goals of ebXML itself.

Delivering on the ebXML Promise

Implementations such as CatXML are delivering on the promise of ebXML to provide open interoperable information content. Previously, organizations may have been capable of sharing and reusing business objects within their own confines, but very rarely achieved reuse across their business partners' systems. Now, new business models created by widespread content-sharing on the Internet are requiring that organizations share content at unprecedented levels. The ebXML initiative focuses on meeting these capabilities.

These technology advances translate into specific business benefits. The ability to reach a large base of small vendor partners is one clear benefit, as evidenced by the U.S. government's EMall initiative. Another benefit is the ability to reach a widely varying supply-chain base in which a large company sends catalog data to many thousands of locations, all of which require specific customization.

A further benefit is the ability to deliver data to a grid of distributed content points. Each point can respond dynamically to requests, so performance can be optimized. Static information can be cached at central locations and only periodically updated, while transient information, such as stock levels, can be directly queried in real time. ebXML helps make all of these benefits possible. The ebXML initiative focuses on the needs of smaller businesses, which the DoD and EMall also address, in part because of federal regulations. But now ebXML can open up collaborative e-business for millions of smaller businesses, and extend the business process improvements and productivity benefits that only larger companies have enjoyed up to now. EMall provides a glimpse of the vast potential that ebXML can unleash.

Part III   Learning More About ebXML

This part of the book lists in one
place many of the references cited
in the book, as well as leads to
more information about ebXML.
We include a glossary of acronyms
used in this book as well as in
e-business overall.

Appendix A

Acronyms

Acronyms Used in This Book

Acronym	Description
ABA	American Bar Association
ANSI	American National Standards Institute
API	Application programming interface
ASC X12	Accredited Standards Committee X12
B2B	Business-to-business
B2C	Business-to-consumer
BFC	BizTalk Framework Compliant
BOV	Business Operational View
Cecom	U.S. Army Communications-Electronics Command
CERN	European Particle Physics Laboratory (French acronym)
CPA	Collaboration protocol agreement
CPFR	Collaborative Planning, Forecasting, and Replenishment
CPP	Collaboration protocol profile
CRM	Customer relationship management
CSS	Cascading Style Sheets
cXML	Commerce XML

DISA	Data Interchange Standards Association
DOM	Document Object Model
DSDM	Dynamic Systems Definition Methodology
DTD	Document Type Definition
D-U-N-S	Data Universal Numbering System
EAN	European Article Number
ebXML	Electronic Business XML
EDI	Electronic Data Interchange
ERP	Enterprise resource planning (systems used for managing multiple business functions in a company)
FSV	Functional Service View
FTP	File Transfer Protocol
GCA	Graphic Communications Association
GDS	Global Distribution System (travel industry online reservation service)
GRACoL	General Requirements for Applications in Offset Lithography
HIPAA	Health Insurance Portability and Accountability Act
HTML	Hypertext Markup Language
HTTP	Hypertext Transport Protocol or Hypertext Transfer Protocol
HTTP/S	Secure HTTP
ICE	Information and Content Exchange
IEC	International Electrotechnical Commission
IEEE	Institute of Electrical and Electronics Engineers
ISO	International Organization of Standards (French acronym)
MIME	Multipurpose Internet Mail Extensions
NAICS	North American Industry Classification System
NVCA	National Venture Capital Association
OASIS	Organization for the Advancement of Structured Information Standards
OMG	Object Management Group
OTA	OpenTravel Alliance
PC	Personal computer

PCX	eProduction eCommerce eXchange
PIP	Partner Interface Process
PROSE	Production Order Specification/EDI (a printing industry EDI specification)
RFC	Request for Comments (IETF documents)
RIM	Registry Information Model
RPC	Remote Procedure Call
SAX	Simple API for XML
SGML	Standard Generalized Markup Language
SMTP	Simple Mail Transport Protocol
SOAP	Simple Object Access Protocol
SQL	Structured Query Language
TDCC	Transportation Data Coordinating Committee
TPA	Trading Partner Agreement
UCC	Uniform Code Council
UDDI	Universal Description, Discovery and Integration
UML	Unified Modeling Language
UN/CEFACT	United Nations Centre for Trade Facilitation and Electronic Business
UN/ECE	United Nations Economic Commission for Europe
UPC	Universal Product Code
URI	Uniform Resource Identifier
UUID	Universal Unique Identifier
W3C	World Wide Web Consortium
WSDL	Web Services Description Language
XDR	XML Data-Reduced
XLink	XML Linking Language
XML	Extensible Markup Language
XPointer	XML Pointer Language
XPP	XML for Publishers and Printers
XSL	Extensible Style Sheet Language
XSLT	Extensible Style Sheet Language Transformations

XML and E-Business Acronyms

Compiled by Betty Harvey, Electronic Commerce Connection Inc., and Glen Burnie, M.D.
www.eccnet.com.

Acronym	Description
AF	Architectural Forms
AFDR	Architectural Form Definition Requirements
AIML	Astronomical Instrument Markup Language
ANSI	American National Standards Institute
ASP	Active Server Pages
ATA	Airline Transportation Association
BSR	Business Semantics Registry
CAD	Computer-Aided Design
CALS	Continuous Acquisition and Lifecycle Management or Computer-Aided Logistics Support
CBL	Common Business Language
CDF	Channel Definition Language
CDM	Content Data Model
CGM	Computer Graphics Metafile
CIDS	Component Information Dictionary Standard
CPFR	Collaborative Planning, Forecasting, and Replenishment
CSS	Cascading Style Sheets
cXML	Commerce XML
cycL	CYC Representation Language
DCD	Document Content Description for XML
DDML	Document Description Markup Language
DHTML	Dynamic HTML
DML	Development Markup Language
DISA	Data Interchange Standards Association or Defense Information Systems Agency
DOM	Document Object Model
DSSSL	Document Style Semantics and Specification Language
DTD	Document Type Definition

EC	Electronic Commerce
ECIX	Electronic Component Information Exchange
EDI	Electronic Data Interchange
ELTA	Encoded Literary Text Analysis
ERP	Enterprise Resource Planning
FIXML	Financial Information Exchange Protocol
FOSI	Format Output Specification Instance
FTP	File Transfer Protocol
GCA	Graphic Communications Association
GCSFUI	General Content, Style, Format, and User Interface
GedML	Genealogical Data Markup Language
GNOME	GNU Network Object Model Environment (GNU is a recursive acronym for GNU's Not UNIX)
HTML	Hypertext Markup Language
HTTP	Hypertext Transfer Protocol or Hypertext Transport Protocol
HyTime	Hypermedia/Time-based Structuring Language
ICE	Information & Content Exchange
IETF	Internet Engineering Task Force
IETM	Interactive Electronic Technical Manual
IMPDEF	EDI Implementation Guide Definition Message (a UN/EDIFACT message)
ISO	International Organization of Standards (French acronym)
JSML	Java Speech Markup Language
KIF	Knowledge Interchange Format
MathML	Mathematical Markup Language
MOF	Meta Object Format
MOM	Message-Oriented Middleware
OAGIS	Open Applications Group Interchange Specification
OASIS	Organization for the Advancement of Structured Information Standards
OBI	Open Buying on the Internet
ODA	Open Document Architecture

ODBMS	Object Database Management System
OFX	Open Financial Exchange Specification
OMG	Object Management Group
OSD	Open Software Description Format
OTP	Open Trading Protocol
PDM	Product Data Model
PGML	Precision Graphics Markup Language
PI	Public Identifier or Processing Instruction
PIDL	Personalized Information Description Language
PML	Pattern Markup Language or Phone Markup Language
PURL	Persistent URLs
RDF	Resource Description Format
RFC	Request for Comment
RIF	Railroad Industry Forum
SAX	Simple API for XML
SGML	Standard Generalized Markup Language
SME	Subject Matter Expert or Small and Medium-sized Enterprise
SMIL	Synchronized Multimedia Integration Language
SOAP	Simple Object Access Protocol
SOCAT	SGML-Open Catalog
SPDL	Standard Page Description Language
STEP	Standard Exchange for Product Data
SVG	Scalable Vector Graphics
SWAP	Simple Workflow Application Protocol
TCIF	Telecommunications Industry Forum
TEI	Text Encoding Initiative
TDML	Timing Diagram Markup Language
UDEF	Universal Data Element Framework
UI	User Interface
UML	Universal Modeling Language
UXF	UML Exchange Format
URI	Universal Resource Indicator

URL	Universal Resource Locator
VAN	Value-Added Network
VICS	Voluntary Interindustry Commerce Standards
VML	Vector Markup Language
VRML	Virtual Reality Markup Language
VXML	Voice Extensible Markup Language
W3C	World Wide Web Consortium
WIDL	Web Interface Definition Language
XFDL	Extensible Forms Description Language
XHTML	Extensible Hypertext Markup Language
XLL	XML Linking Language
XMI	XML Metadata Interchange
XML	Extensible Markup Language
XML4J	XML Parser for Java
XSL	Extensible Style Sheet
XUL	Extensible User Interface Language
YOYO	You're on Your Own

Appendix B

References

The references in this appendix address two audiences. Systems specialists will find sources for technical specifications needed to develop applications. Books, articles, and more general business information on the applicable technologies are for everyone interested in ebXML.

ebXML Technical Specifications

Final, 11 May 2001

ebXML Technical Architecture specification v1.04, approved by the Vancouver plenary on 16 February 2001, www.ebxml.org/specs/ebTA.pdf.

ebXML Requirements Specification v1.06, approved by the ebXML Plenary on 11 May 2001, www.ebxml.org/specs/ebREQ.pdf.

Business Process Specification Schema v1.01, approved by the ebXML Plenary on 11 May 2001, www.ebxml.org/specs/ebBPSS.pdf.

- Document type definition, www.ebxml.org/specs/ebBPSS.dtd.
- Examples, http://www.ebxml.org/specs/ebBPSS.xml.

Registry Information Model v1.0, approved by the ebXML Plenary on 11 May 2001, www.ebxml.org/specs/ebRIM.pdf.

Registry Services Specification v1.0, approved by the ebXML Plenary on 11 May 2001, `www.ebxml.org/specs/ebRS.pdf`.

Collaboration-Protocol Profile and Agreement, Specification v1.0, approved by the ebXML Plenary on 11 May 2001, `www.ebxml.org/specs/ebCCP.pdf`.

Message Service Specification v1.0, approved by the ebXML Plenary on 11 May 2001, `www.ebxml.org/specs/ebMS.pdf`.

ebXML Technical Reports and Reference Materials

Accepted at the ebXML plenary, 11 May 2001

Reference materials are normative references in ebXML specifications. *Technical reports* provide guidelines to help interpret or implement ebXML ideas, or catalogs containing foundation material in ebXML specifications or other technical reports.

Reference Materials

ebXML Glossary, `www.ebxml.org/specs/ebGLOSS.pdf`.

Technical Reports

Business Process and Business Information Analysis Overview v1.0, `www.ebxml.org/specs/bpOVER.pdf`.

Business Process Analysis Worksheets & Guidelines v1.0, `www.ebxml.org/specs/bpWS.pdf`.

E-Commerce Patterns v1.0, `www.ebxml.org/specs/bpPATT.pdf`.

Catalog of Common Business Processes v1.0, `www.ebxml.org/specs/bpPROC.pdf`.

Core Component Overview v1.05, `www.ebxml.org/specs/ccOVER.pdf`.

Core Component Discovery and Analysis v1.04, `www.ebxml.org/specs/ebCCDA.PDF`.

Context and Re-Usability of Core Components v1.04, `www.ebxml.org/specs/ebCNTXT.pdf`.

Guide to the Core Components Dictionary v1.04,
www.ebxml.org/specs/ccCTLG.pdf.

Naming Convention for Core Components v1.04,
www.ebxml.org/specs/ebCCNAM.pdf.

Document Assembly and Context Rules v1.04,
www.ebxml.org/specs/ebCCDOC.pdf.

Catalogue of Context Drivers v1.04,
www.ebxml.org/specs/ccDRIV.pdf.

Core Component Dictionary v1.04,
www.ebxml.org/specs/ccDICT.pdf.

Core Component Structure v1.04,
www.ebxml.org/specs/ccSTRUCT.pdf.

Technical Architecture Risk Assessment v1.0,
www.ebxml.org/specs/secRISK.pdf.

World Wide Web Consortium (W3C) Documents

as of 1 May 2001

The World Wide Web Consortium (W3C) calls its final technical documents *recommendations* rather than *standards*, to distinguish them from full-fledged standards issued by bodies such as the American National Standards Institute (ANSI). W3C uses an open standards process to develop its documents.

Recommendations

Extensible Markup Language (XML) 1.0 (Second Edition), W3C Recommendation 6 October 2000,
www.w3.org/TR/2000/REC-xml-20001006.

Namespaces in XML, World Wide Web Consortium 14 January 1999, www.w3.org/TR/1999/
REC-xml-names-19990114/.

XHTML 1.0: The Extensible Hypertext Markup Language. A Reformulation of HTML 4 in XML 1.0, W3C Recommendation 26 January 2000,
www.w3.org/TR/xhtml1/.

XML Path Language (Xpath), Version 1.0, W3C Recommendation 16 November 1999, www.w3.org/TR/xpath.

XSL Transformations (XSLT), Version 1.0, W3C Recommendation 16 November 1999, www.w3.org/TR/xslt.html.

Proposed and Candidate Recommendations

Proposed and *candidate* recommendations are two levels of review below final recommendation status. Proposed and candidate standards have gone through a public review and resolved outstanding technical issues. Proposed recommendations also have at least a few successful implementations to their credit.

Extensible Stylesheet Language (XSL), Version 1.0, W3C Candidate Recommendation 21 November 2000, www.w3.org/TR/xsl/.

XML Linking Language (XLink) Version 1.0, W3C Proposed Recommendation 20 December 2000, www.w3.org/TR/2000/PR-xlink-20001220/.

XML Schema Part 0: Primer, W3C Proposed Recommendation, 30 March 2001, www.w3.org/TR/xmlschema-0/.

XML Schema Part 1: Structures, W3C Proposed Recommendation 30 March 2001, www.w3.org/TR/xmlschema-1/.

XML Schema Part 2: Datatypes, W3C Proposed Recommendation 30 March 2001, www.w3.org/TR/xmlschema-2/.

XML—Signature Syntax and Processing, W3C Candidate Recommendation 19 April 2001, www.w3.org/TR/2001/CR-xmldsig-core-20010419/.

Notes

Notes are technical documents related to W3C activities and don't represent either an endorsement by W3C or a commitment to pursue work on the subjects they discuss.

The Information and Content Exchange (ICE) Protocol, W3C Note 26 October 1998, www.w3.org/TR/ NOTE-ice.

Simple Object Access Protocol (SOAP) 1.1, W3C Note 08 May 2000, www.w3.org/TR/SOAP/.

SOAP Messages with Attachments, W3C Note 11 December 2000, www.w3.org/TR/SOAP-attachments.

SOAP Security Extensions: Digital Signature, W3C Note 06 February 2001, www.w3.org/TR/SOAP-dsig/.

Unicode in XML and other Markup Languages, Unicode Technical Report #20, W3C Note 15 December 2000, www.w3.org/TR/unicode-xml/.

Web Services Description Language (WSDL) 1.1, W3C Note 15 March 2001, www.w3.org/TR/wsdl.

EDI Standards

ASC X12, Release 4040, December 2000, www.disa.org/Bookstore/Public/ IntroPage.cfm?intCategory=1&intCartID= 0&intUserID=0.

UN/EDIFACT, D.01A Directory—January 2001, www.disa.org/Bookstore/Public/IntroPage.cfm?int Category=4&intCartID=0&intUserID=0 or www.unece.org/trade/untdid/Welcome.html.

Books

Tim Berners-Lee, with Mark Fischetti, *Weaving the Web: The Original Design and Ultimate Destiny of the World Wide Web by Its Inventor* (Harper San Francisco, 1999).

Mark Birbeck, et al, *Professional XML* (Wrox Press Inc., January 2000).

Thomas Friedman, *The Lexus and the Olive Tree* (Farrar Straus & Giroux. June 2000). Friedman, an Op-Ed columnist for *The New York Times,* has written probably the best book on the impact of technology on business worldwide.

Steven Holzner, *Inside XML* (New Riders, November 2000).

Benoît Marchal, *XML by Example* (Que, December 1999).

Articles

In this section, we have tried to identify articles with lasting value. There are plenty of good daily, weekly, and monthly publications discussing current news and events on e-business.

The Economist

"Survey: Software," *The Economist* 14 April 2001, `www.economist.com/surveys/showsurvey.cfm?issue=20010414`. Includes articles about XML for e-business.

Scientific American

Tim Berners-Lee, James Hendler, and Ora Lassila, "The Semantic Web," *Scientific American* May 2001, `www.scientificamerican.com/2001/0501issue/0501berners-lee.html`.

Tim Bray and Jon Bosak, "XML and the Second-Generation Web," *Scientific American* May 1999, `www.sciam.com/1999/0599issue/0599bosak.html`.

Web Sites

You could spend a lifetime reading Web-based literature about XML and e-business. We tried to limit the selections in this section to those directly related to the subject matter of the book.

ebXML

`www.ebxml.org`

For anything dealing with ebXML, of course, start here. Get the latest specifications and news.

XML Cover Pages

`xml.coverpages.org`

Don't even think of starting anywhere else in your search for general XML information. Robin Cover has made it his life's work to chronicle anything and everything dealing with XML and its predecessor SGML.

XML.com

`www.xml.com`

News, articles, reference lists, tool guides. Good for both the techie and newcomer. (Full disclosure: Alan Kotok is a regular contributor to XML.com.)

XML.org

`www.xml.org`

Billed as "The XML Industry Portal," this site is slanted to the activities of OASIS, but is still worth the visit.

United Nations Centre for Trade Facilitation and Electronic Business (UN/CEFACT)

`www.unece.org/cefact`

The international EDI standards body that cosponsored the ebXML initiative.

Data Interchange Standards Association (DISA)

`www.disa.org`

The secretariat for the accredited standards committee X12 as well as Open Travel Alliance, two early and leading ebXML supporters. (Full disclosure: Alan Kotok is an employee of DISA.)

XML/edi Group

www.xmledi-group.org

Good resource on the use of XML for e-business, and independent of vendors. While some of the reading is a little dated, signing up for the listserv gives you access to nearly 2,000 professionals worldwide, many of whom enjoy answering end-user questions. (Full disclosure: David Webber is one of the founders of the XML/edi Group.)

UML Resource Page, Object Management Group

www.omg.org/technology/uml

Specifications on the Unified Modeling Language (UML) and references to articles and tutorials.

Internet Engineering Task Force (IETF)

www.ietf.org

The Internet Engineering Task Force (IETF) provides open standards on the base Internet technology that underpins the Web, email, and FTP. The MIME specifications used in SOAP and ebXML's messaging specifications come from the IETF.

Index

A

ability to apply existing technology (interoperability), 181-182

access levels, registry security, 241

access, indexed repositories' contents, 65

accessibility of XML, 114
Java, 115-116
non-English character sets, 114-115
style sheets, 116-118

accessors, compound type data exchange (SOAP), 200

accommodation of the human element, 186-187

Accredited Standards Committee X12, 31

acknowledgment, receipt of EDI transactions, 147-148

Acknowledgment element (SOAP headers), attributes, 261

acronyms, 297-299
XML and e-business, 300-303

Action layer (RosettaNet implementation framework application layer), 161

activity diagrams, 224
UML, 151

administrative simplification provision (HIPAA), 32

affiliates, 29

agents, as defined in "Fusion of Five" of XML/EDI, 139

aggregate components, 60

agreements
EDI business procedure, 145
trading partner profiles
background information and definitions, 242-243
CPA interactions, 243-244, 251-252
CPP interactions, 246-250

American National Standards Institute (ANSI), 108

analyzing processes, business process specifications, 222-225

ANSI (American National Standards Institute), 108

API (application programming interface), 113, 141, 204
UDDI specifications, 204
inquiries, 204
publishing, 205

C

Y-Z

HOW TO CONTACT US

VISIT OUR WEB SITE

WWW.NEWRIDERS.COM

On our web site, you'll find information about our other books, authors, tables of contents, and book errata. You will also find information about book registration and how to purchase our books, both domestically and internationally.

EMAIL US

Contact us at: **nrfeedback@newriders.com**

- If you have comments or questions about this book
- To report errors that you have found in this book
- If you have a book proposal to submit or are interested in writing for New Riders
- If you are an expert in a computer topic or technology and are interested in being a technical editor who reviews manuscripts for technical accuracy

Contact us at: **nreducation@newriders.com**

- If you are an instructor from an educational institution who wants to preview New Riders books for classroom use. Email should include your name, title, school, department, address, phone number, office days/hours, text in use, and enrollment, along with your request for desk/examination copies and/or additional information.

Contact us at: **nrmedia@newriders.com**

- If you are a member of the media who is interested in reviewing copies of New Riders books. Send your name, mailing address, and email address, along with the name of the publication or Web site you work for.

BULK PURCHASES/CORPORATE SALES

If you are interested in buying 10 or more copies of a title or want to set up an account for your company to purchase directly from the publisher at a substantial discount, contact us at 800-382-3419 or email your contact information to corpsales@pearsontechgroup.com. A sales representative will contact you with more information.

WRITE TO US

New Riders Publishing
201 W. 103rd St.
Indianapolis, IN 46290-1097

CALL/FAX US

Toll-free (800) 571-5840
If outside U.S. (317) 581-3500
Ask for New Riders
FAX: (317) 581-4663

New Riders

WWW.NEWRIDERS.COM

VOICES THAT MATTER

RELATED NEW RIDERS TITLES

ISBN: 0735710201
1152 pages
US $49.99

Inside XML

Steven Holzner

Inside XML is a foundation book that covers both the Microsoft and non-Microsoft approach to XML programming. It covers in detail the hot aspects of XML, such as DTDs vs. XML Schemas, CSS, XSL, XSLT, XLinks, XPointers, XHTML, RDF, CDF, parsing XML in Perl and Java, and much more.

ISBN: 0735711127
363 pages
US $44.99

XML and SQL Server 2000

John Griffin

XML and SQL Server 2000 enables SQL developers to understand and work with XML, the preferred technology for integrating eBusiness systems. SQL Server 2000 has added several new features that SQL Server 7 never had that make working with and generating XML easier for the developer. *XML and SQL Server 2000* provides a comprehensive discussion of SQL Server 2000's XML capabilities.

ISBN: 0735710899
550 pages with CD-ROM
US $49.99

XML, XSLT, Java, and JSP:
A Case Study in Developing a Web Application

Westy Rockwell

A practical, hands-on experience in building web applications based on XML and Java technologies, this book is unique because it teaches the technologies by using them to build a web chat project throughout the book. The project is explained in great detail, after the reader is shown how to get and install the necessary tools to be able to customize this project and build other web applications.

RELATED TITLES

ISBN: 0929652207
360 pages
US $44.95

The Death of e and the Birth of the *Real* New Economy

Peter Fingar and Ronald Aronica

Want to learn more about the business impact of ebXML? We recommend Meghan-Kiffer Press' groundbreaking book. Buy it at online bookstores or directly from the publisher at www.mkpress.com.

Solutions from experts you know and trust.

www.informit.com

New Riders has partnered with **InformIT.com** to bring technical information to your desktop. Drawing on New Riders authors and reviewers to provide additional information on topics you're interested in, **InformIT.com** has free, in-depth information you won't find anywhere else.

- **Master the skills you need, when you need them**

- **Call on resources from some of the best minds in the industry**

- **Get answers when you need them, using InformIT's comprehensive library or live experts online**

- **Go above and beyond what you find in New Riders books, extending your knowledge**

As an **InformIT** partner, **New Riders** has shared the wisdom and knowledge of our authors with you online. Visit **InformIT.com** to see what you're missing.

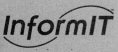

www.informit.com • www.newriders.com

Colophon

This book was written and edited in Microsoft Word, and laid out in QuarkXPress. The fonts used for the text were Bembo, Frutiger and MCPdigital. It was printed on 50# Husky Offset Smooth paper at VonHoffman Graphics, Inc. in Owensville, Missouri. Prepress consisted of PostScript computer-to-plate technology (filmless process). The cover was printed at Moore Langen Printing in Terre Haute, Indiana, on 12pt, coated on one side.